Text Book of Tourism

D.K. Singh

Vice President

Heritage Institute of Hotel & Tourism

Agra

AMAN PUBLICATIONS

NEW DELHI

Published by
Rajiv Jain for Aman Publications
LG-4A, Ganpati Bhawan,
4675-B/21, Ansari Road,
Darya Ganj, Delhi - 110002
PH: 23255012, 23282127
E-mail: sshjbs@yahoo.com

First Published – 2007

ISBN–81–8204–042-6
978-81–8204–042-7

SOLE DISTRIBUTOR
JINDAL BOOK SERVICES
LG-4A, Ganpati Bhawan,
4675-B/21, Ansari Road,
Darya Ganj, Delhi - 110002

Jacket Designed by :
S.M. Graphics

Printed by:
INDUS Press , Delhi, India

Dedicated to the Noble Soul
who
possessed a firm mind
with
delicate heart
My brother
Mr. R. K. Singh (Dadda)

His blessings have always enlightened my path.....

-D. K. Singh
Vice President
Heritage Institute of Hotel &Tourism
Agra

Contents

Preface

Commencing as a struggling industry from its beginnings, tourism in India today is one of the largest enterprises of the Government, bringing in unprecedented revenues, positive nation-image and increased opprtunities for jobs and their growth. Even as the infrastructural situation for supporting and fostering tourism leaves much to be desired, India's numerous attractions as a tourist getaway, and the conscientious effort on the government's part to encourage this trend, has brought tourism to the fore as a major economic activity.

This book has been written so as to assess, evaluate and review the various segments of the tourism industry in India, what they signify and how they can be improved. The "Atithi Devo Bhavah" and the "Incredible India" campaigns launched by India's Ministry of Tourism is reaping rich dividends, and the industry is one of the fastest growing enterprises in the nation. Well-established tour operators and agencies, a growing hospitality sector, well-managed tou guides, transport and other arrangements for visiting places of tourist interest-all of which are needed for rendering tours and travels fulfilling experiences, are very much a part of the way tourism operates in India. Nevertheless, a lot more has to be done, as the industry is still in a nascent stage, and plagued with a quagmire of issues. Tourist safety and exploitation are still amtters of great concern, and other issues like police inefficiency and corrupt bureaucracy further aid problems. Hence, the aim of this book is to present the numerous sectors which contrive to make up tourism, and what measures can be taken to iron out the difficulties in their path. These different segments-travel agencies, tour operators, hotels and accomodations, transport, recreational facilities, restaurants and dining, historical places, etc-have been thoroughly dissected and elaborated upon, emphasizing on what they imply. Based on international trends and managerial styles, which have been modified for Indian conditions, suggestions have been given on how to implement steps for their improvement. Current trends and developments in this field are also examined. Comprehensive and insightful, it is hoped that the book serves well for those in the tourism industry.

1

History of Tourism

Tourism is the sum of the phenomena and relationships arising from the travel and stay of non-residents, insofar as they do not lead to permanent residence and are not connected with any earning activity. The World Tourism Organisation defines tourists as people who "travel to and stay in places outside their usual environment for not more than one consecutive year for leisure, business and other purposes not related to the exercise of an activity remunerated from within the place visited". Tourism has become a popular global leisure activity.

Tourism is vital for many countries, due to the income generated by the consumption of goods and services by tourists, the taxes levied on businesses in the tourism industry, and the opportunity for employment in the service industries associated with tourism. These service industries include transportation services such as cruise ships and taxis, accommodation such as hotels, restaurants, bars, and entertainment venues, and other hospitality industry services such as spas and resorts.

The United Nations classified three forms of tourism in 1994 in its Recommendations on Tourism Statistics: Domestic tourism, which involves residents of the given country traveling only within this country; Inbound tourism, involving non-residents traveling in the given country; and Outbound tourism, involving residents traveling in another country. The UN also derived different categories of tourism by combining the 3 basic forms of tourism: Internal tourism, which comprises domestic tourism and inbound tourism; National tourism, which comprises domestic tourism and outbound tourism; and International tourism, which consists of inbound tourism and outbound tourism.

Intrabound tourism is a term coined by the Korea Tourism Organisation and widely accepted in Korea. Intrabound tourism differs from domestic tourism in that the former encompasses policy-making and implementation of national tourism policies. Recently, the tourism industry has shifted from the promotion of inbound tourism to the promotion of intrabound tourism because many countries are experiencing tough competition for inbound tourists. Some national policymakers have shifted their priority to the promotion of intrabound tourism to contribute to the local economy.

Before people are able to experience tourism they usually need disposable income (i.e. money to spend on non-essentials); time off from work or other responsibilities; leisure time tourism infrastructure, such as transport and accommodation; and legal clearance to travel.

Individually, sufficient health is also a condition, and of course the inclination to travel. Furthermore, in some countries there are legal restrictions on travelling, especially abroad. Certain states with strong governmental control over the lives of citizens (notably established Communist states) may restrict foreign travel only to trustworthy citizens. The United States prohibits its citizens from traveling to some countries, for example Cuba.

Wealthy people have always traveled to distant parts of the world to see great buildings or other works of art, to learn new languages, to experience new cultures, or to taste new cuisine. As long ago as the time of the Roman Republic places such as Baiae were popular coastal resorts for the rich. The terms tourist and tourism were first used as official terms in 1937 by the League of Nations. Tourism was defined as people travelling abroad for periods of over 24 hours.

Health and Leisure Tourism

The history of European tourism can perhaps be said to originate with the medieval pilgrimage. Although undertaken primarily for religious reasons, the pilgrims in the Canterbury Tales quite clearly saw the experience as a kind of holiday (the term itself being derived from the 'holy day' and its associated leisure activities). Pilgrimages created a variety of tourist aspects that still exist—bringing back souvenirs, obtaining credit with foreign banks (in medieval times utilising international networks established by Jews and Lombards), and making use of space available on existing forms of transport (such as the use of medieval English wine ships bound for Vigo by pilgrims to Santiago De Compostela).

Pilgrimages are still important in modern tourism—such as to Lourdes or Knock in Ireland. But there are modern equivalents—Graceland and the grave of Jim Morrison in Père Lachaise Cemetery. During the seventeenth century, it became fashionable in England to undertake a Grand Tour.

The sons of the nobility and gentry were sent upon an extended tour of Europe as an educational experience. The eighteenth century was the golden age of the Grand Tour, and many of the fashionable visitors were painted at Rome by Pompeo Batoni. A modern equivalent of the Grand Tour is the phenomenon of the backpacker, although cultural holidays, such as those offered by Swann-Hellenic, are also important.

Health tourism has always existed, but it was not until the eighteenth century that it became important. In England, it was associated with spas, places with supposedly health-giving mineral waters, treating diseases from gout to liver disorders and bronchitis. The most popular resorts were Bath, Cheltenham, Buxton, Harrogate, and Tunbridge Wells. Visits to take 'the waters' also allowed the visitors to attend balls and other entertainments. Continental Spas such as Karlsbad attracted many fashionable travellers by the nineteenth century.

It could be argued that Britain was the home of the seaside holiday. In travelling to the coast, the population was following in the steps of Royalty. King George III made regular visits to Weymouth when in poor health. At the time, a number of doctors argued the benefits of bathing in sea water, and sea bathing as a widespread practice was popularised by the Prince Regent (later George IV), who frequented Brighton for this purpose.

Leisure travel was associated with the industrialisation of United Kingdom—the first European country to promote leisure time to the increasing industrial population. Initially, this applied to the owners of the machinery of production, the economic oligarchy, the factory owners, and the traders. These comprised the new middle class. Cox & Kings were the first official travel company to be formed in 1758. Later, the working class could take advantage of leisure time.

The British origin of this new industry is reflected in many place names. At Nice, one of the first and best-established holiday resorts on the French Riviera, the long esplanade along the seafront is known to this day as the Promenade des Anglais; in many other historic resorts in continental Europe, old well-established palace hotels have names like the Hotel Bristol, the Hotel Carlton or the Hotel Majestic—reflecting the dominance of English customers.

Winter Tourism

Winter sports were largely invented by the British leisured classes, initially at the Swiss village of Zermatt (Valais), and St Moritz in 1864. The first packaged winter sports holidays took place in 1902 at Adelboden, Switzerland. Winter sports were a natural answer for a leisured class looking for amusement during the coldest season. Organised sport was well established in Britain before it reached other countries.

The vocabulary of sport bears witness to this: rugby, football, and boxing all originated in Britain, and even tennis, originally a French sport, was formalised and codified by the British, who hosted the first national championship in the nineteenth century, at Wimbledon. The Fun Ski & Snow Festival, which has been organised annually by Korea tourism organisation since 1998 and participated by about 10,000 tourists from Asia, is one of the most successful winter tourism products in Asia. The festival provides a variety of events such as ski and sled competitions, ski and snow board lessons, performances and recreational activities.

Majority of the event participants are foreign visitors who come from countries with a warm climate that have no snow. The event offers them opportunities to enjoy winter and winter sports in Korea. In addition, southern South American countries making up the Patagonia region in Chile and Argentina attract thousands of tourists every year. Skiing is extremely popular in the mountainous areas.

Mass Tourism

Mass travel could only develop with improvements in technology allowed the transport of large numbers of people in a short space of time to places of leisure interest, and greater numbers of people began to enjoy the benefits of leisure time. The pioneer of modern mass tourism was

Thomas Cook who, on 5 July 1841, organised the first package tour in history. He arranged for the rail company to charge one shilling per person for a group of 570 temperance campaigners from Leicester to a rally in Loughborough, eleven miles away.

Cook was paid a share of the fares actually charged to the passengers, as the railway tickets, being legal contracts between company and passenger, could not have been issued at his own price. There had been railway excursions before, but this one included entrance to an entertainment held in private grounds, rail tickets and food for the train journey. Cook immediately saw the potential of a convenient 'off the peg' holiday product in which everything was included in one cost. He organised packages inclusive of accommodation for the Great Exhibition, and afterwards pioneered package holidays in both Britain (particularly in Scotland) and on the European continent (where Paris and the Alps were the most popular destinations).

He was soon followed by others (the Polytechnic Touring Association, Dean and Dawson etc.), with the result that the tourist industry developed rapidly in late Victorian Britain. Initially it was supported by the growing middle classes, who had time off from their work, and who could afford the luxury of travel and possibly even staying for periods of time in boarding houses.

The Bank Holidays Act 1871 introduced a statutory right for workers to take holidays, even if they were not paid at the time. By the last quarter of the nineteenth century, the tradition of the working class holiday had become firmly established in Britain. These were largely focused upon the seaside resorts. The spread of the railway network in the nineteenth century resulted in the growth of Britain's seaside towns by bringing them within easy distance of Britain's urban centres.

Blackpool was created by the construction of a line to Fleetwood, and some resorts were promoted by the railway companies themselves—Morecambe by the Midland Railway and Cleethorpes by the Great Central Railway. Other resorts included Scarborough in Yorkshire, servicing Leeds and Bradford; Weston-super-Mare in Somerset, catering for the inhabitants of Bristol; and Skegness, patronised by the residents of the industrial East Midlands. The cockneys of London flocked to Southend-on-Sea, mainly by Thames Steamer, and the South Coast resorts such as Broadstairs, Brighton, and Eastbourne were only a train ride away, with others further afield such as Bournemouth, Bognor Regis and Weymouth.

For a century, domestic tourism was the norm, with foreign travel being reserved for the rich or the culturally curious. A number of inland destinations, such as the English Lake District, and Snowdonia appealed to those who liked the countryside and fine scenery. The holiday camp began to appear in the 1930s, but this phenomenon really expanded in the post-war period. Butlins and Pontins set this trend, but their popularity waned with the rise of overseas package tours and the increasing comforts to which visitors became accustomed at home.

Towards the end of the 20th century this market has been revived by the upmarket inland resorts of Dutch company Center Parcs. Cox & Co, the forebear of Cox & Kings were in existence from 1758 largely entwined with the travel arrangements for the British Army serving around the Empire. While acting as 'agents' for various regiments, they organised the payment, provision, clothing and travel arrangements for members of the armed forces. In the 19th century their network of offices contained a banking and also travel department. The company became heavily involved with affairs in India and its Shipping Agency had offices in France and the Middle East. Other phenomena that helped develop the travel industry were paid holidays:

- 1.5 million manual workers in Britain had paid holidays by 1925
- 11 million by 1939 (30% of the population in families with paid holidays)

NGOs and government agencies may sometimes promote a specific region as a tourist destination, and support the development of a tourism industry in that area. The contemporary phenomenon of mass tourism may sometimes result in overdevelopment; alternative forms of tourism such as ecotourism seek to avoid such outcomes by pursuing tourism in a sustainable way.

International Mass Tourism

Increasing speed on railways meant that the tourist industry could develop internationally. To this may be added the development of sea travel. By 1901, the number of people crossing the English Channel from England to France or Belgium had passed 0.5 million per year. Shipping companies were anxious to fill cabin space that was under utilised. For example, P&O found that the majority of their passengers for India and the Far East joined the ship at Marseilles. Consequently, they marketed holidays based upon sea trips from London to Lisbon and Gibraltar. Other companies diverted their older ships to operate cruises in the summer months.

However, the real age of international mass travel began with the growth of air travel after World War Two. In the immediate post-war period, there was a surplus of transport aircraft, such as the popular and reliable Douglas Dakota, and a number of ex military pilots ready to fly them. They were available for charter flights, and tour operators began to use them for European destinations, such as Paris and Ostend.

Recent Developments

There has been an upmarket trend in tourism over the last few decades, especially in Europe where international travel for short breaks is common. Tourists have higher levels of disposable income and greater leisure time and they are also better-educated and have more sophisticated tastes. There is now a demand for a better quality products, which has resulted in a fragmenting of the mass market for beach vacations; people want more specialised versions, such as 'Club 18 -30', quieter resorts, family-oriented holidays, or niche market-targeted destination hotels. As well, people are taking second short break holidays.

The developments in technology and transport infrastructure such as jumbo jets and low-budget airlines have made many types of tourism more affordable. There have also been changes in lifestyle, such as retiree-age people who living as a tourist all the year round. This is facilitated by internet purchasing of tourism products. Some sites have now started to offer dynamic packaging, in which an inclusive price is quoted for a tailor- made package requested by the customer upon impulse. There have been a few setbacks in tourism, such as the September 11, 2001 attacks and terrorist threats to tourist destinations such as Bali and European cities.

Some of the tourist destinations, including the beach resorts of Cancún have lost popularity due to shifting tastes. In this context, the excessive building and environmental destruction often associated with traditional "sun and beach" tourism may contribute to a destination's saturation and subsequent decline. Spain's Costa Brava, a popular 1960s and 1970s beach location is now facing a crisis in its tourist industry. Sustainable tourism is becoming more popular as people start to realise the devastating effects poorly planned tourism can have on communities.

Receptive tourism is now growing at a very rapid rate in many developing countries, where it is often the most important economic activity in local GDP. In recent years, second holidays or vacations have become more popular as people's discretionary income increases. Typical combinations are a package to the typical mass tourist resort, with a winter skiing holiday or weekend break to a city or national park.

On December 26, 2004 a tsunami, caused by the 2004 Indian Ocean earthquake hit Asian countries bordering the Indian Ocean, and also the Maldives. Tens of thousands of lives were lost, and many tourists died. This, together with the vast clean-up operation in place, has stopped or severely hampered tourism to the area. The terms tourism and travel are sometimes used interchangeably. The terms tourism and tourist are sometimes used pejoratively, to imply a shallow interest in the cultures or locations visited by tourists.

Niche Tourism

Physical activity or sports-oriented niche tourism includes adventure tourism such as mountaineering and hiking (tramping); Backpacker Tourism; Sport travel to do skiing, golf and scuba diving or see a sports event (e.g., FIFA World Cup); and extreme tourism for people interested in risky activities. Learning-oriented niche tourism includes audio tourism and audio walking tours; bookstore tourism, in which travellers visit independent bookstores; creative tourism workshops; educational tourism for classes; ancestry tourism, to visit birth places; Hobby tourism (such as garden tours, amateur radio DX-peditions, or square dance cruises).

The cultural sub-type of learning-oriented niche tourism focuses on cultural and arts activities, including cultural tourism, music tourism, andheritage tourism. The nature and environment-oriented sub-types include Coastal Tourism; Ecotourism (e.g. sustainable tourism in Rainforests or national parks); Garden tourism; and Rural Tourism such as Agritourism.

Lifestyle-oriented niche tourism types include Gay tourism; Gourmet tourism; Wine tourism; Health tourism; Medical tourism; Inclusive tourism for people with disabilities;Mystical tourism (e.g., involving Meditation, yoga,and rituals).

Other Types of Tourism

- Dark tourism includes travel to sites associated with death and suffering, such as the scene of the Hindenburg airship disaster, or to the sites of disasters (Disaster tourism).
- Drug tourism, (e.g., to use drugs in Amsterdam)
- Sex tourism (e.g., to have sex with prostitutes).
- Mass Tourism is an ecotourism policy to minimise the footprint of tourists by concentrating them into a small area. Mass tourism also maximises the use of tourist infrastructure.
- Free Independent Traveler: a sector of the market in which the tourists select their own accommodation and transport, rather than using the established tourism booking system.
- Pop-culture tourism: tourism by those that visit a particular location after reading about it or seeing it used as a location in a film.
- Perpetual tourism: individuals always on vacation; some of them, for tax purposes, to avoid being resident in any country.
- Pilgrimage Tourism: pilgrimages to ancient holy places (Rome and Santiago de Compostela for Catholics,

temples and stupas of Nepal for the Hindus and Buddhist, Mount Athos or Painted churches of northern Moldavia for the Orthodox), religious sites such as mosques and shrines.

- Sacred travel or metaphysical tourism is a form of New Age travel where believers travel to and perform rituals at religious sites
- Shopping tourism promoting shopping festivals such as the Dubai Shopping Festival.
- Space tourism: traveling in outer space or on spaceships.
- Vacilando is a special kind of wanderer for whom the process of traveling and discovery is more important than the destination.
- Visiting Family and Relatives Tourism: traveling to visit persons related by close family ties and combining this with vacation-type activities; distinct from ancestry tourism, which involves genealogical research
- Armchair tourism and virtual tourism: not traveling physically, but exploring the world through internet, books, or TV.

New Trends in Tourism

The World Tourism Organisation (UNWTO) forecasts that international tourism will continue growing at the average annual rate of 4 %. By 2020 Europe will remain the most popular destination, but its share will drop from 60 % in 1995 to 46 %. Long-haul will grow slightly faster than intraregional travel and by 2020 its share will increase from 18 % in 1995 to 24 %. With the advent of e-commerce, tourism products have become one of the most traded items on the internet.

Tourism products and services have been made available through intermediaries, although tourism providers (hotels, airlines, etc.) can sell their services directly. This has put pressure on intermediaries from both on-line and traditional shops. It has been suggested there is a strong correlation between Tourism expenditure per capita and the degree to which countries play in the global context.

Not only as a result of the important economic contribution of the tourism industry, but also as an indicator of the degree of confidence with which global citizens leverage the resources of the globe for the benefit of their local economies. This is why any projections of growth in tourism may serve as an indication of the relative influence that each country will exercise in the future.

Space tourism is expected to "take off" in the first quarter of the 21st century, although compared with traditional destinations the number of tourists in orbit will remain low until technologies such as a space elevator make space travel cheap. Technological improvement is likely to make possible air-ship hotels, based either on solar-powered airplanes or large dirigibles. Underwater hotels, such as Hydropolis, expected to open in Dubai in 2006, will be built. On the ocean tourists will be welcomed by ever larger cruise ships and perhaps floating cities.

Information Technology and the Tourism Industry

The tourism industry is made up of three major components: namely,

(i) Transport sector, which includes air, water and surface transport,

(ii) Accommodation sector, all types of establishments that offer lodging to visitors (Hotel, Motel, Guest houses, caravans etc.)

(iii) Attraction sector which comprises manmade and natural attractions which are developed to satisfy visitors educational, recreational, aesthetic needs etc.

Transport sector

Transport provides the essential link between tourism origin and destination areas and facilitates the movement of holidaymakers, business travelers, people visiting friends and relatives and those undertaking educational and health tourism. Before setting out on a journey of any kind, every traveler makes sure which Transport Company has a good safety record. To this effect, airplanes coaches and even taxis are equipped with good communication equipment. An Airplane flies with the help of modern information technology equipment which provides information ranging from weather, altitude and other information to the pilot to communication made during emergency by the pilot with other airplanes and air traffic control stations.

In-flight entertainment is also a product of information technology, video games, video films are examples. In the case of buses/coaches and taxis, in many countries with developed tourism business, they are equipped with radio communication systems for various uses. For example, the driver or the tour guide updates the Tour Company headquarters about the progress of the tour throughout the touring period. This communication ensures the safety of tourists. Fast and easy information flow is of paramount importance to build confidence in the travelling public. In recent years, the confidence built due to the use of modern IT has been demonstrated by a tremendous increase in the number of travelers worldwide.

Accommodation sector

In the accommodation sector also the contribution of

information technology is prominent. Any individual or group wishing to travel to any part of the world now has an easy access to the accommodation service providers. A visitor can access an information about the kind of hotels at the destination, their ranges of product, the price and other relevant information without leaving his/her office or home. What one has to do is to ring up a travel agency and get the expert advice. This will help any visitor greatly as to where to stay during any kind of away from home. Here the information can be obtained aided by still or moving pictures in order to give an exact feature of an accommodation, facilities and services of ones choice.

At a destination also visitors are at ease during their stay in every respect, in getting information about their business, family or other information back home. They are also at ease to relax with the videos and television entertainment programs, which nowadays are part and parcel of many accommodation units.

Attractions sector

In the case of attractions both manmade and natural attraction owners need to communicate or inform their customers and potential customers about their production. Information about the kind of attraction, where they are located and how to get there is of vital importance. The attraction owners particularly the national tourist offices discharge their duty of promoting their country's tourist attractions using the information technology products. Information through promotional videos, Internet web Sites, television advertisements and travel documentaries are the main information dissemination tools.

Travel Intermediaries

One of the unique characteristics of tourism products is the need of the role played by the so-called travel intermediaries. These travel intermediaries are travel agents, tour operators, conference organisers booking agents etc. They are so important again because of the nature of the tourism product, perishablity and intangibility. This means service products including tourism, cannot be stored for a litter sale, and cannot be inspected for their quality before purchase respectively. This entails a very big effort for marketing and distribution of these products.

Tourism product supply is fragmented both geographically and as product component, coupled with their relatively low capital volume, individual components cannot afford to market and distribute their product for the dispersed potential and actual customers on their own. Let us take an airline company as an example. An airline company, which flies many destinations, can have a representative but cannot have so many offices or product distribution channels in all routes it serves. Or, in Addis Ababa itself for example, Ethiopian Airlines has few offices to distribute and market its product.

However, one can also buy Ethiopian Airline ticket from many other travel agencies in the city. One can imagine if the airline can run these many say sixty offices on its own which are usually with high fixed costs. This makes the travel agents an indispensable partners both in efficiently distributing and marketing the product and substantially reducing the cost of operation for the airline. As these are working on commission basis, the cost of operation for the airline is relatively low. These travel agencies are performing this indispensable task of being intermediary by the use of computers and computer reservation systems (CRS).

Computer reservation systems

The airline CRS systems were the pioneers of computer

applications in the 1950s and are now virtually indispensable to airlines because they enable their revenue streams to be maximised by efficient inventory control. However, these days, hotel and car hiring companies by renting the service from the airline companies are also employed these systems. The technology works by using computers of special kind and leased telephone lines.

The travel agent is connected on line to the central host computer system or CRS. The host computer is almost always a mainframe with massive database attached. The mainframe host polls each travel agent terminal every second or so, to see if it has any messages to send. In this system it is possible that airliners, Hotels and car rental companies can talk to the travel agent and vise versa. This system contributes to a great extent in increasing sales volume and giving precise information on the availability and selling the products efficiently ensuring substantial profit gain.

Global Distribution Systems

Global Distribution Systems (GDSs) are systems which distribute reservation and information services to sales outlets around the world. Unlike the CRSs used solely by an airline or hotel chain, GDS distribute more than one CRS to users who are usually travel agents. GDSs were formed from the airlines of several CRSs, each of which had its airline backer. Once formed, there was a period of some consolidation and shakeout, after which four main GDSs emerged. These are Amadeus, Galileo, Sabre and World Span. These world leading GDSs are switches or simply computers that are connected on the one side to many different supplier systems and on the other side to many end users.

The end users of switch comprise travel agents with a single reservation system to support the sale of airline seats and related travel products such as hotel-and car hire, via a single computer terminal, usually a Personal Computer. All the GDSs, are owned by a group of airline companies. Eleven carriers of different countries for example own Galileo and there are 500 participating airlines companies.

GDSs require massive investment because they are extremely large computer systems that link several airlines and travel principals into a complex network of PCs, telecommunications and large main frame computers. It is not important here to go into the complex operation how these GDSs are working. However it is pertinent to say that GDS are the macro version of CRSs with a specialised and improved information technology for the distribution of Travel products.

2

Tourism Products: Definition and Meaning

Tourists want something different from their daily lives. Because most visitors come from modern cities, the experience of spending time in a small town or a rural area is attractive and meaningful to them. This is even more so if the area has a particular ethnic background, its history is well told, and its natural heritage is explained in a compelling way. Fredericksburg, Texas, is a good example. Some people, including a few residents, may think things are overdone in Fredericksburg. However, Fredericksburg's tourism provides a strong economic base that maintains property values, personal incomes, and tax revenues. Although there are some negative impacts of tourism in Fredericksburg, critics should consider what the town would be like without its tourism economy. Visitors want a sense of authenticity. If things are overly contrived visitors will be offended by the "tourist trap."

What are the essential elements of a heritage tourism product that can be found in virtually any small town? The primary parts of a heritage product are historical events, ethnicity, architecture, natural features, and the daily life of the community, but it is the story of these that makes them into an experience for the visitor. Some ways to discover and use each of these essential elements are briefly described below.

Historical events: Every place has a history. People came from somewhere and settled there for some reason. They started farms and businesses. They fought in wars and with each other. Some of them became famous and some infamous. We should not think of "history" as it is often taught in schools—the presidents, generals, and battles. Instead, we should think of social history. Why did people come to this place and how did they live here? How did the town get its name? Where did they get their water? Did they build dams and mills on the river? How did they make their living? What kind of daily life did they have? What were their triumphs and tragedies? Did a fire, flood, or tornado destroy the town? How and why did the people rebuild? What happened when the railroad came? Did the town have to move to the railroad or did the town develop because of the railroad? These are the stories of the lives of people who made the town, and visitors are inherently interested in the human story.

Ethnicity: In Texas, everyone came from somewhere else and therefore represents an ethnic heritage. "Native Americans" probably came from Mongolia. Hispanics, African Americans, French, Irish, Scots, English, Germans, Polish, Russians, Syrians, Lebanese, Czechoslovakians, Norwegians, Dutch, and on and on make up the people of Texas. Why did people come from Norway to Bosque County? What is the story of the Jewish people in many small towns? Why is Guadalupe, one of the most common Spanish names, based on the Arabic word "wadi?" All of these stories can fascinate visitors.

The Institute of Texas Cultures in San Antonio is a treasure of information about the great variety of Texas ethnicity. Ethnicity becomes a product not just in the stories, but in how those stories are told. Festivals, dance, music, food, dress, architecture—all of these are ways that ethnicity is expressed.

Architecture: Some small towns may not have a single building designed by a "real" architect, but that does not mean that there is no architecture there. On the contrary, every building is a piece of vernacular architecture—often much more interesting and creative than famous architecture, and certainly more representative of the place. Some of that vernacular architecture is now well known.

Natural features: Just as every place has a history, every place also has natural features. Maybe they are not as dramatic as the Grand Teton Mountains, but they are real and important. Without the land, water, air, and sun there would be no life, so how do those things go together to make life in your town or region? What were the characteristics of those features before European settlement? How did the Native Americans use the natural features? How has modern culture changed them? Are there places with particularly scenic views or watchable wildlife?

What kinds of agriculture are practiced in the region? Many people have never seen corn or cotton in the field, not to mention trees heavy with grapefruit. They don't understand grazing and range management or irrigation. All of these things, that may be so ordinary to local residents, can be memorable experiences for the visitor. Most of us who live in rural places forget that seeing a white tail deer is a major nature experience for someone from Houston or Dallas.

Daily life of the community: The heritage, ethnicity, and architecture of Europe are major attractions, but so is daily life there. Millions of Americans go to Europe each year to sit in sidewalk cafes in Paris, live in rural villages in southern England, or ride mopeds in Rome (bless their souls!). In the same way, daily life in the Texas towns can be an attraction for visitors from cities. The livestock auction, the hardware store, the barbeque joint, the local rodeo, even six-man football, are all unique experiences for visitors.

Tourists are people and like to be treated like people—that is, with respect, consideration, and friendliness. Thus, one of the best tourism products you can provide is to simply be nice to your visitors. Talk to them. Let them ask you questions and give them respectful answers, even if the questions seem dumb.

Hospitality: The eating and sleeping service offered to visitors—is another way to provide meaningful experiences based on the historic, ethnic, natural, and cultural characteristics of a community or rural area. Eating should be an experience. The barbecue restaurants in Lockhart and Luling are tourist destinations because they are authentic expressions of daily life in those towns. Restaurants do not have to be ethnic in order to express the character of a place and to provide a meaningful experience. They just have to be "local." They must show a connection to the place. This may be expressed by the owner's collection of historic local photographs or their obvious support for the local school athletic teams. Even the chain restaurants can achieve this "localness" by choice of décor.

Lodging is as important as restaurants in expressing the local character of a place. The architecture should be consistent with the town and region. The décor should be consistent with the place. How often have you been in a motel in a desert region that was decorated with pictures of ocean scenes? That does not create a valuable product for the visitor. A meaningful product is a cohesive experience. Bed and breakfast establishments are especially important as overall heritage tourism products. The visitor is staying in someone's home and should have an experience that makes them feel like they have lived in the town, even for one night.

National and state parks, which have done heritage tourism for more than one hundred years, place major emphasis on what is called interpretation. Guided trails, ranger talks, booklets, videos, maps, and visitor centers are all part of the interpretive programs of parks. Heritage tourism in small towns and rural areas must also provide interpretation because visitors will not see or understand most of the heritage tourism products described above unless someone "interprets" them to the visitors.

While it would be difficult for someone not to be awestruck by the Rocky Mountains or the coast of Maine, the Rio Grande Valley takes a little explaining to help visitors recognise what is there and to have memorable experiences. There is an entire profession of heritage interpretation. Many people make their living as interpreters. They may be formally trained or they may be self-taught. There is a professional association, the National Association for Interpretation that offers certification courses. But what is interpretation, how can people learn interpretive methods, and how can interpretation be used to develop heritage products in your town or region?

There are some formal definitions of interpretation, but basically interpretation is telling the stories of a place. Those stories may focus on history, ethnicity, architecture, natural characteristics, daily life, or all of these. The stories may be told by individuals talking to groups, or by music, drama, art, printed material, video and audio, signs, displays, and many combinations of such methods. But whatever the topic or method, interpretation must speak to the needs and interests of the visitor and must stimulate their interest.

Interpretation is not classroom teaching. It is not about conveying a certain set of facts to the audience. It is about arousing their interest and curiosity about the place by somehow connecting the characteristics of the place to their lives, background, and interests. The purpose of interpretation is to provide a memorable experience (product) to the visitor, not to prepare them to pass the final exam.

Interpretation is not difficult if you love your place and your visitors. You want to show your visitors a good time by sharing your excitement and understanding of the place they are visiting. Good interpreters do not have to have university degrees or high school diplomas. They don't have to be experts on history or zoology. Certainly they have to know some things, but they also have to know how to say they don't know, and stimulate the visitor to want to find out. Chicken or the egg—product or market?

Standard business practice says develop your product to meet a market demand. Research the market and give them what they want. Clearly, that's essential. You must have someone who will pay for your product. However, developing heritage tourism products does not follow the textbook practice. First, there are some major constraints on the kinds of products you can develop or want to develop. Texas will not be able to offer hiking on glaciers or the heritage of the Italian Renaissance—we just don't have those things, even if that is what the market wants. Likewise, many towns may not want to turn their ethnic heritage into a commodity and landowners may not want birdwatchers on their land. So the first step in product development is to determine what you have that may be a product and then determine if you want to offer it as a product.

After you identify your potential products, you have to determine if someone will pay for them and how much they will pay. This may be difficult because there are few comparables to use for analysis. For example, when Dan Brown decided to offer hummingbird watching on his ranch outside Christoval, Texas, he had almost no examples to draw on. He knew birdwatching was popular on the Texas coast, near a large population. How could anyone know if people would drive several hours to Christoval? Sometimes in heritage tourism product development you simply have to hope that if you build it, they will come, as they have with the Dan's Hummerhouse.

Part of the attraction of a heritage product is its uniqueness, but because the product is unique it may be very difficult to find comparables. This presents a major problem for financing heritage product development. Lenders need assurance that the business venture will be successful, but the lack of comparables can make it difficult to provide such assurance.

Tourism Policy

A comprehensive tourism policy highlighting the importance of tourism and the objectives of tourism development for the country was promulgated by the Government in 1982. The policy envisaged developing many attractions in India for tourism through well-planned, well-defined and fully-integrated national programmes. It specified the responsibility for tourism development as a common endeavour of all agencies vitally concerned with tourism at central and state levels, including public and private sector enterprises; airlines, railways and road transport systems; municipal and local bodies as well as cultural and educational institutions. It further provided an action plan based on a "travel circuit" concept to maximise the benefits of tourism.

The plan proposed to achieve intensive development of selected circuits, dispel the tendency of concentration in a few urban centres, encourage the diversification of tourist attractions and open economically-backward areas which have many tourist attractions. Tourism was recognised as an industry by 1986 and became eligible for incentives and facilities, including taxincentives, subsidies, priorities in the sanctioning of loans by state financial institutions and preferences in providingelectricity, water and sewerage connections.

Employment in the tourism sector was also expected to double by the turn of the century. The basic strategy for increasing the tourist flow includes improvement of infrastructure facilities in identified circuits and destinations, development of special tourism areas, diversification of tourism products, development of pilgrim tourism and a package of incentives for attracting private investment to the tourism sector. It is now being proposed to increase tourist arrivals to 5 million by the turn of the century. This would mean substantial expansion of tourism infrastructure facilities like hotels, restaurants, tourist coaches, cars, air taxis, entertainment facilities and so forth.

The strategy for achieving the national objective is to establish all inclusive "Special Tourism Areas" and undertake intensive infrastructure development for identified circuits and destinations. Since most infrastructure elements and the delivery systems are within the puNiew of the state Governments or private sector, tourism infrastructure is being developed mainly with financial assistance to state/U.T. governments and by providing various incentives to private entrepreneurs.

The most frequent pattern of funding which has continued over successive plan periods is known as "normalfunding". Under this pattern, the Central Department of Tourism meets almost the entire expenditure, except the cost of land and interior decoration in the case of construction projects. A new method of funding by way of grant-in-aid towards project cost was introduced during 1992-1993. In this scheme, 28 per cent of the project cost is provided by the central government and 12 per cent is provided by the state government.

The balance of 60 per cent has to be raised as a loan from financial institutions or banks. This method of funding is applicable to projects requiring large investments. It is expected that the state governments would be able to mobilise more resources from financial institutions for investment in tourism projects through this method.

PRIVATE ENTREPRENEURS

Hotels and tourism-related activities have been declared as a priority sector for foreign investment. As aresult, foreign equity participation in tourism projects is automatically allowed up to 51 per cent, and higher percentages of foreign equity can be approved on a case-by-case basis.

Tourism industries are also eligible for a number of incentives, such as interest subsidy, income tax exemption, reduced customs duty, etc. There are specific incentives being provided by the Central Department of Tourism. One specific incentive is for approved hotels up to the 3-star category and heritage hotels outside the four metro-cities which are eligible for an interest subsidy for loans from the Industrial Finance Corporation of India, Tourism Finance Corporation of India and State Financial Corporations.

The rates of interest subsidy are (a) 5 per cent for 1 to 3-star category hotels in areas identified for intensive development; (b) 5 per cent for heritage hotels outside metropolitan areas; and (c) 3 per cent for all other 1 to 3-star category hotels outside metropolitan areas. In order to encourage the owners of heritage properties to convert palaces, forts, havelis, etc. of any size into heritage hotels, a capital subsidy scheme was introduced since May 1993. Under the scheme, a capital subsidy of 10 per cent of the project cost or Rs.500,OOO, which ever is less, is available for developing any structure of 75 years or older as a heritage hotel.

Domestic travel agents and tour operators are given assistance to develop markets abroad. Assistance isgiven for market research, promotional visits abroad, and so forth. An Investment Facilitation Cell has been set up in the Department of Tourism to provide assistance to prospective entrepreneurs.

Product Development

India has been mainly conceived as a cultural tourist destination, but it has diverse tourist attractions which need to be developed. A conscious policy has, therefore, been adopted to diversify and improve tourism products of India, including cultural tourist attractions. The schemes implemented through state governments for product development are:

- Promotion of fairs and festivals, rural craft, melas, etc.
- refurbishment of monuments and environmental planning;
- flood lighting/son et lumiere (SEL) shows;
- development of pilgrim centres;
- development of adventure sports facilities;
- designation of special tourism areas; and
- development of specific circuits through external aid.

A national strategy for the development of tourism has recently been developed for synergising the activities of different infrastructure sectors, the state governments and the private sector for tourism development. The specific components of the strategy include:

- Infrastructure development;
- Product development and diversification, including development of mega-tourism resorts;
- Entrepreneurial development and promotion of self-employment opportunities;

- Enhanced tourist facilitation;
- Human resources development;
- Research and computerisation;
- Promotion and marketing;
- Environmental protection and cultural preservation;
- Provision of incentives; and
- Monitoring and evaluation and strengthening of organisations.

The word tourism encompasses all activities of persons travelling to and staying in places outside their usual environment for not more than one consecutive year for leisure, business and other purposes. These activities make demands for goods and services, and the establishments which provide such services are considered as part of the tourism industry.

Mobile Technologies

Tourism is an activity of great importance both economically and in terms of the pleasure it gives to holidaymakers worldwide. Nearly all individuals in the western world take some sort of holiday away from home every year, although the number of days differs across and within different countries. Tourism is also an activity that can divide rich and poor, through a negative or parasitical effect that damages places: 'touristification'. The cities, Edinburgh and Glasgow, are the second and third most popular cities for tourists to visit in the U.K., after London.

Summer is a particularly busy time of the year for both cities, with the Edinburgh Festival a major tourist attraction. Some of the tourists are predominantly independent travellers, who had mostly arranged their own travel although some used the assistance of a travel agency. While the package tour market is obviously a very important part of tourism, since this group suffers more acutely from problems of organisation. While a major proportion of independent travellers are 'backpackers', young people travelling for a prolonged period of time before entering paid employment, independent travellers are a diverse group with a wide age range.

One example is that tourists often need to use public transport to get between places. To do this they need to solve a number of practical problems, such as finding where bus stops are, finding out which bus to get, and so on. The most important part of tourism for the purposes of designing new tourism systems. This emphasises the decisions that tourists make and the information they use to make these decisions.

Problems and Remedies

The first, seemingly straightforward, problem which tourists face in an unfamiliar place is what to do. Unlike work, where tasks are often determined (in part) by an overall goal or by other people's plans, tourism is much more open-ended. Tourism encompasses a broad range of activities such as sightseeing, relaxing, shopping, visiting friends and visiting family. Indeed, since tourism can be part of business travel, the boundary between work and leisure is often blurred. Yet whatever tourists do, they must at least make some sort of decision about what to do, often in advance. This decision must take into account the time it takes to get to different places, as well as balancing the attraction of different sites.

When one reaches a tourist site one has to be careful about how one acts, since behavioural norms can be different in different countries. Ignorance about local customs is an oft mocked feature of tourists. Even straightforward activities such as buying goods can be organised differently in different countries, compounded with the problems of working with a new currency, and avoiding being exploited, or just 'looking stupid'. Along with what and how, tourists have to manage when they do different activities.

Tourism is usually constrained in time, because of the need to return home. Time is also a problem in that tourists work with organisations that provide services: opening times must be co-ordinated with the times of public transport, such as trains or buses. This is compounded by the 'pre-booking problem'. Many facilities require pre-booking, so decisions need to be made before one has been to a place. In visiting a city many of the attractions are distributed around the city. There is therefore a need to minimise the times spend travelling between places, understand what one might see and do along the way, and group together attractions which are close together.

In doing so tourists must also navigate public transport, often with limited information, or unfamiliar road systems. Lastly, an important part of a holiday is sharing that holiday with others who are at home. Although the tourist fascination with taking photos or videos has been often criticised, it displays how visitors are not isolated individuals but are part of a social group. Tourists record and represent experiences in the form of photos and stories, to remind themselves of the visit and to share with others after they return home. This is a valuable part of tourism.

The most successful tourist technology is the camera, specifically designed for this 'taking the visit back home'. The popularity of Internet cafés for tourists also suggests that email sent back home is becoming a significant part of the tourist experience. These 'problems' are not a negative part of tourism. Travelling and finding out where to go is part of the very enjoyment of tourism. Tourism transforms what might seem mundane activities into something enjoyable or even romantic. Train journeys, for example, are a common resource for the travel writer, and bus and underground travel can have their own pleasures (such as the smell of the train's tires in the Parisian metro, or the electronic sounds of the Tokyo subway).

Particularly in city visits, walking between places is an important part of being in a place, with 'treet life' being one of the easiest ways to access the natural life of locals. These pleasures are a whimsical yet crucial part of the enjoyment of tourism. So, in solving these problems tourists are not simply looking for some optimal solution. Instead, solving these problems is part of the enjoyment of the experience; finding a nice café or reading a map, for example, is enjoyable in itself.

Accordingly, the solutions that tourists have to these problems are often finely tuned to both the problem and the enjoyment of working through the problem. One method that tourists use to solve their problems is sharing the visit with other tourists. Tourism is very much a social activity. A tourist generally travels with others, e.g. as part of a family group, and statistics from the US show that 79% of leisure visits involve groups of two or more.

Since leisure travel is predominantly group-based, there is considerable intra-group interaction and collaboration. The first tourist holds an "A to Z" street guide and is looking through it. While the second tourist glances around the railway station, the first tourist finds the correct page of the map. Then the second tourist takes out her glasses to look at the map, glances at the map and then points at an exit sign in the train station that names the street to which the exit leads. They then give the street guide a last look, pick up their bags and leave the station. Even in this simple excerpt one can see a division of labour between the two tourists. The second tourist looks around the station to find the exit, while the first tourist tries to find the correct page on the map. She holds the map so as to make both the map and her progress in using it available to her companion.

On finding the station, she describes the location of the station to her friend, and the friend adds the name of the street reached via the exit. With these two items of information, they now know where they are on the map, where the exit will take them and how to proceed to their destination. Reading the map is done here in such a way that it can be 'checked' by the first tourist's companion. If she makes a mistake (which is easy to do), or if they later find themselves lost, the companion can intervene. The job of remembering the route is thus shared by the two tourists. Together they use the environment to move between the map and a course of activity. The sign in the station is used to link the map with where the station exit leads.

Along with these collaborative advantages of working together, visiting with others is not without its own overheads. With the collaborative 'working out' in this clip there is also an implicit negotiation going on. The two tourists are deciding what they are going to do as well as how. Visiting with others involves considerable co-ordination in this way. The desire to visit different attractions, or simply to see different museum exhibits, means that tourist groups often split up and then need to co-ordinate getting back together. This can present considerable challenges since tourists are highly mobile. It is in these situations that mobile phones become a useful tool, in that calls can be made between individuals or sub-groups.

A more local form of this co-ordination problem also takes place in particular sites where individuals go to different rooms, or different exhibits, and they need to locate their travelling companions. This is particularly the case for tourists with children, since children sometimes run off, and must be carefully watched to see that they come to no harm. In the incidents researchers observed, mothers spent considerable time shepherding children around museums, in particular, collecting all the children together before leaving the museum. For these parents a large part of their holiday was 'managing' the group and making sure that nobody got lost.

A second way in which visits are shared is through meeting other tourists. The standard jokes about holiday romances displays something of how meeting other people is an integral part of many tourist experiences. In part, these opportunities come from the lowered barriers to social contact. Individuals are 'on holiday' from many of their home commitments. The facilities that tourists use, such as hostels, trains and buses, also can also afford social contact. One reason behind these social contacts, and certainly a common conversation topic, is the exchange of stories and advice on where to go and what to visit.

Role of Guidebooks

A second way tourists solve their problems is the use of published information. The two most quintessential tourist publications are the guidebook and the map. These are often used in combination when tourists navigate and find out about what to do in different places and how to get between them. While both have been subject to computerisation, this has had only limited success.

In part, this limited success can be put down to a lack of knowledge about how maps and guidebooks are actually used by tourists. Studying the use of these conventional paper publications can reveal some of the advantages of paper publications and how to better design their digital equivalents. Guidebooks come in many different forms, from free handouts to Michelin and Baedeker guides. One reason why guidebooks are so useful to tourists is that they catalogue, in a structured and relatively standardised form, relevant aspects of the places that tourists visit. They list accommodation (with phone numbers), attractions (with opening times), recommended bars and restaurants, and so on. This standardisation can make strange places feel considerably safer to tourists by reducing their uncertainty.

Guidebooks also offer short 'guides to action . highlighting differences in everyday activities that might cause embarrassment. In use, however, this information needs considerable interpretation-guidebooks need to be 'put in their place'. What the guidebook says has to be combined with other information, in particular information on maps, or advice from locals. Tourists holding a map and a guidebook, and using these in combination.

In particular, guidebooks were collaborative artefacts, conversation would take palce around the guidebook with tourists pointing at the guidebook, and then pointing either at a map or in a direction, so as to link together the establishments being discussed with their position. The tourists go through a number of descriptions of where the house is and what it is like to help them find it with eventually the age helping them to find the house "its probably the old one". These descriptions help the tourists to find the house, along with informing them about what they are visiting.

Even with a map, a guidebook, and the assistance of a local, the tourists need to work the guidebook to 'place' the old house on the street they are actually on, and overcome some of the confusions of streets which change name, the difference between how a street is named on a map and a name that locals use. In this way, tourists take the information held in guidebooks and combine this with information they find from particular places, such as street names or train timetables in a railway station. This is how guidebooks are 'put in their place'.

In designing technologies for tourism also pay attention to a second aspect of guidebooks: their physical form. Pages in guidebooks can be easily bookmarked by placing one's fingers into the pages at multiple points in the book, and opening the book on a particular page. While this might seem a trivial operation, it supports jumping between different pages quickly so as to compare and combine information, with the fingers acting as bookmarks. This is important, since much of the work of tourists is this very comparison and combination-as in combining information on maps with descriptions.

Different publications can also be arranged so they are in the visual field at the same time. Conversations over accommodation at the TIC would often take place with the guides laid across the serving desk, with staff helping visitors through the guides to show where different sorts of accommodation in the city were. In this way, the format of the paper guide allowed both staff and visitor to interact around the guide.

Role of Maps

Maps have of course been a well-researched artefact in fields as widespread as cognitive psychology and cultural studies. The specific topic of way-finding has been explored in depth. One finding from these studies is that map users are significantly better at tasks that involve configuration information than those without maps, sometimes better even than local people with years of knowledge of a place. However, perhaps surprisingly, there is little work that has examined the in-situ, non-experimental use of maps.

As Correll and Heth argue, there is a need for work which studies "humans navigating real world routes" since little work has looked at the 'naturalistic' use of maps: how they are used in situ without an experimental task.

Tourists using maps in situations where they did not know exactly where they are going, but only had an idea of a particular area that they were heading towards. This was usually because they believed that they would find something interesting in that area, although they had no specific attraction in mind.

Alternatively, tourists used maps to go towards a specific type of attraction, such as a café, but with no specific café in mind-they would head towards a street where they thought there would be cafés. Tourists also often only had a rough idea of where they were, and would use a map to locate or orient themselves so as to head in a 'roughly correct' direction, rather than along a specific route. So, in using a map, tourists might not know where they were, might have little idea about their orientation, might not know where they were going, and might even be unsure about what they were looking for.

So, map use is often less about explicit route planning and more about wandering a city in a 'roughly correct' manner. The routes that tourists used were more directional than specific, with tourists frequently stopping en route, using the map to find the direction to walk in, and then setting off again.

A second feature of map use is their combination with guidebooks. A key aspect of this is how tourists combine characteristics and geography in an attempt to simultaneously solve the problems of where things are and what things there are. One way of doing this that researchers observed exploits the 'ocial zoning' of cities. As any frequent visitor will know, one of the most effective ways to find a restaurant in an unfamiliar city is to simply wander around a central area.

Although by no means a perfect way of finding particular amenities, walking around exploits the tendency of certain facilities (such as bars and restaurants) to be clustered in particular area. In this way, one can also judge establishments by their appearance and menu, as one walks past. These 'clusters' are exploited in tourists' use of maps. When choosing where to go to, it is often safer to pick an area with more than one potential facility.

Researchers observed tourists heading towards a 'restaurant zone' of a city, often with one restaurant in mind, but with the flexibility to go elsewhere should that restaurant prove to be busy or unsuitable. By combining maps and guidebooks, tourists can look for 'clusters' of facilities in particular areas and go towards these particular areas rather than (or in addition to) heading towards a specific establishment. This is not to say that maps are never used for working out how to get to specific places or attractions, but observations showed some of the problems that tourists had in doing this.

Following a route on a map involves considerable interpretation as one moves around a city. A tourist has to link between the map and what they see of streets and landmarks. When staff in the tourist information centre gave directions, they combined two different methods. One set of directions was given by drawing a line on a map-a portable and abstract version that can be used by a tourist to find their destination. Staff combined this with 'howing' in physical space where the destination was and how to get there: saying "it's behind us on Argyle Street" while using an arm movement to point in a specific direction.

A last point about maps' use concerns how they are frequently read in advance of getting to the place the map describes. This was a common use of maps researchers observed. A major aim of using a map is to learn about a place sufficiently that one can get around without using a map, learning about a place by looking at where the streets go, the names of the streets and potential landmarks.

Applications of Technologies

Although tourism presents a number of barriers to introducing new technology—in particular the need for devices to be sufficiently mobile—tourists have already adopted many new technologies, e.g. the web, mobile phones and digital cameras. This suggests that there are opportunities for new tourist systems which fit tourist practice. An important part of tourism is sharing the visit with others.

One problem that tourists face is co-ordinating their activities while they are separated—in particular getting groups back together again. One application that would assist this is a handheld- or phone-based system that allowed tourists to communicate their location to each other. So, if a group splits into two, they could choose to 'tie' their locations together so that each subgroup would be able to see where the other was.

'Tying' in this way could support synchronous awareness without running into difficult privacy problems. In addition, technology could support tourists showing the routes they took and things they did when they meet up again. This could allow them to make recommendations to their companions and also to other tourists who they meet. These ideas are developing in the City system, a system that supports co-visiting between PDA users in different location, along with web and VR users in other locations. This system allows a tourists' visit to be shared with others over the Internet.

Each user can see where others are, communicate over an audio link, use hypermedia related to their locations in the city centre, and share information about their visit. A second aspect of sharing visits is collaboration between tourists who do not know each other. One recommendation here is for technology to support sharing comments and reviews on different tourist attractions.

However, it is important here to make this an interactive experience between tourists; exchange of information is as much about meeting other tourists as it is exchanging information. This could be supported by using public machines or message walls where tourists can meet as they exchange information.

Electronic guides and maps

Electronic guidebooks and maps have been a popular application area for mobile technology, with existing system generally following a similar format to paper guidebooks, augmented with GPS. There are a number of limitations with this design. In particular, the rich affordances of paper guidebooks suggests that to be successful, electronic guidebooks must offer compelling advantages over their paper equivalents. Simply copying content into an eBook is unlikely to be successful if that content is much harder to use.

One innovation that electronic guidebooks could support is in making connections between where attractions are and what they are. Electronic guidebooks should expliclty support the comparison of information, allowing users to quickly move between related pieces of information. Partly due to the limited screen size, mobile systems seldom offer this feature.

Pocket internet explorer, for example, only allows the user to load one web page at a time. One solution to this could be to produce paper maps which are designed to be used with an electronic guidebook. This would remove some of the disadvantages of the small screen by allowing users to juxtapose the PDA and the map in their visual field. In addition, by using the cameras increasingly common in devices, users could point out areas of interest on the map in a way that was apparent both to the system and to one's friends, triggering on-screen display of information.

Mapping systems could also support more of the 'wandering' behaviour of tourists; for example, showing at a glance whether a tourist is going in the right direction rather than simply displaying a pre-determined route. Indicators could show close by attractions, cafés, areas or main streets to support surreptitious discovery. These sort of representations move beyond supporting wayfinding to supporting the broader range of tasks which tourists undertake when navigating.

So, such a representation would support going between one shopping district and another, while looking for a café. In cases like this it is not the exact route that is important, although walking in the right direction is, but a more general sense of learning about the city as one wanders around.

Tourism Planning

Planning is necessary for tourism to develop in a way that is beneficial, sustainable, and not detrimental to the environment, culture, and community. Integrate tourism planning into your overall community planning. In communities with some tourism, development efforts often begin with an existing organisation such as a chamber of commerce, retail association, or economic development group. The organisation may provide initial leadership to planning efforts. Leadership may also come from tourism businesses, individuals, or elected officials. Planning will help community set goals for tourism and provide guidelines for development. Steps are given below:

Define tasks and roles: The committee should begin its work by deciding who will lead it and how tasks will be assigned and completed. You'll also need to establish a funding source for the planning process. In most communities, funding is provided through an existing organisation such as the chamber of commerce or economic development group. Or, your committee may seek funds from local government or from regional or state granting resources.

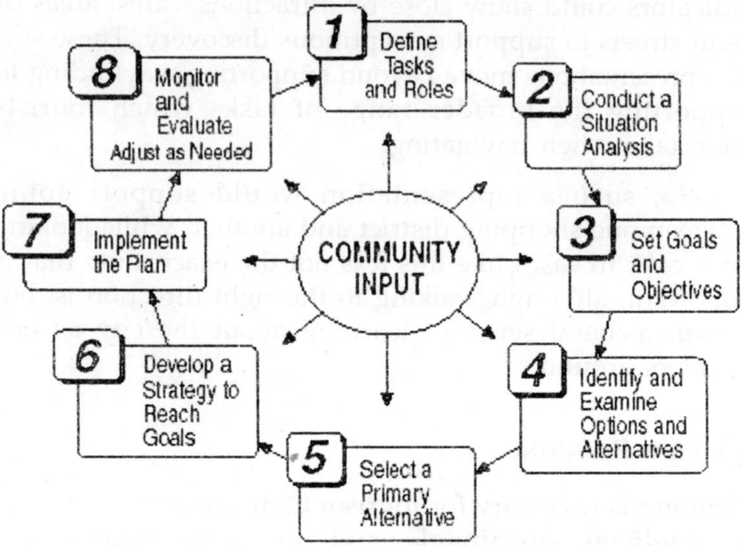

Figure 1. The Community Tourism Planning Process

Next, determine your time line. This will help you get active participation, generate community support, and show results. Communities just starting the process can expect to spend up to two years to create and begin implementing a tourism development plan. The sample time line provided in the preface can help you.

Conduct a situation analysis: The situation analysis is the research aspect of planning. It involves gathering information about community resources, current and potential target markets, and your competition. You need to inventory and objectively assess the quantity and quality of what you have to offer in order to focus tourism development effectively. An important part of your situation analysis should be an overview of trends in external "environments" (Figure 2) that might influence your tourism development efforts.

You will also want to identify and consider tourism trends. For local tourism trends, consult regional and state tourism organisations. For international trends, consult the World Tourism Organisation, World Travel and Tourism Council (WTTC) and Travel Industry Association of America (TIA). Assessments of existing attractions and services as well resident and business attitudes toward tourism is a key part of your situation analysis.

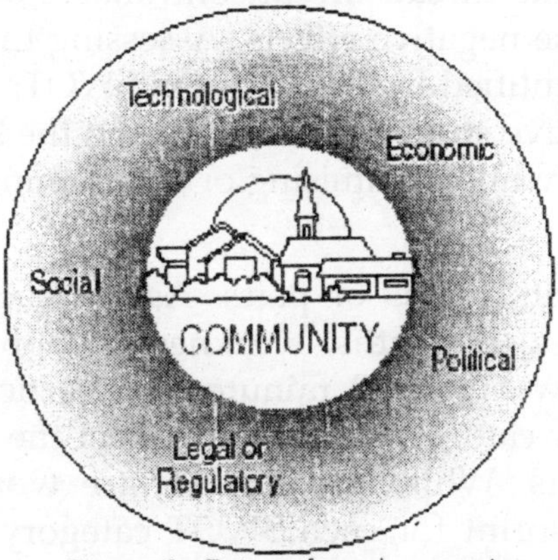

Figure 2. External environments

The situation analysis should also include a profile of the current visitor market, estimated numbers of tourists visiting your community, and the economic impact. Visitor profile information includes:

- an average of the total tourist visitation (preferably by season)
- estimates of daily and total expenditures by visitors
- demographic information (age, education, income, residence)
- trip-specific information (activities, attractions visited, accom-modations, purpose of trip, satisfaction levels).

Economic profiles are useful in determining what role tourism plays in the community's overall economy (e.g., jobs, personal income, number of businesses, tax revenues).

Finally, identify the internal strengths and weaknesses and external opportunities and threats for the community. Internal strengths are resources or capabilities that help achieve stated goals.

Internal weaknesses are deficiencies in resources or capabilities that may prevent you from achieving your goals. Opportunities are outside factors that may be beneficial, while threats are uncontrollable outside factors that may cause negative effects. Assessing these elements, frequently identified by the acronym SWOT, will help you develop effective strategies that focus on the strengths and opportunities while minimising or overcoming weaknesses and threats.

Divide into teams or pairs. Assign each one of the four categories (strengths, weaknesses, opportunities, or threats). Allow about 20 minutes for participants to list things in their categories that may affect the community's tourism efforts. While participants are working, post a piece of newsprint for each SWOT category on the wall. At the end of the 20 minutes, ask participants to call out their responses. List them on the newsprint, consolidating similar responses as appropriate. When finished, discuss the findings and implications.

Set goals and objectives: Setting goals and objectives means stating clearly what tourism will bring to the community. Goals are the broad statements about the community's vision for tourism. They establish long- and short-term targets you hope to achieve as a result of tourism development. Goals may relate to economic, social, or environmental needs. Some examples:

– to create long-term sustainability for natural, cultural, and social resources

- to identify and create partnerships within the region
- to create job opportunities and economic benefit
- to preserve local culture and indigenous arts.

These are then translated into objectives. Objectives explain how you will achieve the goals. They address the concerns and strengths inherent in the goals. Good objectives are clear, concise, measurable, and include a specific action within a set time frame.

Identify and examine options and alternatives: Prioritise your goals and objectives according to the internal and external factors you identified through the situation analysis. Then, using your goals and objectives as a guide, generate a list of options and alternatives for tourism development projects and strategies. This is the time for creative thinking and brainstorming. There is no single "right" alternative. Next weigh alternatives according to the opportunities and potential for success they offer in achieving your goals. Consider resources, time lines, market trends, and community needs.

Goals and objectives will evolve and become more focused as your involvement with tourism and tourism planning grows. For example, in the early stages of tourism development, goals may involve establishing organisational structures and collecting information. Selecting goals that produce short-term success might be an effective strategy for building community support early in your development program. There are many methods to identify and prioritise goals. The nominal group process is a method that allows everyone in a group to have input.

Select a primary alternative: The primary alternative is simply the one(s) that you decide to move forward with. There is no "right" alternative.

Develop a strategy to reach goals: The selected alternative will now guide the development of strategies and specific actions to fulfill the goals and objectives.

Implement the plan: Now that you have drafted a plan, it's time to implement it. Follow through with your planned strategies.

Monitor and Evaluate: Monitoring and evaluation of your efforts is critical. It allows you to measure how well you are meeting your goals, and to make adjustments if necessary. Evaluation will help you identify what is or isn't contributing to the progress of your tourism efforts.

Evaluation must be continual to be effective. Build evaluation measures into each effort from the beginning. Establish measures to evaluate quantity and quality of outputs, time lines, and the effectiveness of the selected alternative. Regular monitoring and evaluation enables you to identify weaknesses or problems so that corrections can be made before they become unmanageable. Regular monitoring also provides a basis for comparison, and for forecasting future trends.

Tourism in Developing Countries

Tourism is a potential source of growth and development in poor countries. It is a major world industry. It is growing faster in the developing world than elsewhere. Tourism makes a substantial contribution to their GDP and is a higher share of exports there than in OECD countries. Many of the countries in which tourism is important are among the poorest and least developed in the world.

Tourism data are collected and analysed by organisations such as the World Tourism Organisation (WTO/OMT) and the World Travel and Tourism Council (WTTC), while crosssectoral data on trade flows are collected by the United Nations Conference on Trade and Development (UNCTAD) and Balance of Payments data are produced by the International Monetary Fund (IMF). The most limited definition of tourist services is that of the World Trade Organisation (WTO), which includes only hotels and restaurants, travel agencies and guides. This definition, based on producing sectors, is designed to cover services provided internationally which may be regulated (and therefore which need to come under the General Agreement on Trade in Services—GATS) and which are not included in other categories.

While these are a major component of tourism, and for some purposes the question of what is regulated internationally will be important, the WTO definition clearly excludes a great many activities which are commonly purchased or used by 'tourists' and includes some (restaurant meals or hotel conference facilities for non-visitors, for example) which are not. An alternative approach is to measure the activities of particular types of people. This is the basis of the WTO/OMT definition, of spending by people away from their homes. It corresponds to the normal balance of payments definition, of spending by tourists, and to what is measured by most national surveys of tourists. National sources give more detailed data according to their different specialisations.

For some purposes, other types of data (regional data, information about particular activities or data from types of supplier) can supplement these. The international and macro-economic data allow us to compare countries and to compare tourism to other exports or other sectors. The more specific data help us to understand the details of its impact. The international tourism data are built up from information on movements of people and some country data on their spending. International balance of payments data, although some use the same surveys, are based on what is spent, not who spends it.

Since data on services tend to be less accurate than those on trade in goods, tourism and other services data in balance of payments information are often less carefully estimated and checked than in those sources that are dedicated to tourism. Balance of payments data also, of course, exclude data on domestic tourists, an increasingly important part of the sector in many developing countries. The World Tourism Organisation defines tourism as 'the activities of persons travelling to and staying in places outside their usual environment for not more than one consecutive year for leisure, business and other purposes'. This broad definition of tourism is then broken down into six categories according to the purpose of the trip:

1. Leisure, recreation and holidays
2. Visiting friends and relatives
3. Business and professional
4. Health treatment
5. Religion/pilgrimages
6. Other

Tourists can also be divided into international tourists and domestic tourists and into overnight tourists and same-day visitors. Official statistics tend to focus on 'international visitors'. Each classification may be useful for looking at the effects of tourism or at expectations for how it will grow. Business travel, for example, will respond to some factors which are different from those driving leisure travel. Within the conventional understanding of tourism, as leisure trips of days or weeks, there are a range of possible activities, with potentially different impacts on the country by creating different demands on it.

Other distinctions possible are between 'high quality' (in the sense of high spending tourists) and low or between 'high impact' (in either the sense of integrated into the non-tourism activities of the country or in a specifically poverty or environmental sense) and low. Much of the basic infrastructure of all these (accommodation, food, and travel) are the same and therefore a high proportion of the effects, are constant, but not all.

If we are studying 'pending or activity by tourists', not just 'production in the hotel and other tourism sectors', we need to know absolute numbers of tourists, not just estimates of spending, partly because for many supplier industries information on numbers will be the only firm information on which to base estimates of tourism's impact, but also because concern about the environmental and other non-economic impact is often based on the quantity of tourists, not the value of services. We also need to know from which countries they come, because surveys show that different nationalities use different services with different impacts.

The WTO/OMT has done a great deal of work on the refinement of the technical standards used to collect and report the data. However, not all countries are members of the WTO/OMT and the reliability of the data varies from country to country. The most basic statistic is international arrivals. But some countries do not report international arrivals figures and may have no effective mechanism in place for collecting them. Where the figures do exist, they have a number of limitations in assessing the potential significance of tourism for pro-poor growth:

- By definition these do not reflect the strength and significance of domestic tourism.
- National data have limited utility in assessing the importance of tourism in different localities within a country. At the local level there is no standard mechanism available for the collection of data that can inform decision making—hotel occupancy figures are sometimes used as a proxy indicator but are commercially sensitive, time-consuming to collect and under reporting can have tax advantages for accommodation owners.

- Visitor arrival figures focus on volume rather than value. It is the amount of time each tourist spends in any location and the amount of money he or she spends on accommodation, transport and other goods and services as well as the overall volume of tourists that determines the economic impact that will be felt. Even where figures on average daily spend and in-country tourism expenditure are calculated however, they do not generally provide any information about the potential for pro-poor tourism unless this is specifically analysed (e.g. by focusing on expenditure on goods that are, or could be, produced locally).
- Figures on visitor numbers often say little about the potential of the industry for pro-poor development. In West Humla, Nepal, for example very small numbers of tourists have a significant impact on local livelihoods.
- The form of tourism and the extent of access to tourists by local people as well as the volume of tourists define opportunities for pro-poor tourism. If tourists arrive in a destination or at an attraction in coaches in the evening, drive straight to the hotel and eat dinner without venturing out, and in the morning pack and depart by coach to visit a cultural monument before driving on to their next overnight stop, there are very few opportunities for poor producers to sell to tourists—what ever volumes they arrive in.

Beyond visitor arrival statistics, a Tourism Satellite Accounting (TSA) system has been developed by the World Tourism Organisation and the World Travel and Tourism Council to estimate the economic value of tourism at the national level. Satellite accounts involve the 'rearrangement of existing information found in the national accounts' in order to estimate the significance of sectors such as tourism that are not accounted for separately. Including the sectors from which tourists or their suppliers buy inputs is logical in examining the nature and tourism.

But it is not legitimate then to use the data to compare the size of tourism to other sectors, because all sectors buy from others, and therefore aggregating sectoral accounts is double- (or multiple) counting. And there are limitations of this system in determining the potential of tourism for pro-poor growth. Aside from the fact that the development and reliability of satellite accounts is heavily reliant upon the quality of the data available, as with visitor arrivals statistics the analysis is generally carried out at the national level and again is not disaggregated at the destination level. Apart from the WTTC approach, other methods for assessing the impacts of tourism tend to be specific to sites, disciplines and researchers.

To fully understand the economic impacts of tourism—on poor people, on the local economy, on the national economy, on national poverty levels -would require a considerable amount of data and a strong methodology. For example, while most effects of an increase in tourism revenue lead, eventually, to an increase in national income, the direct consequences for the distribution of this among households (and within households) are not necessarily the most favourable for reducing poverty. Poverty may decrease for some and even increase for others. An increase in tourism provides a direct increase in income to those who supply the hotels, transport, and other services, and also to the host country through tax revenues and perhaps some service charges.

It then provides indirect increases in income to others through the spending of the direct income. How these changes are distributed will determine the direct impact of tourism on poverty, thus distribution needs to be assessed. A major potential impact comes from how policy makers react to the increases in income: if they have a pro-poor orientation, they can both redistribute the income (through taxes and public spending) and influence its original allocation (e.g. by regulating the types of tourism). If a high share of the increased income is easily available to the government in taxes or easily taxable sectors, then this will increase its ability to act.

Important impacts may occur through physical changes, such as development of infrastructure or use of natural resources, rather than through monetary flows. Therefore data on total tourism impact, information on where this comes from, and consideration of different types of impact, are important.

Merits and Demerits of Tourism

Tourism is not a panacea for economic development. In any context decisions about whether or not tourism–domestic or international–presents viable opportunities for local economic development need to be made locally in the context of the other opportunities which exist for propoor development. As with other industrial sectors, economic growth as a result of tourism development does not necessarily result in poverty reduction. However, tourism does have some advantages over other sectors for delivering pro-poor growth:

- Tourism delivers consumers to the product rather than the other way round. This opens up huge opportunities for local access to markets for other goods and services. Development strategies can enhance potential links to local enterprises and poor producers.
- Tourism does not face tariff barriers, although taxes on air travel can have a similar effect.
- Tourism has considerable potential for linkage with other economic sectors–particularly agriculture and fisheries. Realising these linkages will increase the

proportion of tourism revenue retained in the host country.

- There is a possibility of other types of linkages, for example demand for tourism may add sufficiently to another sector's demand for the combination to provide a basis for introducing local provision of goods or services, e.g. transport.
- It may create initial demand for a good or service that can then itself become a growth sector. In furniture, both Jamaica and Kenya provide examples where furniture firms whose first major market was hotels have developed to provide other consumers.
- Tourism provides opportunities for off-farm diversification. Tourists are often attracted to remote areas with few other development options because of their high cultural, wildlife and landscape values.
- Tourism provides relatively labour-intensive opportunities. It is more intensive than manufacturing and non-agricultural production, although less labour-intensive than agriculture. Its relation to the economy as a whole therefore depends on the relative weights of agriculture and manufacturing: this suggests that it is more likely to be among the most labour intensive sectors of the economy in more developed countries.
- Tourism employs a relatively high proportion of women and can contribute to gender equality. This is, however, less true in developing countries where there is higher male unemployment than in developed countries.
- Tourism can provide poor countries with a significant export opportunity where few other industries are viable. The large number of countries for which tourism receipts are important is evidence that it is a much less demanding sector in terms of initial conditions than many other commodities available to

developing countries. In particular it is more widespread than most agricultural goods, which are its superior in labour intensity. It appears to be more like manufactures, where comparative advantage can be created through a combination of identifying a possible product and creating a specialised demand.

- Tourism products can be built on natural resources and culture, which are assets that some of the poor have.
- The infrastructure associated with tourism development (roads, electricity, communications, piped water) can provide essential services for rural communities which would otherwise be excluded from general infrastructure provision.
- It appears to have relatively few market distortions (either as barriers to entry or trade policy rents). It is particularly sensitive to marketing skills, and also to public sector action (or inaction).
- It has a high income elasticity, and therefore offers a relatively rapidly growing market. Tourism may be expected to perform 'better' than traditional commodities, but not necessarily better than newer exports such as manufactured products.
- It can take different forms, using different inputs, and is therefore available to a wide range of countries (and regions within a country).

At the same time, tourism operates in a market economy and it is subject to international market forces. New destinations emerge and others decline because they are undercut on price or become unfashionable. Countries dependent upon undifferentiated products like the traditional beach, sun, sand and sea holiday are particularly vulnerable. It is relatively easy for tour operators to respond to new opportunities and to switch operations when new destinations come in at a more competitive price. Political instability and security concerns (both domestic and international) also have an impact on tourism.

Countries with significant domestic and regional tourism industries tend to suffer less because these are not affected by declining numbers of air travellers in the face of terrorism fears but internal security issues can also pose a threat. Experience suggests that tourism numbers rapidly recover from terrorism and other events, although not uniformly so. Seasonality is also a notable feature of the tourism industry. Whether tourism is seasonal and whether the seasonality is compatible with agricultural work in particular are likely to affect its pro-poor potential.

Risk is reduced if countries (as well as individual households) are not overly dependent on any one economic sector and in the case of tourism, which is vulnerable to changes in consumer preferences, undercutting from new competitors and recession in originating markets, on any one market. The constraints described above are not unique to tourism but affect many other industries. There are also myths surrounding tourism and the view that tourism is not a worthwhile or 'erious' local economic development strategy is widely held.

To a large extent this view is a result of a failure to recognise the heterogeneity of the industry, but there is also a view that services, and tourism in particular, are not 'erious' development drivers, like agriculture and manufacturing. It is therefore often neglected and subject to policies and priorities designed for other sectors. It is rarely singled out as strategically important, because of either its potential effects as a pole of development for other industries, or its poverty effects.

Therefore, when it comes into potential conflict with the interests of industries that are regarded as national priorities it is tourism whose interests come second. But this 'neglect' is in the context of a much greater acceptance that government has a direct interest in the outcome than would be true for most other predominantly private industries. Most countries have a tourism ministry, even if it is 'tourism and...', not just tourism; most other sectors do not. This puts tourism in an odd, intermediate position; the government has an interest, but no clear perception of what that interest should be.

In contrast to the view that linkages are an important advantage, there is a widely held view that tourism's effects are dissipated by 'leakages'. Unusually high levels of leakage are often cited as one of the major disadvantages of tourism as an economic development sector—for example UNEP (undated) notes levels as high as 70 per cent in Thailand and 80 per cent in the Caribbean. It is clear, however, that the amount of leakage will depend greatly on the form of tourism and the nature of the economy and no standard figure can sensibly be applied across the globe.

In small countries and islands (for example Mauritius), a share of spending goes on imports, but that is equally true of other industries in small countries and islands. In larger and more developed countries (for example South Africa and Jamaica), the shares are much smaller. The most important point about 'leakage' is that it can be used to identify opportunities to create economic linkages within the host country—some of which could have the potential to benefit poor producers. Other criticisms of tourism and the answers include:

- Foreign private interests drive tourism, so it is difficult to maximise local economic benefit: There is no evidence that levels of foreign ownership are higher than for comparable sectors. It is clear that many small enterprises and individual traders sustain themselves around hotels and other tourism facilities and that these SMMEs are not foreign owned. There is often confusion about levels of foreign ownership; local ownership is often masked by franchise agreements and management contracts.

- Tourism can impose substantial non-economic costs on the poor through loss of access to resources (particularly beaches), displacement from agricultural land and social and cultural disruption and exploitation: The losses can be substantial for the poor and minimising them is an important PPT approach. However, many forms of development bring with them disadvantages of this kind.
- Tourism is vulnerable to changes in economic conditions in the originating markets, which cause major swings in the level of tourism in the destinations, and international visitor arrivals are also vulnerable to civil unrest, crime, political instability and natural disaster in the destination: It is not clear that the volatility of export markets for tourism is significantly greater than for other commodities. The destination has some control over civil unrest, crime and political instability.

Five developing countries were in the list of twenty major tourist destinations according to international visitor arrivals statistics in 2000. The volume of arrivals to the top destination in the developing world – China – was only just over 40% of the volume to the world's leading tourism destination – France. That developing countries feature within the list of the top 20 destinations is a relatively recent phenomenon. Only 15 years earlier China, for example, received only 1.3 million arrivals due to its restrictive travel policy.

More established destinations like Mexico have seen very similar growth rates when compared to France, i.e. a doubling of arrivals between 1985 and 2000. Compared to other developing country exports, this gives them exceptional prominence. While developing countries receive 42% of tourism spending they only supply 25% of traditional primary commodities. Developing countries have a surplus on tourism trade (they are net exporters).

Sustainable Tourism

Tourism is also a major generator of wastes. In most tourist regions of developing countries, sewage, wastewater and solid waste disposal are not properly managed or planned. Lastly, tourism is also responsible for a considerable proportion of increased volumes and mileage in global transport and hence the associated environmentally damaging pollutant emissions. The tourism industry has not shown sufficient willingness to (internalise or) compensate the cost of conservation of bio-diversity in, for instance, protected areas, even though they can profit from it.

Tourism is also a powerful agent of change. International tourism acts as a catalyst for the transition from traditional ways of life to so-called modern, Western forms of society. Accordingly, tourism often brings with it the introduction of new behaviour trends and norms. Very often, these are contrary to traditional norms existing in the host community, and can come into conflict with its cultural identity and threaten the traditional value systems there. The problem is that the investors seem to have a lack of cultural understanding of the invested society.

There is a need for an increased awareness that establishment of new hotels etc. will have its consequences on the society and the people who live in it. Tourism has become associated with violation of human rights. Many destination countries have experienced an increase in criminality, prostitution, alcohol and drug abuse as a consequence of tourism. Furthermore, child labour is commonplace in the tourism industry (particularly in the informal sector). According to estimates made by ILO

(International Labour Organisation), between 3 and 19 million children and teenagers work in the tourism sector.

A particularly abominable form of violation of human rights is child slavery and despicable abuse of children taking place in the booming sex industry in many countries. In these countries, tourism has led to an incredible increase in prostitution and also in the exploitation of children. The tourism industry has not yet come up with a general condemnation of these violations of human rights.

The tourism industry is characterised by a high degree of monopoly, which implies a concentration of services and profits into very few big transnational corporations. In many countries, tourism facilities mostly belong to foreigners. Furthermore, in local host communities in many countries a relatively small number of people are involved in the tourism industry in host communities in many developing countries. Very often, there is a lack of qualified manpower in the locality. Hence, most employees are recruited form the big cities, neighbouring countries or even from the country of origin of the investors.

Multiplier effects from tourism are less significant than is often assumed. One reason is that tourism industries purchase most of their inputs (materials, products or services) in their country of origin. As a result, a considerable amount of foreign exchange revenues leaks from the destination countries. The more goods, services, physical capital and human capital a country must import for its tourism services, the higher the leakage. Very often the investors are not approaching the local community to see what it actually can provide.

In addition to this, the General Agreement on Trade in Services (GATS), with its liberalisation of global trade and services, is increasingly undermining the possibilities of individual countries and regions to control their tourism industries and the possible economic gains from tourism. The tourism industry should engage in promoting sustainability as a hallmark for investors. More specifically, investors in tourism should strive to adopt environmentally sound technologies or other measures to minimise the consumption of local ground water.

In the case of water utilisation, such measures might be water saving equipment, desalination systems and collecting and utilising rainwater. Using other types of resources in a sustainable manner is, of course, also crucial. There is a need to use ecological materials and installation of renewable sources of energy systems (solar energy) in all new buildings and new construction.

Furthermore there should be an acceleration of installation or solar/wind power in all public work projects of communities where tourism will be introduced. To prevent or minimise the impact of chemical inputs in soil, water and health, one should start utilising sound ecological methods, including IPM (Integrated Pest Management). Ecological methods need to be applied in all areas utilised for tourism, including in the maintenance of golf courts, gardens and recreational facilities.

Pollution of ground and coastal waters must be prevented, and recommendations must be made (perhaps even legislation) for tourism investors to invest in proper sewage treatment facilities. Appropriate waste disposal systems and ways to separate garbage into organic and non-organic waste should be developed. Organic waste can be composted and possibly reused on hotel gardens or even for local farming. This could be done through collaboration with local residents. Residents could organise themselves and manage the allocated dumping sites, and hence benefit from the system in receiving payment from the hotel for services rendered.

A system to separate the different materials, and recycle some should be in place at the landfill site, thus reducing the waste even further. To avoid degradation of the natural environment, tourism projects can help finance protected areas and safeguard ecologically sensitive regions against further environmental deterioration. By empowering local populations and have them participating in the entire process, sustainability will be ensured as it becomes accepted by and adjusted to the local communities.

Also, a protected area might certainly be a suitable tourist-attraction, where tourists can experience amazing nature and learn about conservation and traditional uses of natural resources in the area. Investors in tourism should always respect the traditional land tenure system in the area and the traditional user-right systems of resources. In regard to this, the communication and consultation with the local communities about resource-use is important.

Tourism investors should not exclude local people from using local resources, and thus take away what they depend on for maintaining their well being. The tourism industry can and must take initiatives to implement that polluter(s) pay a principle (or other forms of internalisation of externalities) for pollution related to tourism operations. This may be organised and carried out through local tax systems or through funds established by the tourism industry for local community development. However, the paid principle should be applied for minor pollution only and should not be developed into a possibility for investors to pay a symbolic fine for imposed irreversible negative impacts on the local environment.

Inaccurate and/or mild environmental legislation in destination countries may possibly attract more foreign investors contributing to fast economic growth and development, but with environmental damage as a consequence. To avoid the dilemma, destination countries will have to choose between economic development and environmental protection international. Multinational enterprises must be committed to follow the environmental standards of their home country should these be stricter than those at the destinations.

The tourism industry should promote projects, which are compatible with the cultural identity of the local population's way of life. Furthermore, the tourism sector should always make sure it acts in accordance with the cultural heritage, and respect the cultural integrity of tourism destinations. This might be accomplished by defining codes of conduct for the industry and hence providing investors with a checklist for sustainable tourism projects. Establishing and developing tourist training programmes could be one way of managing codes of conducts for the tourists.

Here, tourists can be informed and educated about the destination for their travel both before and after their arrival at the site. At the site, tourist information centres can be established through funding from the investor. The information given to tourists should include codes of conduct regarding appropriate behaviour and clothing. It is reasonable to assume that people's offending behaviour is largely a consequence of ignorance rather than intention. Consequently, information and facts about the destination, ways of life, history, cultural heritage is crucial to help tourists get along.

It is an absolute must that tourism investors do not engage in or promote child labour and prostitution. Moreover, it is appropriate that the industry commit themselves to a global campaign against such and any other violation of human rights. Evaluating the sustainability of the tourism development, in regards to cultural and human rights aspects, is highly recommended for those responsible for the tourism projects. As with the case mentioned earlier of preventing environmental degradation, this must be carried out through communication and consultation with the local communities.

By devising local training programmes and establishing educational projects, the tourism industry can ensure that qualified local people are employed in their projects. One should train the local people instead of foreigners to become guides due to their knowledge of the area and resources. The investors should be responsive to the kind of knowledge, abilities and skills found in the local communities. Very often such knowledge and skills are well fitted to be used in tourist activities be it fishing trips, nature trails, souvenir sales or dancing courses for tourists etc.

To constrain foreign exchange leakage, those responsible for the tourism projects should ensure that local inputs are purchased for their projects. A proper examination of local resources available will be beneficial for both the industry and the local residents. Usually, there is considerable local willingness to start producing new products if a market for these products exists. The tourism sector should also adopt measures to prevent foreign exchange leakage by a commitment to re-investment of a fair share of the locally accrued profit.

Initiatives towards more local community development projects should also be appropriate. The tourism industry should promote the establishment of small and medium-sized tourism enterprises which, compared to large-scale hotels etc., have far more moderate impacts on the environment. It is the industry's responsibility to act as a model for communities to show that it is possible to do business whilst protecting natural resources.

The industry should also promote and support local communities to start tourism-related businesses and grant access to low interest loans. It is the responsibility of the tourism sector to ensure total transparency in all transactions, and to prevent tourism projects from being used as projects for laundering illicit money, as well as to refuse using bribes as a means to obfuscate or avoid government rules and regulations. There should be a global boycott against those investors involved in such or other types of illegal activities.

Empowerment of residents at tourist destinations, through local participation, may be facilitated by providing written and legally binding contracts between local people and tourism investors. The contracts will help to avoid broken promises, which too many examples and previous experience prove to be a huge problem. In addition to the mentioned examples (providing proper information for tourists and establishing training programmes for residents), the tourism industry, through for instance the WTTC or the WTO with NGOs in the selection panels, could issue awards especially for sustainable tourism projects as an encouragement for investors.

Within the industry, it is important that both small and large-scale tourism operators are included in the collaboration and that they participate in solving problems related to tourism development. A sustainable development of the tourism industry can only be ensured through participation of all local residents in the destination countries. There is a need for a willingness and ability for the partners to work with this kind of bottom-up approach.

Governments in both destination and countries of origin of tourists and investors are responsible for providing appropriate legislation for sustainable tourism development, and to follow up the tourism projects with sufficient monitoring and appropriate sanctioning. Exchange of successful experiences of sustainable tourism projects is an important factor in this connection. Lastly, an interdisciplinary approach to the problem is necessary:

using local, regional and/or international consultative forums.

Role of Consumers

International tourism plays an ambivalent role in contributing to cultural exchange and sustainable development. On the one hand, it involves a highly buffered, short-term consumer experience of other locales. Tourists can pay and leave, remaining isolated from negative impacts at the local level. On the other hand, tourism may increase recognition of the importance of respecting cultural diversity and developing an identity as a world citizen. It offers opportunities to educate consumers regarding responsible tourism and sustainable development.

Consumers can play a major role in the transformation of societies towards sustainability. While mass tourism in the past was rather producer-driven, the industry today is becoming increasingly consumer-driven. In highly competitive tourism markets, well informed, responsible consumers can put increasing pressure on the industry to behave more responsibly. A number of official proclamations have affirmed every individual's right to rest and leisure including tourism. However, tourism remains an unobtainable luxury for the majority of the world's population.

Tourists primarily originate from affluent industrialised societies where tourism has become a mass phenomenon. Tourists' values, attitudes and behaviour are determined by their social environment, cultural identity and way of life which may be in conflict with local customs. Tourism is heterogeneous in nature, made up of many different types of traveller, seeking a wide range of tourism products. Demand is influenced by irrational factors, e.g. fashion and trends. Demand depends on the availability of time and money, on images, perceptions and attitudes.

Tourists have various needs, desires and motivations, both of a 'push' and 'pull' nature. While household incomes in major touristsending countries are declining, industry sales projections continue to grow, indicating increasing competition. The consumer mind is set on discount prices and "buy now/pay later" options. This poses serious threats, as prices already lag far behind any realistic accounting of tourism costs and impacts. Many of the demand patterns in tourism reflect the unsustainable lifestyles of industrialised consumer societies.

Tourism acts as an agent in exporting these life-styles and consumerist attitudes to less industrialised societies via demonstration effects and modelling. Tourism increases demand for imported consumer goods in the destinations, with detrimental effects on the environment, due to the ecological costs of transport and the high amount of waste generated. Increasing imports also reduce local/national economic gains, due to foreign exchange leakage. The over-consumption of resources by tourists and tourism infrastructure (e.g. the excessive use of water, firewood or food) is incompatible with sustainable development.

The carrying capacity of natural environments is often exceeded with the addition of tourism demands. Tourist demand for resources (land, water, energy, food) may also compete with the needs of local people and may increase social inequality, gender inequality and injustice. Tourist transport, especially air travel, is highly energy intensive and causes pollutant emissions. Many tourism activities such as skiing, boating, mountain hiking, motorised water-sports (e.g. jet skies), and trekking represent stress for fragile ecosystems.

Tourists often lack information and awareness about their impact in a different culture and environment, about their impacts on socio-economic and socio-cultural development, and about the environmental costs of tourism. While tourists may be open to learning, they are often unaware of inappropriate behaviour and have little guidance on how to improve them. Others may refuse to adapt to local life-styles (even when informed) insisting on their freedom to behave as they want. While the tourism industry may be willing to improve their products and services, there is a conflict between the industry's pursuit of economic gains and social and environmental responsibility.

The industry lacks information on the requirements of sustainable tourism and on how to integrate economic forces with environmental and social requirements. Tourists shopping for escapism generally abide by one fundamental consumer ethic: receipt upon payment. Consumer advocates may intervene where inferior customer service is delivered. However, the sustainability of corporate practices is self-regulated. This conflict of interest within the industry, and consumers' low awareness of tourism impacts, have led to a widespread abuse of 'green' labeling.

The mass media, especially television through films and reports about events, sights, etc. in other parts of the world, are increasingly influential on travel decisions and consumer behaviour in the destinations. However, these programmes often serve primarily as advertisements, painting images of destinations, rather than providing relevant information for potential travellers. There is a lack of reliable and appropriate (e.g. age and gender segregated) research data on the determinants of tourist demand, motivation and behaviour.

Few countries, whether tourist-sending or tourist-receiving, collect such data that are helpful under sustainable development criteria. Most studies of tourist behaviour focus on mainstream markets or market segments, rather than assessing or modelling sustainable alternatives. Governments in many tourist destinations and local communities have little or no information on what to expect from tourism and the incoming tourists, and how to influence and control tourism and guide tourist behaviour; They are controlled by international/global institutions, the industry and the consumers.

Governments of the affluent countries are only beginning to look at the issues of outgoing tourism. They are not yet sufficiently aware of their responsibility and methods to influence tourist behaviour by political and legal guidelines/criteria and appropriate planning and policies. Trade unions have fought successfully for shorter working hours and more vacation. However, they need to take more responsibility for helping to create a leisure industry that is more sustainable. Consumer behaviour can and must be influenced by:

- Fighting unsustainable forms and aspects of tourism, at the various levels, by sanctioning unacceptable behaviour and discouraging inappropriate consumer behaviour.
- Promoting responsible and sustainable patterns of behaviour, at the various levels, by promoting best practises and encouraging responsible consumer behaviour. There are different types of instruments and remedial measures available:
    a) Legal measures (rules, regulations, sanctions);
    b) Market based instruments, such as taxes to influence market prices;
    c) Promotion of and (financial) support for best practice;
    d) Industry self-monitoring/codes of conduct;
    e) Information, education and research.

3

Components of Tourism Products

Though there are many definitions for tourism, it could be simply defined as a "travel and stay of a non-resident". In order to travel to a particular area there must be a reason. For example a person may travel for leisure, business, visiting friends and relatives, health, education etc. He/she chooses a destination for one or the other reason. Transport is necessary to travel and accommodation to stay at the destination. So, tourism as an industry has three major components: Attraction, Accommodation and Transport.

In the developed world, today, all these components have reached at their zenith in satisfying their customers' needs aided by modern technology. These components have also came a long way to offer a range of products which suit the needs of multitude tourists around the world, and are still working hard to cater to an ever changing test of them.

Tourism is ranking the top ahead of all other categories of international trade. This is evident from the statistical information compiled from all over the world by WTO (World Tourism Organisation). The number of international arrival shows an evolution from a mere 25 million in 1950 to 657million in 1999. The trend shows a tremendous increase both in the number of tourists and income in the coming years. With respect to the income generated through tourism, in 1998, international tourism and international fare receipts (the receipts related to passenger transport of residents of other countries) together accounted for an estimated US$ 532 billion. This growth of tourism activity clearly marks tourism as one of the most remarkable economic and social phenomena in the world.

Structure of Tourism Industry

The tourism industry is multi-tiered, from those responsible for promotion to those who serve the consumer directly. The industry comprises the following organisational structures:

National Tourism Offices

The main responsibility for promotion of a country's tourism attractions lies with government-funded tourist organisations such as national tourism offices. National tourism offices collaborate with hotels and air carriers to raise finance for destination promotion programmes. They devote much of their overseas efforts to establishing relationships with tour operators and travel agencies. They support new developments or new tours by providing introductions and influencing development plans affecting destinations, as well as legislative or financial policies. They provide support for familiarisation trips, hold promotional events and produce research data.

Tour Operators

Tour operators (outbound providers), tour agencies, and ground operators (in-country or inbound providers) are on the front line of the industry. Tour operators are companies that sell tours to customers, either directly or indirectly through travel agents. Tour operators vary in size. Many of the smaller firms handle specialised markets such as eco-tourism and adventure travel. They provide travel agents with marketing support, for example by offering familiarisation visits for staff members.

Tour operators often go to the same locations, and promotional materials and brochures tend to look alike. Tour companies try to differentiate their destinations with gradations of challenge or price, for example at ski resorts, where accommodations may be more or less luxurious and the skiing may be more or less difficult.Although Tour Operators respond for only about 12 % of global tourism flows, they can help bridge low travel seasons by providing a steadier market, develop new destinations and can help define service and infrastructure needs at local level.

Travel Agencies

In contrast, travel agencies handle a wide variety of travel packages available from tour operators and airlines. In Europe and in North America, a high percentage of tours are marketed to the public through travel agencies. In Europe, travel agencies dominate the supply of holidays and largely determine the information on which most clients base their holiday decisions. Large tour operators select travel agents to represent them on the basis of the agency's productivity. Local individuals, national groups, international enterprises or any combination of the three may own travel agencies.

Although website sales to individual consumers are on the rise, generally, travel agencies sell tours from brochures and the computerised reservation systems of major tour operators. Therefore, brochures are pivotal to the business. However, so many brochures are available, that travel agencies simply cannot stock the full range. What winds up on their display cases is a function of the commissions paid by tour operators, the efficiency of their reservation systems, and the strength of the business relationship.

In general, travel agencies are not prepared to offer information from outside the core package tours that they sell. Related to tour operators are ground operators, or in-country operators who handle logistics or ground operations. They handle tourist groups from the moment of arrival off the plane or boat, until departure. They can also sell tours in the countries in which they are operating. Ground operators are mostly based in capital cities and are usually welleducated host nationals who can speak several languages.

In some countries a key to increasing a site's popularity is to have reliable ground operators working with tour operators in Europe or North America. A scarcity of ground operators, while unlikely to deter independent travellers, may discourage consumers of organised tours who depend on their services.

Tourism Markets

The tourism market comprises three general classifications:

- the independent travel market,
- the speciality activity market, and
- the general package-holiday market.

Independent travellers are not part of organised groups but travel alone or in small groups of friends. They travel either out of a general interest or because they want to practise a certain activity in a new and different environment. Most independent travellers are young, adventurous, willing to use rustic accommodations, eat traditional foods, and take public transport. Independent travellers get much of their information on a tourist destination either from friends who have visited the area or through guidebooks, newspaper and magazine articles, or, increasingly, from the Internet.

Many in the tourism industry discount these tourists because they tend to travel cheaply, falling into the category of the budget-conscious "backpacking crowd". In reality, independent travellers are "explorers" who are often responsible for popularising a destination. Their financial input is often enough to enable local businesses to expand and improve rustic accommodations for more demanding tourist groups. Such travellers, often young, are more willing to use local goods and services, and interact more with the community outside the supervision of an organised tour, which unfortunately may cause negative social impacts.

Speciality tourism firms organise trips for clients wishing to participate in a specific activity such as bird-watching, wildlife viewing, photography or archaeological, historical and cultural tours. Also in this category are adventure travel firms offering activities such as backpacking/ trekking, white water rafting, kayaking, canoeing, rock climbing and sport fishing. Other speciality firms organise field research trips for scientists. These firms attract groups of paying volunteers who sign up to work as field assistants on projects such as archaeological digs and wildlife monitoring programmes.

In addition, this market includes organisations and universities with special interest travel programmes. For example, the World-wide Fund for Nature and many museums organise tours for their members. These tours generally help to raise funds for a particular cause or project. These groups generally sub-contract to other tour operators to handle the travel arrangements. Speciality tour operators commonly use host-country ground operators for in-country logistics. These national firms, based in the country in which the tour is operating, provide all services (transportation, hotel accommodations, guides, etc.) from arrival to departure.

Some speciality firms in North America and Europe handle ground operations in a foreign country for themselves, but they tend to be exceptions to the rule. Managers should be aware that many speciality companies are small and go in and out of business rapidly. The general package-holiday market attracts groups wishing to see an area and its culture but without a specific interest in a defined activity or subject matter. These tourists tend to be interested in general sightseeing and shopping, and may be interested in cultural attractions such as museums, ruins or other well-known or documented historical sites.

Tourists in this market tend to want the standard services and amenities offered by most general tours. They will probably not be satisfied with the services that a rural community can offer; more often than not, general international tour groups want comfort, ease of access, security and more upscale accommodations and food.

Tourism is more than ever before divided into market segments defining different types of experiences. Specialised holidays cater to people's particular interests, such as sailing, bird-watching, photography or archaeology. Markets or market segments have been developed around the different activities. Specialised holidays have become so popular that whole new categories of travel have emerged, including ecotourism, adventure travel, heritage tourism and cultural tourism. A trek in the Himalayas is now likely to be considered adventure travel, and a week visiting cultural sites in India as cultural tourism.

Eco-tourism is one of the most frequently cited categories of the "new" tourism: It is defined by the International Ecotourism Society as, "responsible travel to natural areas that conserves the environment and sustains the well being of local people." A number of activities have been labelled eco-tourism, including bird- and whale-watching, helping scientists conduct conservation research, snorkelling off coral reefs, game viewing and nature photography. Eco-tourism is linked to and overlaps with heritage tourism and cultural tourism. Surveys show that eco-tourists tend to be young and highly educated, with professional and managerial occupations.

Eco-tourism trips tend to be longer, with fewer people in the typical tour group. Researchers report that eco-tourists are more likely to use small independent hotels, as opposed to mass tourists, who tend to stay at chain hotels. As would be expected, the eco-tourist is interested in a more natural environment, preferring less crowded destinations that are off the beaten track and that offer challenging experiences. At the site level, the demands of eco-tourists and mainstream tourists may overlap and be difficult to differentiate.

Some eco-tourists, for example, may demand condominiums, not campgrounds, for lodging. People on a bird-watching cruise to Patagonia could be considered eco-tourists but may have demands similar to those of tourists on an expensive Caribbean islands cruise. In practice, eco-tourism connotes a travel ethic, promoting conservation behaviours and certain economic policies. Examples are, an emphasis on low-impact techniques for viewing wildlife and a preference for hiring local guides.

Adventure tourism includes a wide range of outdoor activities: Adventure tourists engage in activities that are physically challenging and sometimes dangerous, or perceived to be so. Examples are sports such as trekking, mountaineering, white-water rafting and scuba diving. Adventure tourism does not necessarily require expensive facilities and infrastructure, but it does require good organisation, guides, transportation services, basic accommodation in the field, and opportunities for more comfortable accommodation at the end of the tour. Adventure travel is a rapidly growing sector of the speciality tourism market.

Cultural tourism is frequently used to describe certain segments of the travel market: It may be associated with visits to historical, artistic and scientific or heritage attractions. The World Tourism Organisation (WTO) has two definitions of cultural tourism. In the narrow sense, cultural tourism includes "movements of persons for essentially cultural motivations such as study tours, performing arts and cultural tours, travel to festivals and other cultural events, visits to sites and monuments, travel to study nature, folklore or art, and pilgrimages."

In the broader sense it is defined as "all movements of persons, because they satisfy the human need for diversity, tending to raise the cultural level of the individual and giving rise to new knowledge, experience and encounters." Because culture is subjective, definitions of cultural tourism tend to be either too wide or too narrow, limiting their practical use in the field.

Heritage tourism is a broad category that embraces both eco-tourism and cultural tourism, with an emphasis on conserving natural and cultural heritage: It is a category or market segment that includes visits to historic sites, museums and art galleries, and exploring national and forest parks. Heritage tourism, because of the large number of activities it covers, is difficult to define and measure. In recent years city planners interested in urban regeneration have adopted the term to describe many tourism programmes, a strategy that has received support from business and banks.

Many other tourism terms reflect environmental ethics and local interests. Environmental preservation concerns have given rise to what is known as green tourism, conservation-supporting tourism, and environmentally aware or environmentally sound tourism. Generally, such tourism favours minimal environmental impact and emphasises concern over environmental issues. Urban and rural tourism categories have also been created. However, since few countries have made the distinction, quantification has been difficult.

Different Types of Tourist

Seeking definitions that would be more useful in practice, researchers have concentrated on tourists' behaviours and preferences. Definitions and their related market segments, such as adventure travel or cultural tourism, tend to group people into broad categories based on a range of activities. These definitions and activities necessarily overlap, making it difficult at the site level to differentiate between types of tourism.

For example, eco-tourism and heritage tourism combine aspects of both culture and nature, as do most speciality tours. So for instance, trekking in the Himalayas is considered an adventure travel activity, but most trekkers visit Buddhist or Hindu cultural sites at the same time. Bird-watchers visit archaeology sites and frequently engage in trekking.

The broad definitions of the international markets are too comprehensive to be used for site-specific decisionmaking. An effective way of addressing this overlap for research, policy and site management purposes is to classify tourists according to their motivations, behaviours and desired experiences. Researchers have developed several categories of tourist behaviours and preferences. For example, tourists may be classified according to the intensity of experiences they are seeking or the ruggedness of the conditions they desire or will accept, including the kind of accommodations expected. Thus:

- Hard-core tourists join tours or groups travelling specifically for educational purposes and/or to take part in environmental or cultural projects, such as wildlife monitoring.
- Dedicated tourists want to visit protected or cultural areas and understand local natural and cultural history.
- Casual tourists consider natural and cultural travel as an incidental component of a broader trip.

Another system that is useful for classifying preferences differentiates between "hard-class" and "soft-class" travel. This classification relates to the ruggedness factor, mostly concerning the degree of challenge involved and the comfort level of accommodations. These categories include:

- A hard-class experience that is physically difficult with an element of danger. For example, it may require walking miles into the back country, climbing a technically difficult mountain, or sleeping in rudimentary shelters.
- A soft-class experience means lower risk and more luxurious accommodations. For example, a tented safari may involve physically challenging conditions while offering amenities such as gourmet meals and comfortable transport.

ACCOMMODATION

The concept of carrying capacity addresses the question of how many people can be permitted into an area without risk of degrading the site and the visitors' experience of it. It has generally been broken down into three categories: physical, ecological and social.

- Physical carrying capacity, called "facility carrying capacity" by the World Tourism Organisation, mostly has to do with available space the number of beds available to overnight guests, how many cars would fill a parking lot, how many campers in a campground, seats in a theatre, and so on. Concomitant to such considerations is the question of fresh water and electricity supply.
- Ecological carrying capacity is the degree to which an ecosystem is able to tolerate human interference while maintaining sustainable functioning. A curvilinear relationship may exist between use and impact at a site, and wide variations in ecosystem resistance and resilience make ecological carrying capacity difficult to predict.
- Social carrying capacity is psychological and socio-cultural and refers to the limit beyond which the number of people in an available space would cause a decline in the quality of the recreational experience and the users' satisfaction. Overcrowding is a prime example of a socio-cultural carrying capacity issue. Since different user groups have different social expectations and because of complicated issues related to cultural resistance and resilience, this factor is also difficult to assess.

Monitoring Issues

The shift to LAC-type methodologies has highlighted the importance of monitoring: Managers need to know when desired conditions are being threatened, for example, with increasing water pollution in a stream or when waiting lines become too long at an entrance. A well-developed and regular monitoring programme can provide resource managers with data to justify sometimes controversial actions such as limiting the number of people allowed into a site at a time. Monitoring visitors' likes, dislikes and travel patterns, as well as their impacts, can help identify and justify needed actions in the changing tourist industry.

The most difficult aspect of monitoring is ensuring that it is carried out on a regular basis: Managers are faced with many pressing day-to-day problems and often have little time or desire to carry out monitoring exercises. However, monitoring is effective only if it is done regularly; if it cannot be sustained, its usefulness is severely limited. well as their impacts, can help identify and justify needed actions in the changing tourist industry.

Many types of monitoring procedures are possible depending on the level of accuracy desired and available resources: For example, soil erosion on a nature trail can be measured in several ways. One method is to identify eroded sections by walking the trail and counting variations in width, perhaps caused when visitors seek to avoid muddy sections. Another is to establish permanent checkpoints at problem areas along the trail to measure soil loss.

Each approach has advantages and disadvantages. Examining trail conditions in a general fashion does not give a precise measurement, but provides a good overview. On the other hand, while permanent monitoring plots will provide a more accurate measure of soil loss, the method is more expensive and time-consuming. The differences in approach can also be illustrated with bird population counts.

One inexpensive method systematically records the number of bird sightings by local guides. A more accurate but expensive method of tracking population changes involves catching specimens with nets or setting up a transect, or a fixed corridor along which species are counted on a regular basis. Fewer options exist for monitoring socio-economic conditions such as crowding and community attitudes. Most socio-economic information is obtained through questionnaires or interviews, work that is labour-intensive and time-consuming.

A monitoring procedure should be selected on the basis of what questions need to be answered and how much time and funding is available to carry out the work.At the Great Barrier Reef in Australia, travel distances made monitoring each campsite in detail prohibitively expensive. Managers decided instead on the more cost-effective tactic of sampling a cross-section of camping areas. Finally, all monitoring programmes should be evaluated to determine how well they measure the indicators. This evaluation should also determine how large a measured change must be for management to be confident that it is the result of visitor impact and not errors in data collection.

Monitoring of historic monuments must take into account values of integrity and authenticity: Indicators of structural or engineering conditions cannot translate into an overview of the complete health of a site since they do not reflect values of integrity or authenticity. While it is important to monitor the use of a facility and visitor satisfaction, experts say more monitoring is needed to measure the effectiveness of communicating a site's historic significance.

Simple monitoring systems with built-in incentives may be the most feasible and best approach for a sustainable programme: Given the many difficulties in sustaining a monitoring programme, consideration for the practical needs of site managers, tourism officials and private operators will improve chances of success. Monitoring can be incorporated into maintenance activities, or local guides can carry out monitoring functions. Tour operators interested in tracking visitors' preferences may be prepared to finance surveys. Government officials may also want the information because it can directly affect national tourism initiatives. Experience has shown that a simple monitoring programme is better than none at all and can be more effective than costly ones.

For example, with historic buildings and other built cultural sites, a simple report with notes and photos has been found to be far more useful than detailed, item-by-item reports on conditions. Short, simple reports covering general problems and a few specific problem areas allow staff to determine which properties require the most attention and to offer guidance to their agencies.

Site staff are given a checklist of items to monitor. The monitor notes any changes made to the property since the last visit, any problems related to general maintenance or repair, any potential problems, and any contemplated changes and repairs. Four categories are monitored: exterior, interior, the area around the building and the rest of the grounds.

Marketing Plan

One of the most important steps a business or community can take to improve the effectiveness and efficiency of their marketing efforts is to develop a written marketing plan. This plan will guide their marketing decisions and assist them in allocating marketing resources such as money and personnel time. The plan should include:

- the overall business objectives-what you want to accomplish;
- an assessment of the market environment-what factors may affect your marketing efforts;
- a business/community profile-what resources are available,

- market identification (segmentation)--the specific groups or clientele most interested in your product;
- the marketing objectives for each segment;
- the marketing strategies (or mixes) for different markets you target-the best combination of the 4 Ps (product, price, place, promotion) for each segment;
- an implementation plan-how to "make it work;"
- the marketing budget-how much you have to spend; and
- a method for evaluation and change.

Marketing Strategy

The marketing strategy, or mix, should be viewed as a package of offerings designed to attract and serve the customer or visitor. Recreation and tourism businesses and communities should develop both external and internal marketing mixes for different target markets.

External Mix

The external marketing mix includes product/service, price, place/location, and promotion.

Product: Earlier we said the principal products that recreation and tourism businesses provide are recreational experiences and hospitality. The factors that create a quality recreational experience often differ among people. A quality experience for one skier might include an uncrowded, steep slope. To another it might be a good restaurant and a chance to socialise.

Decisions on what facilities, programs and services to provide should be based on the needs and desires of the target market(s). They should not be based on the preferences of the owner/manager or necessarily on what the competition is providing. Recognise that a recreational/tourism experience includes five elements: trip planning and anticipation; travel to the site/area; the experience at the site; travel back home; and recollection. Businesses should look for ways to enhance the quality of the overall experience during all phases of the trip. This could be accomplished by providing trip planning packages which include maps, attractions en route and on site, and information regarding lodging, food and quality souvenirs and mementos.

Recreation and tourism businesses should also view their service/product in generic terms. Thinking of products/services in this manner helps focus more attention on the experiences desired by customers and also the facilities, programs and services that will produce those experiences. For example, campgrounds are the business of providing recreational "lodging" not just campsites to park an RV or set up a tent. Marinas should provide recreational "boating" experiences, not just slippage.

Location and Accessibility/Place: Too many tourism businesses and communities fail to recognise their role in improving travel to and from their areas. They focus instead on servicing the customer once they arrive at the site/community. A bad experience getting to or leaving an R/T site can adversely affect a person's travel experience. Ways to help prevent this include:

- providing directions and maps;
- providing estimates of travel time and distances from different market areas;
- recommending direct and scenic travel routes;
- identifying attractions and support facilities along different travel routes; and
- informing potential customers of alternative travel methods to the area such as airlines and railroads.

Potential businesses should also carefully assess alternative locations for:

- distance and accessibility to target markets;
- location of competitors with respect to target markets;
- modes of travel serving the area; and
- other attractions and activities that might induce travel to the area.

Pricing: Price is one of the most important and visible elements of the marketing mix. When setting prices it is important to take into consideration all of the following:

- business and target market objectives;
- the full cost of producing, delivering and promoting the product;
- the willingness of the target market to pay for the product or service you provide;
- prices charged by competitors offering a similar product/service to the same target market(s);
- the availability and prices of substitute products/services (for example, campgrounds, motels, and bed and breakfast are all substitutes for lodging);
- the economic climate (local and national); and
- the possibility of stimulating high profit products/services (such as boats) by offering related services (such as maintenance) at or below cost.

When establishing prices, R/T businesses should give attention to pricing strategies which may encourage off season and non-peak period sales, longer stays, group business, and the sale of package plans (combination of room, meals, and recreational facilities).

Promotion: Promotion provides target audiences with accurate and timely information to help them decide whether to visit your community or business. The information should be of importance and practical use to the potential or existing visitor and also accurate. Misrepresentation often leads to dissatisfied customers and poor recommendations. Don't make claims you cannot live up to.

Developing a promotional campaign is not a science with hard and fast rules. Making decisions regarding which type or combination of promotion types to use (personal selling, advertising, sales promotions, or publicity) is not always easy. If, however, you follow a logical process and do the necessary research, chances for success will be improved. It will be necessary to make decisions regarding:

- Target audience—the group you are aiming at;
- Image—that which your community or business wants to create or reinforce;
- Objectives-those of the promotional campaign;
- Budget—the amount of money available for your promotion;
- Timing—when and how often should your promotions appear;
- Media—which methods (television, radio, newspaper, magazine) will most effectively and efficiently communicate your message to the target audience; and
- Evaluation—how can the effectiveness of the promotional campaign be determined.

Internal Mix

Marketing services such as recreation and tourism differ from marketing tangible products. Recreation and tourism businesses must direct as much attention at marketing to customers on site as they do to attracting them. In this respect, internal marketing is important because dissatisfied customers can effectively cancel out an otherwise effective marketing strategy.

The success of internal marketing is dependent on creating an atmosphere in which employees desire to give good service and sell the business/community to visitors. To create such an atmosphere requires the following four important elements:

– *Hospitality and Guest Relations*– An organisation wide emphasis on hospitality and guest relations, including a customer oriented attitude on the part of the owners and managers as well as the employees. If the owner/ manager is not customer sensitive, it is unlikely the lower paid employees will be.
– *Quality Control*– A program which focuses on improving both the technical quality (the standards associated with what the customer receives) and the functional quality (the standards associated with how the customer receives the service). All employees who come into contact with customers should receive hospitality training.
– *Personal Selling*– Training the staff in the selling aspects of the property (business) or community. This also includes rewarding them for their efforts. By being informed about the marketing objectives, and their role in accomplishing those objectives, they can help increase sales.
– *Employee Morale*– Programs and incentives aimed at maintaining employee morale. The incentives can be both monetary and non-monetary.

A customer oriented atmosphere usually results in customers that are more satisfied, do less complaining and are more pleasant to serve. This helps build employee morale, their desire to provide good service and their efficiency.

Budget

Successful marketing requires that sufficient money and personnel time be made available to implement activities comprising the marketing strategy. A marketing budget is a financial plan which shows the total amount to be spent on marketing during different times of the year and how it is to be allocated among alternative activities. Separate marketing budgets should be developed for each marketing mix strategy. The separate budgets should then be aggregated to develop an overall marketing budget.

If the total amount is too great it will be necessary to modify the overall objectives and the target market objectives, narrow down or drop target markets, or adjust marketing mixes. The final budget should be realistic given your objectives. When deciding on a marketing budget, consideration should be given to the job that needs to be done as defined by the objectives. Basing marketing budgets on some percent of sales or what the competition spends usually leads to over spending or under spending.

Decisions should also be based on the costs, projected revenues, and desired profitability of different activities, not just costs alone. Successful marketing activities will generate additional revenues which can be projected based on the marketing objectives (such as increase off season stay by 5%). Although budgets should be viewed as flexible plans, every effort should be made to adhere to them. Revisions in the budget should only be made after careful consideration of the likely impact of the change on the marketing mix and accomplishment of your objectives.

Implimentation

Many well designed marketing plans fail because they are poorly executed. Businesses, agencies, and communities can increase the likelihood of successful implementation if they:

- identify specific tasks which must be accomplished;
- assign people or departments specific responsibility for different tasks;
- provide employees with information on the marketing plan (rationale, objectives, strategies);
- develop time lines and deadlines;
- adhere as much as possible to the budget; and
- regularly monitor and evaluate progress.

Evaluation

It is important that marketing efforts be continually evaluated. This will improve the effectiveness of marketing strategies by quickly identifying differences between actual results and expected performance and determining likely reasons for the success or failure to realise objectives. A framework for evaluation would include:

- *determining which elements of the different marketing mixes are most important to evaluate.* It is rarely possible or cost effective to evaluate all elements;
- *establishing performance standards to compare against actual results.* Marketing objectives, if properly formulated, should serve as performance standards;
- *development of formal and informal methods for collecting data on actual results.* There are many ways different elements of the marketing mix can be evaluated. For example, promotions can be evaluated with money off coupons. Special information request forms, telephone numbers to call or post office box numbers to write to can identify the area the request is coming from. Also, formal (written) and informal (face-to-face)

surveys can be used to determine the promotional material the customer used in planning the trip;

- comparison of results with objectives;
- determination of needed change(s).

Effective Tourism Marketing Program

Step-by-step instructions describe how to inventory attractions, assess current marketing efforts, find existing market research, determine target markets, determine tourist motivators, develop promotional goals, determine campaign themes, find an advertising media, develop public relations and gather the correct data for an evaluation.

Inventory of Attractions and Accommodations: The first step in developing effective marketing plans is to inventory the attractions a community has to offer tourists. A community must know what it has to offer or sell before plans can be laid for marketing the product. These can include natural, manmade, historical, cultural or ethnic, festivals, special events and recreational attractions.

Assessing Current Marketing Efforts: Listing current advertising efforts for all attractions is necessary to assess the present promotional campaign's successfulness, and to develop new campaigns.

Market Research: Market research is an important part of developing a market plan. Several important pieces of information are needed to develop a market plan. These include:

- An inventory of tourist attractions in the area, region, or destination
- Market trends
- Tourist motivations
- Tourist profiles, including expenditures

It helps to review other successful marketing plans, remembering that a marketing plan should meet the individual needs of the area, region or destination for which it was developed. Learning from previous mistakes is a key to developing better programs.

There are two types of research data that can provide this information. The first is primary research gathered through phone calls, surveys, or other interviewing techniques. Secondary data has been compiled by outside organisations. Be careful when using secondary data; confirm the reliability of the source.

Target Market: Trying to appeal to everyone is a common mistake made in marketing. Not everyone looks for the same thing in a destination, and every destination cannot be all things to all people. Target marketing, focusing on a particular segment or segments of the market,allows for a more effective marketing plan. Market research will define the market segments, which will find those tourists most interested in what a community has to offer. Data on past visitors can indicate the type of tourist or the geographic region on which to focus. A target market can be a geographic region, a type of tourist, a combination of the two or any grouping that makes sense.

Determine Tourist Motivators: The fifth step is detemine tourist motivetors. Tourist motivators should be studied once a target market has been defined. Discovering where and why tourists travel is important when focusing advertising. Enticing the tourist to chose a historical destination because of its mystique, or choosing a full-service resort where every need can be catered to requires different motivational factors.

Developing Promotional Goals: Establishing goals provides the basis to determine what a community wants its marketing and promotion program to accomplish. Goals should be well thought out and be measurable, and can also serve as controls. Writing down goals provides directional guidelines. It can be difficult to get feedback on promotional goals, but with specific goals set, an evaluation and feedback plan can be implemented. This will gather the necessary data for the evaluation process, which can determine the successfulness of a community's plans and program.

Determining a Campaign Theme: A campaign theme should emphasise the image aimed at tourists in a given area. Remember, always capitalise on the positive aspects in the area, region or destination. Campaign themes should be developed for a clearly defined target market. For example, New Mexico's promotion, "More to Explore... New Mexico USA," targets nonresidents, and capitalises on the fact that New Mexico is a part of the United States, although many tourists think it is a part of Mexico. A campaign focusing on New Mexico residents, on the other hand, would emphasise what their home state has to offer. It could incorporate a theme of "Travel Close to Home."

Advertising Media: Determining which advertising media to use should not be done until after the target market is identified. Once the market has been determined, the tourist profile of the target market can be matched to the audience profile of specific advertising media. Most advertising media can provide an accurate profile of their audience. Some advantages and disadvantages of various forms of advertising media are listed below.

Newspapers

Advantages	Disadvantages
High reach	High waste factor and inability to target
High geographic concentration	Limitations on creative format
Good frequency	Relatively poor reproduction quality

Tangibility	Clutter
Short lead times	Short life span
Relatively low cost	High cost of national coverage
Ability to communicate detailed information	
Ability to place in most appropriate location	

Magazines

Advantage	Disadvantages
Tangibility	Limitations on creative format
High audience selectivity	Clutter
Good reproduction quality	Low reach
Long life span and good pass-along rate	Low frequency
Prestige and credibility	Low frequency
Ablity to communicate detailed information	Long lead times
	Relatively expensive
	Difficulties in geographic targeting

Radio

Advantages	Disadvantages
Relatively low cost	No visual communications
Audience selectivity	Inability to transmit complex messages or detailed information
High frequency	Short life span
Short lead times	Shared attention

Television

Advantages	Disadvantages
Potentially high reach	High total cost

High persuasive impact	Short life span
Availability of uniform national coverage	Inability to transmit detailed information
Some geographic and demographic selectivity	

Direct Mail

Advantages	Disadvantages
Audience selectivity	Junk mail syndrome and high discard rate
Highly flexible	Relatively high total cost
High level of personalisation	Limitations on creative format
Ability to measure responses	
Low Cost	
Tangibility	
Short lead times	

Outdoor/Transit (Billboards, posters, painted bulletins)

Advantages	Disadvantages
High reach and good frequency	High waste factor and inability to target
Geographic selectivity	Relatively long lead times
Long life span	Inability to transmit complex or detailed messages
Large size	Not prestigious
	Limitations on creative format

Public Relations: Public relations can be an excellent way to promote a community or attraction. Public relations activities are uniquely different from advertising. Advertising is paid, but public relations uses free public exposure to ensure goodwill. Public relations can use radio,television or newspapers. Public relations efforts not only can be used to promote the destination to tourists, but also to promote the community itself.

It can help create a feeling of pride in the community by educating the local community about what it has to offer tourists. This can develop a feeling of pride for the residents when they are asked to describe their community to tourists. Instead of seeing tourists as invaders, they will be seen as an economic boost to the local economy.

Developing an Evaluation Plan: This is the 10th step. An evaluation plan requires detailed planning during the initial stages of a marketing plan. Establishing measurable goals in a marketing plan is the first step in this evaluation. From this step, decide what information is needed to prove or disprove the accomplishment of the goal. If methods to gather the information are established at the beginning, all needed information for evaluation will be available at the end.

One of the most difficult parts of an evaluation is uncovering all the information that is needed, especially if an organised system is not included at the beginning. The second most difficult part is convincing everyone of the importance of such an evaluation. It is the key to the entire marketing plan that says, "Yes, it worked" or "No, it didn't work." An evaluation can show if the wrong audience was targeted or the plan conveyed the wrong message. Evaluation also provides the information needed to improve marketing. Great care should be taken to incorporate an evaluation plan into the marketing plan.

Another important part of an evaluation is the conversion study, which compares the number of inquiries to the number of people who actually visit. The conversion study is conducted by using the list of inquiries generated over the specified time frame, randomly choosing a sample, then performing a follow-up telephone or mail survey. Other information that can be collected along with a conversion study, when it is determined that the inquiring person has actually visited, is:

- Place of residence
- What time of year visited
- Transportation
- Estimated expenditures during trip
- Purpose of trip
- Would you visit again

These questions help establish a tourist profile. Information that needs to be collected for a proper evaluation of a marketing plan is:

- Advertisement cost
- Advertisement dates
- Number of times an advertisement was run
- Advertisement agency costs (if any)
- Media in which advertisement was placed
- Number of inquiries received from each advertisement
- Request fulfillment costs (mailing costs, envelopes, mailing brochures)
- Follow up information

Gathering this kind of data provides information to determine the effectiveness of advertising. When follow-up information on actual visitation and expenditures is obtained, advertising effectiveness can be further evaluated.

- *Number of Inquiries*—The number of people who requested information through the advertisement.
- *Ad Costs*—The cost of placing an advertisement in the advertising media.

- *Ad Cost Per Inquiry*—Ad cost divided by number of inquiries.
- *Request Fulfillment Cost Per Inquiry*—Request fulfillment cost divided by number of inquiries: includes mailing, brochure, and envelope costs.
- *Ad Agency Fixed Cost Per Inquiry*—Ad agency fixed cost divided by number of inquiries.
- *Total Cost Per Inquiry*—Total costs divided by number of inquiries.

Data collection methods should be decided on and in place before any advertising is done. Thus, all needed information will be available when evaluation procedures start. Suggested advertisement monitoring methods include:

- A phone answering script that determines the caller's name, address, phone and type of information requested.
- Coding advertisements so inquiries received are easily tracked to a specific advertisement.
- Monitoring guest registrations for visitor's points of origin.

Funding: Once the marketing plan has been developed, there must be funding to support the implementation of the plan. Learning to budget the expenses that will be incurred with the marketing plan is the first step. Funding sources want to know from the beginning how the money will be spent. Determining how much money to spend is not the hard part; determining where to get the money is. Non-profit organisations such as Convention and Visitors bureaus and Chambers of Commerce may have access to the Cooperative Advertising Program offered through the State Travel and Tourism Department, which provides matching funds. Lodgers' taxes are another source of funding. This money is usually administered by local government. Other funding sources at the local level are member fees, banks and utilities.

Tour Operators

These people are solely into marketing the concept of travel. They plan and `sell' trips to individuals and groups. They book tickets—for air, rail, sea or road travel, arrange hotel reservations or guest houses, hire taxis etc. Besides domestic, all travel agents undertake international bookings and special business tours or conferences. Tour operators are mostly into travel management. They organise and put together package trips and holidays. These could be for incoming tourists from abroad or outbound tours or even domestic travellers. They can offer special packages, which could include such diverse attractions as deep-sea diving, snorkelling, Himalayan trekking or even camel safaris in the Thar Desert.

Working in this field means dealing with people directly on a daily basis. Helping people plan their itinerary, providing ticketing services to company executives, co-ordinating with the airlines, railways or transport company staff, arranging passports and visas, booking hotels—all these require not only a great deal of mobility but also regular contact with representatives of the various services. One must be up-to-date on rules and regulations governing foreign travel, documents required, hindrances if any; so as to correctly advise the clients. All the staff, be it in marketing, counter sales or guide services must be knowledgeable about the places their clients intend to visit—the best way to reach your destination, places to visit, facilities available etc.

Major areas of work in a travel agency include counter work, marketing and management. Counter work involves helping clients with their itineraries, chalking out travel routes, procuring tickets, arranging for passports and visas, making hotel reservations, organising cargo transport and the like. Counter clerks must be able to have easy access to timetable information and be extremely accurate with the information provided to clients. A small slip on their part could result in embarrassing or even disastrous consequences.

Marketing area includes advertising and an aggressive promotion of the agency to potential customers. Procuring steady business for the company is their major job. The management staff deals with the administration of the agency. The managers co- ordinate and streamline the work of the clerks and select brochures of the various tours and packages available with them, among other things.

Major Functions

- *Planning*: The planning of the tours is done by the tour directors or once-in-a-while by experienced counter clerks. Planning involves chalking out the tour programme, working out the cost, confirmation of accommodation and other facilities like food and entertainment, and consulting tourist officials.
- *Sales and Reservations*: The staff has to ensure that travel brochures are on display at agencies. They also take bookings from travel agents or individuals.
- *Representatives/guides*: These are freelancers mostly whose job involves accompanying tourists to their destination and looking after their needs while travelling. A smattering knowledge of different languages can be useful as well as a general awareness and history of the place visited. This job can be easily done by students or even office workers and others who are interested in travelling. Tour operators or local tourism departments often employ professional guides who have a thorough knowledge of the history

and cultural significance of a place. Many tour operators, nowadays specialise in areas such as adventure tourism, beach tourism, mountain holidays etc.

– *Entry*: A basic diploma in travel and tourism management can be advantageous to a person seeking to work in this field. Advertisements appear from time to time for jobs available in travel agencies and tour operating companies or for a position in a government department or corporation. In general, the minimum requirement for entry into this industry are: (i) 10+2 and fluency in the spoken language up to tourist guide level. (ii) for higher positions, a graduate degree in any discipline with a specialisation in history and architecture or geography and archaeology can be a great asset as is the knowledge of one or more foreign languages. If one is applying for a government post, he/she has to clear a written test, a personal interview and a medical examination. On-the-job training is provided to all new entrants.

– *Training*: With the demand for trained people increasing by the day, it is wise to gain some insights into the field through professional training. There are a number of institutions in the country which offer training courses on different aspects of the industry. There are equally good correspondence courses too.

– *Career prospects*: A career in travel and tourism can be exciting and full of fun. Not only is it flexible, but certain jobs in the field can provide excellent travelling opportunities. Job prospects include working in: travel agencies as tour operators, in airlines (domestic and foreign) transport and cargo companies, travel consultancy services and in the government run tourism departments. With enough experience and capital, one can even start one's own travel consultancy.

The tourism industry is thus a high-growth industry which can only expand with time, what with more and more people finding the means and the inclination to discover new places and seek new adventures. At the rate the industry is growing, it is certain to be the industry of the 21st century, providing ample job opportunities to all kinds of people at all levels.

Air Carriers

Tour operators enter into long term contracts with air carriers, hotels and other suppliers for the provision of bulk travel services. Discrete travel services are then assembled into a package tour featuring round trip transportation, seven nights accommodations, ground transportation and tours of local sites. The package tour is marketed to the general public through travel agents. Tour operators are principals and responsible to consumers for the provision of the component travel services of each tour package.

Tour Operators' Performance Indicators

The Tour Operators' Initiative, in cooperation with the Global Reporting Initiative (GRI), has developed a Sector Supplement to the GRI 2002 Sustainability Reporting Guidelines providing Tour Operators' performance indicators. Forty-seven indicators have been developed to measure tour operators' performance in addressing the environmental, economic and social impacts of their business operations.

The tour operators' supplement adds to, but does not replace, the 2002 GRI Sustainability Reporting Guidelines' section on performance indicators. The tour operator's sector supplement applies only to businesses dedicated to organising holiday packages, that is a pre-arranged combination of accommodation, transport and other tourism services not ancillary to transport or accommodation and accounting for a significant proportion of the package, when the service covers a period of more than twenty-four hours or includes overnight accommodation.

The supplement was not designed to capture sector-specific aspects of the various service industries associated with a package, such as transport, accommodation, and other tourism services. The tour operator's performance indicators are divided into categories that reflect the life cycle of the holiday product: from the planning stage, to the development and delivery of the product. The indicators have been grouped under five categories:

- Product management and development (PMD) includes actions related to the choice of the destination as well as the type of services to be included (e.g., the use of train vs. plane).
- Internal management (IM) reflects all the operations and activities that take place in the headquarters or country offices (e.g., use of office supplies, production of brochures, direct employment).
- Supply chain management (SCM) addresses actions related to the selection and contracting of service providers.
- Customer relations (CR) summarises the actions taken to deal with customers, not only with regards to the responsibility to serve them and reply to their comments, but also the opportunity to provide information and raise consumer awareness regarding sustainability.
- Cooperation with destination (D) includes all activities and decisions related to destinations that tour operators make beyond the production and delivery of their holiday package. This mainly includes efforts made by tour operators to engage in dialogues with

destination operators about the impacts of tour packages, and philanthropic activities.

During the process of developing the supplement, the participants began to develop 'guidance notes' listing recommended best practices, as well as more specific instructions on the sustainability issues to be taken into account for three specific indicators. The guidance notes have not been officially reviewed and approved as part of the GRI framework and represent the experience and recommendations of the TOI and the members of the Multi Stakeholders Working Group.

The Tour Operators' Initiative (TOI) entered, in Summer 2001, an official agreement with the Global Reporting Initiative (GRI), to produce the tour operator's specific supplement to the GRI 2002 Sustainability Reporting Guidelines.

A key element of the agreement was the recognition that the tour operator specific supplement will be developed in full consultation with all the relevant stakeholders. Key stakeholders' representatives were then selected in consultation with relevant experts, and a Multi-Stakeholder Working Group (MSWG) was established.

The Multi Stakeholder Working Group included twelve tour operators members of the Tour Operators' Initiative, as well as representatives from Non Governmental Organisations, trade unions, tourism board, local authorities, tour operators' suppliers, consumers' associations, from various regions of the world.

The tour operator's sustainability reporting performance indicators were developed according to the following work plan:

— *Step 1*: preparation—by the members of the MSWG—of First Draft of the sustainability reporting performance indicators for the selected areas of activity/impact.

- *Step 2*: First Draft of the Tour Operators' Sustainability Reporting Performance Indicators—addressing internal and supply chain management and customers' awareness—posted on the web for public comments, and sent to key stakeholders and organisations for targeted comments.
- *Step 3*: Second Draft of the Tour Operators' Sustainability Reporting Performance Indicators prepared by the MSWG, accounting also for external comments received in Step 2. This Second draft prepared during the second Multi Stakeholder Working Group Meeting will also include an additional set of indicators addressing tour operators' impacts and influence on destinations.
- *Step 4*: Second Draft of the Tour Operators' Sustainability Reporting Performance Indicators—addressing internal and supply chain management, customers' awareness and activities at destinations—posted on the web for public comments, and sent to key stakeholders and organisations for targeted comments.
- *Step 5*: Third and Final Draft of the Tour Operators' Sustainability Reporting Performance Indicators finalised by the MSWG, accounting also for external comments received in Step 4.
- *Step 6*: preparation by the MSWG of the vision paper: how the performance indicators will be further developed in the following years.
- *Step 7*: submission of the final draft of the Tour Operator's sector performance indicators to the GRI Board of Directors for approval.
- *Step 8*: Approval by the GRI Board in September 2002 and publication of the Tour Operator's as a supplement to the updated GRI 2002 Sustainability Reporting Guidelines by mid-2002.

4

Meaning and Definition of Hospitality

Hospitality refers to the relationship process between a guest and a host, and it also refers to the act or practice of being hospitable, that is, the reception and entertainment of guests, visitors, or strangers, with liberality and goodwill. Hospitality frequently refers to the hospitality industry jobs for hotels, restaurants, casinos, catering, resorts, clubs and any other service position that deals with tourists.

Technologies in Hospitality Industry

Technology is a tool that has made humans more productive. Technology really doesn't replace people, it changes their responsibilities, their coverage, and, it probably adds people, just in different places. A decade ago a new PMS could have cut down staff at the front desk but added an information and systems manager. Today, a good CRM system will cut down on the number of reservationists the chain may employ but may add staff at the property level to fulfill the now known requests of guests.

This decade's challenge to a hotelier to be successful will be to provide a satisfying and unique visit each time that guest stays in that brand's hotels. The newest technology may tell us the fiber count a particular guest wants on his or her pillow cover, but it will be the people, using the technology, that will make the difference. Soon, your staff may be walking around the hotel with a wireless earpiece telling them the name of each guest as they approach.

Hospitality has a human factor. It is a service industry. In the law of supply and demand, the consumer demands to stay at a hotel where the service outshines that of its competitors. All of this new technology coming out is great. But don't think that it will decrease your staffing while increasing occupancy. Instead it will generate a need for staffing in areas you never previously considered. In order to make CRM work most effectively, for example, you will need to have staff query your guests. These employees will need to be "people oriented," able to speak and listen well, able to work with consumers that may be too busy to respond or unable to determine what the options are and which ones are the best for them.

Then, employees will be needed to load the data, manage the systems, and train the individual hotels and so on. More employees may be required to fulfill the demands of the guests at the hotel level, such as evening and night shift housekeepers and technology butlers. Service must be greatly enhanced by technology. The technology driving the improvement to service must be transparent to the consumer. To do this, people must be involved. Good people. All of this new technology is a good thing. It gives us another reason to communicate with our guests, to provide them with a product that they find value in. To be successful, it forces us to touch our customers, one human to another.

Telecommunication Service

The early 1980s marked the beginning of an era of profitable hotel telephone departments. The advent of call accounting systems enabled hoteliers to easily mark up calls to a profitable (some say too profitable) level. Guests had little choice back then but to use the guestroom phone and grumble about the cost. This era has come to an end. With few exceptions, most hotels have seen between a 15 percent and 25 percent drop in telephone revenues over the last five years. The main reason for this decrease is guest choice.

The guest now has a variety of choices for communicating including fax over the Internet, e-mail, cell phones, calling cards and now even Internet-based phones. All these alternatives offer a less expensive means of communicating than using the traditional hotel guestroom phone and other services such as fax. A fax machine in the guestroom was considered a premium amenity for many years. With the Internet explosion, however, the machines have seen less use. While some hotels continue to enjoy a reasonable revenue stream, others have reported declines in revenue.

E-mail and Internet faxing have contributed to the drop in usage. Calling cards have led the shift from 0+ to 1-800 dialing. This shift not only has depleted revenue from commissions but also ties up much needed trunk lines. Modem calls are also another source of PBX congestion, but contrary to popular belief, not as much as calling cards. Cellular phones have become so widely used that some cell phone providers have had trouble keeping up with the demand. AT&T's one-rate plan was so successful that for a time subscribers were unable to complete calls in certain areas. These problems have now been addressed for the most part.

What is of concern to hoteliers attempting to eke out a profit in telecom is the proliferation of nationwide cell phone plans that include no roaming or long-distance charges and nights and weekends free. A typical example is the all-digital plan from Sprint, which includes 600 anytime minutes, e-mail and Internet access (limited), and 5,400 night and weekend minutes (nights begin at 9 p.m.). The cost of this plan is $60 per month. A guest on such a plan has an average cost of about 5 cents per minute for long distance, depending on the mix of anytime vs. night and weekend. Assuming that the wireless reception quality is acceptable, it is very difficult for the hotel to compete on a cost basis.

High-speed Internet access (HSIA) is fast becoming an expected amenity. With more guests carrying laptops than ever before and Internet business activity rapidly increasing, the guest must have the best connection available. HSIA also relieves the congestion on the PBX caused by modem calls. While some revenue-sharing business models have proven unsuccessful, there are realistic approaches to installing and providing HSIA on at least a break-even basis, if not generating a small profit.

Self-Contained Guest

Another concern among hoteliers is what can be termed the self-contained guest. Typically, this guest carries a notebook computer, a small printer, a cell phone and perhaps a pager. The guest has spare batteries for the phone, an antenna booster that enhances reception and the ability to connect to the Internet wirelessly. The guest sends and receives faxes over the Internet or with a direct dial wireless connection. The phone receives voicemail messages when in use or turned off during charging. Theoretically, the self-contained guest needs no hotel telecommunications services.

Hotels are unable to compete on price with devices that the guest has brought with him. What the hotel can do is offer a better experience at a reasonable price to entice guests to use the hotel's telecom infrastructure. No matter what cell phone the guest may carry or what service provider is used, no wireless connection is as good as a land-line connection. Given a choice, most guests would prefer to use the hotel phone if they can afford to.

Wireless Internet connections, while improving, offer an experience that is, at best, the speed of a dial-up connection. Generation 3 cell phones promise better connections, but that is some time in the future. Therefore, it is not possible for the guest to attain anywhere near the quality wirelessly that a high-speed Internet connection furnished by the hotel can provide.

Some hoteliers have recognised this advantage in quality by offering package plans. One small hotel chain is offering unlimited local calls and high-speed Internet access for $9.95 a day. The take rate on this package has been as high as 25 percent. Other chains are tying such packages to their loyalty programmes. The guest must first enroll in the programme to be eligible for the packages. This approach has led to an increase in enrollment. Such packages can require a two-way interface with the call accounting system. This two-way interface allows the call accounting system to recognise package plans vs. normal call accounting billing for other guests.

Other properties are looking at the feasibility of offering fixed-rate long distance, such as 12 cents per minute. This is a variation from traditional hotel long-distance pricing, but is more attractive to the guest. No matter what strategy a property takes in the telecommunications department, one thing is for certain, it needs to be a different one from the past. Given the hotel's advantage in quality over the guest's portable devices, the proper packaging of services will lure even the most avid self-contained guest back to using the hotel's telecom services.

Wireless Technology

While many advances have been made in the industry regarding wireless technology with each advance comes its own list of challenges. When considering a wireless application currently a hotel is faced with a lack of standards across the industry, concern about the payback of the new system and the fact that the current second generation (2G) of wireless applications is sluggish. Dan Phillips said that many of the applications that are being brought into the hospitality industry are technologies that have been developed outside the hotel industry and are being retro-fit to accommodate the needs of hospitality.

When searching for a wireless applications Phillips cautioned that a technology should be brought in to enhance the guest experience and make a hotel more profitable and competitive. Additional challenges to wireless are acceptance of the technology, security of the system and the cost of the new technology. While the security issues can be, and should be, addressed with your perspective provider, the cost issue is one that should be addressed based on the particular application. Antonio Dimilia estimated that a wireless high-speed access system could save up to one-third the cost of rewiring an existing hotel.

The non-invasive installation of such a system also can be considered a positive cost advantage as guestrooms would not be taken out of service or guests inconvenienced with an invasive installation. While some wireless applications cost less than similar traditional solutions other wireless technologies have up front costs with the anticipation of return on investment coming through its administrative use or as a revenue generator over time.

According to Dimilia some additional considerations include whether the solution is expandable for future enhancements, does the provider guarantee a level of service and does the provider understand the needs of the guest. Needless to say hoteliers need to carefully consider the vendor's business model to ensure continued support and service 12 months down the road. If the business model doesn't make sense the vendor may not be able to continue its service to your hotel.

A wireless solution currently in action is the MACH-1 (Mobile Access to Carlson Hospitality) system from Carlson Hospitality Worldwide. MACH-1 is completely wireless, running on a Compaq iPAQ system and is used for business information, guest profile information and for management notifications. It is designed to alert management of specific business information, such a VIP at check in or if more than a certain number of guests are waiting for rooms to be cleaned and released or any of a number of triggers defined by management.

Bill Lashley, of Inter-American Data a property management system company servicing large hotels and casinos, believes that the infrastructure for wireless technology is the most important consideration. He mentioned hardware challenges from multiple device communications to a consortium of vendors to develop solutions that continue to need to be overcome. He feels that the technology and cooperation is already ready and available. Inter-American Data has successfully used wireless technology in its Opryland Hotel and The Venetian installations for data collection and check in purposes. He mentioned other practical applications including housekeeping and baggage handling.

Carlson's David Sjolander believes that wireless technology will follow a standard cycle. Based on the Gartner Group hype curve Sjolander charted the emergence of wireless over the following points: technology trigger to the inflated expectations, the trough of disillusionment, the slope of enlightenment, and the plateau of productivity. Following this cycle wireless has already passed through its inflated expectations around the time of BlueTooth hype and is currently working toward the slope of enlightenment, which means that we can expect that there will be a plateau soon where productivity and acceptance of multiple applications will emerge.

Electronic Distribution Channels

The number of reservations flowing to hotels through the electronic distribution channels - the global distribution systems and the Internet - is growing steadily. Once a minor contributor of bookings, they are now primary business sources and grow more important with every passing month. This productivity growth has heightened emphasis throughout the hotel industry on using the electronic distribution channels effectively and maximising their potential. Every director of sales and marketing faces the challenge of understanding, prioritising and managing these electronic outlets on behalf of his or her property.

The Hotel Electronic Distribution Network Association (HEDNA) reported that in 1999 the global distribution systems delivered over 43 million bookings with a value in excess of $12.5 billion. GDS booking growth continues at about 10 percent a year. Everyone has his or her own stories of the impact of the Internet. Some large chains are experiencing 200-300 percent growth annually. Some small, boutique properties report that over 75 percent of their bookings now come from the Web.

Regardless of the Internet's current reservation production for your hotel, it bears only modest resemblance to the broader and ever-expanding impact it will have in the future. As the number of people who have Internet access approaches 100 million in the United States and 200 million worldwide, research repeatedly indicates that consumers are turning to the Internet for travel-related information. They may not book online (although they will eventually), but they are already comparing you with your competitors before they pick up their telephone to call your CRO or drive up to the front door of your property.

As a hotel sales and marketing professional your limited resources are allocated to presenting your property in the sales channels that will be the most productive for you—be they print ads, direct mail, public relations, sales calls or electronic distribution channel participation and advertising. You strive to select the most cost-effective and compelling channels, that will in turn bring guests to your door and put heads in your beds. This resource allocation process requires assessment of each potential business source's target audience, opportunities for participation, probable production and costs. This applies to electronic distribution just as it does to other sales options. Narrowing the focus to the electronic distribution channels, the two broadest categories are global distribution systems (GDS) and Internet web sites.

Web sites, like the GDSs, require several types of information in order to sell lodging - availability, rates and product description. In some cases, web sites link to existing sources of this information and need not be manually maintained by on-property staff. This is true of web sites for which data is provided by - or powered by - the hotel chain or representation company's central reservation system, a switch company or one of the GDSs.

Often the decision to participate in a CRS-, switch- or GDS-powered site is made at the chain or representation company level. In other cases, no arrangement or permission is gained. In some cases, the information is redisplayed by an associated onward distribution site. Web sites are no different from any other distribution or advertising medium in that they have specific user demographics. Site sales representatives should be able and prepared to describe those demographics to you. You in turn must decide if that constituency matches a priority market segment for your hotel.

If a site is not powered i.e., does not draw its availability, rates and descriptive data from a CRS, switch or GDS, then the responsibility falls to the property to maintain the information on a day-to-day basis. This commitment cannot be taken lightly. Even the simplest of systems takes more time to maintain than the sales patter for the site generally suggests. Some hotel staffs take the position that only occasional maintenance need be given, such as when occupancy begins to build they turn off these sites. In doing so, they shortchange a valuable opportunity for last room sale. This is occurring more frequently than most general managers and directors of sales are aware.

The web site maintenance situation is improving, but widespread relief is months, and for most hotels, years off. PMS vendors are adding functions to allow a direct link to property web sites, so that a hotel can use its PMS as the real-time booking engine on its web site. Elsewhere, web site operators are beginning to develop PMS interfaces to allow automated downloading of Internet reservations to the PMS, and later, uploading of availability data. Additionally, master databases are in design, which will allow a one-time updating of a single master data file those updates will be instantly communicated to all of the web sites where you are listed.

Difficulties in first evaluating and later maintaining your hotel's information on travel web sites do not diminish their importance and a hotel's need to participate in them. The Web is quickly becoming a mainstream promotional and sales medium. It is essential to have a strategy for the extent and manner to which your hotel will participate in the Web and then the processes to ensure that strategy is applied on a day-to-day basis.

Once your have chosen to list your hotel on a site, that and every other site where you are listed should be reviewed on a regular basis to verify that the data for your property is accurate, complete and compelling. If it is not, correcting the deficiencies needs to be a top priority. Next comes a commitment to maintain the same rates and availability data on the web sites as in all of your other sales vehicles - the front desk, the reservations office, the chain's reservations centers and the GDSs.

Differentiating the Web from the GDSs is the presence on the Internet of not only traditional "shop and buy" travel sites but also specialty sales sites. These sites, whose use may be appropriate from time to time by your hotel, specialise in selling distressed inventory. They operate using several models - discounted prices, auctions, reverse auctions and consolidators.

Like the GDSs, web sites offer supplemental promotional opportunities. Preferred placement of your listing in sites or search engines, banner ads and additional on-screen graphics are just a few of the extra cost options. As you decide to list your hotel's inventory on a site, inquire about the site's promotional possibilities. For the sites where participation has been arranged at a corporate level, ask the individual in your corporate office to provide you with a description of the opportunities offered by each of the sites.

Electronic distribution and, in particular, the Internet is a complex and quickly changing sales environment. In the end, the powerful and productive sales tool called electronic distribution can be effectively employed because fundamental marketing principles apply to it just as they do in every marketing decision.

Meetings

A meeting is a planned event in which a group of people

gather together to accomplish something Meetings can be planned in Hotels, cruise ships, convention center, colleges or at several locations by teleconferencing. Variable number of people attend meetings depending on the type of meeting. Many specialised services technologies and facilities are used at meetings. There are three types of meetings: Association meetings, Corporate meetings, Trade shows and expositions

Association Meetings

May be made up of trade groups, social groups, Labour Unions, Service associations Generally hold one annual meeting to elect office bearers, plan budgets and activities. Some large associations employ a full time meeting and travel department. Meetings range from 1 day to 1 week. Besides annual meetings there are national regional or international conventions. Annual meetings planned well in advance due to large number of delegates. Proper site selection is vital as Attendance is voluntary Adequate exhibition space is an important planning characteristic.

Corporate Meetings

- *Management meetings*: Largest category in corporate meetings. Financial reviews, strategic planning sessions are held during management meetings
- *Training seminars*: Ranks second in the number of meetings held. Large companies prefer to take their staff offsite and conduct training sessions.
- *Sales meetings* are essential for teaching new(national 3.6 days 104 attendees; and regional meetings 2.5 days and 42 attendees)
- *Professional and technical meetings* (2.3 days 62 people)
- *Incentive trips*: Offer combination of meeting and recreation Stockholders meetings (1 day, 95 owners attend)

– *Other corporate meetings* (press conference etc.)

Trade Shows and Expositions

An exhibition of products and/or services held for members of a common or related industry. Not open to the general public

Difference between Hospitality and Meetings

Two major distinctions separate the meetings business into its own specialised classification within the hospitality industry. One is the size of the group. The second is the function of the group. Although the size of a meeting, convention, or exposition can vary—from a handful of delegates to thousands of registrants—the exact number (whether 2 or 200,000) is not the primary distinguishing factor.

As a whole, meetings, conventions, and expositions are groups utilising convention hotels and facilities. They often reserve space months, even years, in advance and negotiable package deals that may include rooms, meals, events, local tours, and entertainment. Therefore, the number of participants, the group's needs, its length to stay, and the number of meetings and conventions scheduled are all determinants of "size."

Second, it is the function of the group that also distinguishes meetings, conventions, and expositions from other aspects of the industry. These groups have very specific, defined purposes and agendas (for example, planning policy, exchanging ideas, presenting services) with decisive outcomes in mind. Business, leisure, and other hospitality travelers and guests have more general purposes (for example, sightseeing or finding a place to stay between business appointments).

Hospitlity Revenue

Conventions, meetings, and expositions are a major and growing enterprise, not just for the people who work in the business but also for the communities that reap the economic benefits of such meetings. Up to now, however, there has been no way to measure the exact size of the convention business. Some estimates indicate that meetings and conventions increased fourfold in the years between 1980 and 1989, with a full 43 percent increase just from 1987 to 1990.

In 1992, the International Association of Convention & Visitor Bureaus (IACVB) employed Deloitte & Youche, a multinational public accounting and consulting firm, to determine a straightforward and statistically valid measure of the economic impact that conventions have on the average city. Between June 1992 and June 1993, seventy-three cities were the subject of a study involving more than five hundred events worldwide. Deloitte & Touche analysed responses from more than 17,000 meeting delegates, associations, exhibitors, and exposition service contractors before it reached its final conclusions.

No one factor caused the growth of the meetings industry. A number of factors are responsible, but explosive growth in information and easy availability of airline travel head the list.

Perhaps, the primary reason for growth in the industry lies in the major reason people hold meetings, conventions, and expositions: to communicate information. People attend meetings, conventions, and expositions to exchange idea and knowledge. In the last thirty years, availability of information has explored. Computers have made it possible to gather, manipulate, and disseminate a wealth of information on every conceivable subject.

Certainly, no one can keep up with all that information. In fact, most people can't keep up with the information in their own field. They attend meetings, conventions, and expositions to learn what's happening in their field, to describe what they are doing, and to trade ideas. This is as true for the hair stylist as it is for the scientist. As more information has become available over the years, it has become necessary to hold more meetings, conventions, and expositions to keep pace.

Another major reason for growth in the meetings business is accessibility to air travel. In 1970, the airlines introduced the 747 jumbo-jet, and for the first time large numbers of people could travel from one point to another —no matter how far—quickly and efficiently. Since that time, no destination has been considered "off limits" for the meeting industry, which in turn, has made national and even international meetings, conventions, and expositions possible.

At about this same time, one of the biggest changes between the airline and the meetings business took place—the formation of a trade association called Meeting Planners International (MPI). MPI formed a task force to retain similar privileges of free passage for meeting planners that the major carriers offered travel agents. In the wake of rising fuel costs, the airlines were more than willing to accommodate this new and growing business as a way to increase their passenger load—and their profits. Besides the introduction of the jumbo jet, the deregulation of the airline industry in the early 1980s also directly effected the meetings business.

Deregulation stimulated price wars between airlines, and airfares plummeted, making travel to and from meetings, conventions, and expositions more affordable. As a result, the airlines began catering specifically to the meetings business by offering package deals and negotiated fares. Recently, however, the struggling airline industry changed its policy. Airlines pulled back on special deals, putting planners in the position of demanding—sometimes without success—reduced fares and other perks for meeting attendees. Now, though, things are changing again in the other direction.

As the meeting business grew, other businesses, organisations, and jobs grew to meet its needs, and in turn they made it easier for the meetings business to grow. Specifically, the growth of the lodging industry, convention centers, convention bureaus, conference centers, meeting technology, and the jobs of meeting planner and ground suppliers spurred on and were spurred by the expanding meetings business.

Convention Centres

There is another growing niche serving the changing needs of the industry: the convention center. During the past twenty-five years, convention centers have been synonymous with lodging industry expansion. Space, accessibility, and storage facilities have made convention centers a one-stop arena for meetings, conventions, and expositions. Convention centers and convention hotels (hotels that include lodging with exhibit and meeting facilities) are now all-inclusive places that have moved beyond the old four-walls, and a ceiling concept of accommodation.

The Coliseum in New York City was probably the first convention center built to accommodate groups of varying size. Completed in 1958, the Coliseum offered flexibility: soundproof movable walls to subdivide large areas, designated registration areas, a variety of lighting options, and truck ramps to the lower exposition floors. Now, hundreds of cities around the world boast their own convention centers. Because of the convention center boom of the last decade or so, many have argued that the market has reached total saturation.

Convention and Vistiors Bureaus (CVBs)

Yet another factor affecting the meeting business is the relationship between planners and convention and visitors bureaus (CVBs). According to the IACVB, a convention and visitor bureau is a not-for-profit umbrella organisation that represents a city or urban area in soliciting and serving all types of travelers to that city or area – whether they visit for business, pleasure, or both. In other words, a CVB has three primary purposes:

- encourage groups to hold meetings, conventions, and expositions in the city or area the CVB represents;
- assist groups with meeting preparations and offer services during the course of the convention, exposition, or meeting; and
- encourage tourist to visit and enjoy the historical, cultural, and recreational opportunities that the city has to offer.

CVBs worldwide orient visitors to host cities, act as liaisons between suppliers and meeting planners, and offer convention and meeting management services. CVBs are indispensable in that they attract meetings, conventions, and expositions that might otherwise never be interested in a particular city or region. The task of the CVB is not an easy one. There are unusual requests to fulfill, demands to be met, and schedules to adhere to. Like other segments of the hospitality industry, convention and visitors bureaus face much competition within their segment of the hospitality industry. They, too, must compete regionally, nationally, and internationally for hospitality dollars.

This, however, can be a distinct advantage for the meeting planner. While most CVBs can recommend suppliers, secure hotels, and act as a liaison between a group and the community, they also can provide the meeting planner with materials, tour arrangements, and on-site assistance. Simply, put, CVBs work for the visitors and meeting planners, as well as for the city—at no cost. It is important to remember that the meeting planner is the "organiser" and that the CVB is the "assistant." CVBs help visitors learn more about the host city and its area attractions. At the same time, they also help the planner make best possible use of all services and facilities the city has to offer.

Conference Centres

The continued evolution of conference centers has also been greatly influenced by the incredible growth of the meetings business. Formerly, conference centers were usually sparse rooms, barren of everything except chairs and necessary audiovisual equipment. The fitness boom in the 1970s, however, hit even this part of the industry. No longer were conference participants content to sit for hours and hours with no diversion. Conference centers jumped on the fitness bandwagon and began designing their centers to be more resort-oriented. With recreational and physical exercise facilities available, conference centers now cater to even broader audiences. And they no longer cater to them just on land.

Floating conference centers -conference centers aboard ships—are a recent development. Ships are fitted with meeting rooms and auditoriums and offer such technical amenities as closed-circuit television and videoconferencing. Airport meeting rooms are another variation on the theme. Not all conference centers are available to the public. Some are owned by corporations and are used only by these corporations. Others, however, are owned by corporations that use the facilities but also rent them out. And still others, owned by universities, are accessible to the public.

TECHNOLOGICAL ADVANCEMENTS

The electronics revolution of the last few years has given the meetings and convention industry maximum flexibility with respect to meeting presentations. Videos, 360-degree projection techniques, multi-image presentations, computers, and unique sound system have all become commonplace. Technological advancements within the industry have opened up a world of different ways to communicate that make meetings, conferences, and conventions more interesting to attend and easier to arrange.

Video Technology

Before the mid-1970s, the term "video" was virtually nonexistent. With the advent of such technology as the video projector, video has now become synonymous with the meetings business. There are video-enhanced speakers, multi-image video walls, instant replay, and "live projection."

Teleconferencing: In the 1980s, technology advanced beyond video into teleconferencing. Satellites, commonly used to beam news coverage worldwide, made it possible to link separate groups and speakers. In 1980, Holiday Inn broadcast the first national teleconference, linking two thousand participants in thirty-three meeting sites.

Computers: Computers are used in virtually every aspect of the meetings business -including reservations, meeting workshops, and demonstrations. For example, a computerised information network enables CVBs to exchange impotent demographic and historical information on potential meeting sites with other CVBs worldwide. Clearly technology is an indispensable part of the meetings business. Videoconferencing, computer applications, and other technology will continue to advance as quickly as the technological innovations will allow.

Meeting Planners

The role of the meeting planner began to evolve about twenty years ago and has progressed as the meetings industry has grown. The meeting professional plans and organises the details that make the meeting, convention, or exposition operate smoothly. Certainly no event is produced single-handedly. But without the support of the many planners within the industry, the growth and success experienced by the meetings industry would have come more slowly.

Ground Suppliers

Finally, the arrival of ground suppliers in the 1970s (those who handle details on tours, transportation, sight-seeing, banquets, and hotel registration) began a significant change within the industry. While ground suppliers were primarily "shuttle operators" in the first few years of their existence, they have grown into programme planners offering, for example, special events for spouses of meeting participants, on-site sports tournaments, and motivational speakers.

5

Hospitality: Products and Services

A hotel is an establishment that provides paid lodging, usually on a short-term basis. Hotels often provide a number of additional guest services such as a restaurant, a swimming pool or childcare. Some hotels have conference services and meeting rooms and encourage groups to hold conventions and meetings at their location. There is no hard and fast rule differentiating motels from other hotels, although a "Motel" is clearly suggesting that it is aimed at motorists. This may simply mean that it is a hotel with good access to the road network (on a motorway or ring road) so that a long car journey need not be interrupted for long by town-centre traffic.

In other cases the designation is simply an attempt to make the most of a poor location inconvenient for town-centre services and attractions. Classically, though, a Motel is a hotel which is made convenient for people who, for whatever personal reason, wish to be able to have quick access from the outside world (especially from their parked car) to the hotel room—without passing the scutiny of a receptionist or fellow guests. This is usually arranged by having rooms (sometimes in individual chalets or even trailers) arranged around the car park with room doors opening directly to the outside rather than to an internal corridors.

Because of constant changes, staying current just with who is offering what and where can be difficult for the guest. The necessity for classifying hotels came about when hotels began to differ from one another enough to appeal to different group of people. Long gone are the days when the guest had two choices—luxury hotels or budget hotels. Hotel entrepreneurs such as Kemmons Wilson created a third option when they built facilities intended to serve middle-class families. These property classes had clear-cut boundaries in the beginning.

Potential guests knew they could expect more services at a luxury hotel than a budget motel, and something in between at a midpriced hotel. As the economy in general boomed and room supply increased, hoteliers focused on setting themselves apart from the crowd by offering specialised accommodations. No longer just a place to sleep, hotels were appealing to conventioneers, business groups, and special-interest groups.

Descriptive hotel classifications helped potential guests locate suitable lodgings, and as such, became a valuable marketing tool. As this diversity flourished, so did competition for customers and brand loyalty. As properties continually upgraded their services, boundaries between the descriptive labels blended into one another. Old systems of classification were not as clear.

For instance, the Marriott brand, once recognisable as a midpriced hotel, began to include hotels classified as economy (Fairfeilds Inns), business (Courtyard), extended-stay (Residence Inns), all suite (Marriott Suites), and upscale (Marriott Hotels and Resorts). Other chains also began to cater to a myriad of guests—from business to pleasure travellers and from individuals to groups.

Consequently, lodging classification became more complex. Facilities were then grouped according to size, amenities offered, price, type of guest (business or pleasure), or type of hotel (luxury, full-service, or economy, extended stay to name a few). Many facilities fit two or more categories, and did so in order to attract different types of guests.

Motels and hotels are the most widely recognised forms of lodging. They can be found almost anywhere—from the center of a huge metropolis to the streets of a small town. For the most part, hotels and motels attract transient guests who need a place to stay for a night or two while travelling for business or pleasure. Hotels that specialise in residence or extended-stay accommodations serve guests looking for more permanent lodging. From the age of grand hotels to the troubled 1990s, the hotels has been the most fabled type of lodging.

Varying greatly in style and service, most hotels share a similar structure. They generally have more than two stories with guest rooms located along common hallways. Guests rooms usually have a bed, bath, telephone, and television. In addition to housekeeping, services may include luggage assistance, access to a business center for use of a photocopier or fax machine, and availability of recreation facilities, restaurants, or bars. Hotels are most often located in or near business districts, travel destinations, and airports.

Motels offered fewer amenities and were less expensive to build and operate than downtown hotels. The lower rates, basic accommodations, roadway locations, and lack of a central lobby were well-suited for the new overnight automobile traveler. Motels are generally less formal than hotels. Guests usually carry their own luggage, and free parking is available, often adjacent to the guest's room. Many motels provide swimming pools and restaurant service. Guests who prefer to save money may opt for a budget motel that has smaller rooms, no pool, and fewer amenities.

Unlike regular hotels, all-suite hotels rent only suites, often combing living space with kitchen facilities, or a bedroom section with an attached parlour. To keep rates competitive with other hotels, many all-suite hotels have small lobbies and no public meeting rooms. Some do not offer restaurant or bar facilities. As the market has expanded, through, some all-suite hotel hotels have reintroduced public areas and limited foodservice. Amenities such as free breakfast, cocktail hour, and access to an on-premise health club keep Summerfield Suites Hotel in San Jose, California, at a 98 percent average occupancy rate.

Convention hotels provide meeting and banquet facilities for large groups (usually five hundred or more) booked in their guest rooms. Because they target groups, these hotels need large lobbies to accommodate group arrivals. They also have a high percentage of double-occupancy rooms and emphasise food and beverage services. Convention hotels may also offer concierge floors to cater to individual guests' needs.

At one time, hotels differed distinctly by the services they offered. Recognising that all guests do not expect the same services nor have the same amount to spend on lodging, the hotel industry offered a variety of services at different prices aimed at particular markets (groups whose members have similar expectations and budgets). Familiarity with these labels is helpful in understanding guest perception as the transition is made from one system to another. Also, classification's short history shows how dynamic the industry is and how important service is at all levels. Classifying hotels by service contains four broad categories: luxury, full-service, limited-service, and economy.

Luxury Hotels

Traditionally, independent hotels offer the finest

accommodations money can buy. Luxury properties are descendants of the grand hotels, featuring expensive, lavishly decorated public areas and the high levels of customer service. They offer the finest cuisine and the full range of amenities from shampoos and hair dryers to private Jacuzzis and fireplaces. Whether parking your car, carrying your luggage, or delivering room service, staff members—including concierges, bell persons, front desk attendants, and wait staff—are well-trained and efficient. Luxury resorts offer the finest entertainment and recreational facilities available. A part of luxury properties' attraction is their ability to perpetuate an exclusive image by charging high rates.

Full Service Hotels

Full-service hotels generally offer clean, well-decorated hotels with meeting and restaurant facilities, a limited room-service menu, and a variety of recreational activities. Although not as extravagant as the luxury properties, fullservice hotels generally have large, attractive public areas. The ratio of service of the concierge or other staff may be limited to designated VIP floors. Some all-suite and extended-stay hotels with good-sized public areas also fit into the full service category, with amenities like in-room coffeemakers, microwave ovens, and refrigerators.

Limited Service Facilities

Usual offerings included simple, clean rooms with a telephone, free cable television, swimming pools, and an adjacent restaurant. Staff services, other than housekeeping, were limited, but some offered a few extra amenities such as complimentary shampoo and lotion to distinguish themselves from the economy properties. The remaining all-suite hotels fit into this category because of their limited services and amenities, and small public areas.

Once offering only the basic bed and bath facilities, economy properties focus on "more values for the dollar" with clean and low-priced lodging. Economy properties generally did not offer meeting and recreational facilities or food and beverage services, with the possible expectation of a vending area featuring prepackaged snacks and video games. Staff was limited to only those required to provide basic front office services, security, and housekeeping services. Generally, the smaller guest rooms of the economy hotels offered one or two double beds and a separate bathroom equipped with no more than towel and soap.

Restaurant Industries

The restaurant industry runs the gamut from gourmet restaurants to hot dog stands. The restaurant industry includes many 'different types of facilities and markets.

Social and economic trends have emerged to shape the restaurant industry. The most profound trend is the working woman. With a larger income, women view restaurants not only as an affordable way to dine, but also as a convenience for themselves and their family. Restaurants provide an alternative to the added stress of arriving home from the office and dropping everything to cook the family's evening meal.

The increase in household incomes has created a desire and convenience for people to spend time dining away from home or ordering takeout meals. The association cites households with a pretax income of $30,000 or more spends a larger amount of time dining out. In short, the increase in working women has created a larger household income in which people can afford to eat away from home.

The mere convenience of avoiding a night of cooking over the stove after a long day at the office is enticing to many women and their families. This trend is expected to remain long-term as people's lives continue on a fast-paced schedule. Whether it's driving a son or daughter to a school function or staying late at the office, sitting down at home for a meal with the entire family is hard to come by. From a promotional products perspective, understanding the driving forces behind the changes in the restaurant industry will enable eatery owners to properly target the audience they decide to pursue. The restaurant industry has two distinct audience segments: full- and limited-service operations. Both segments attract a certain clientele as well as various promotional products.

Full-Service Restaurant

The full-service segment of the restaurant industry can be categorised as sit-down restaurants that cater to the customer with a sense of personal attention. For example, an Italian restaurant with a hostess, a choice of wines and Italian music playing softly in the background is a full-service experience. Many full-service restaurants are competing for customers, not only in the full-service market, but with the fast-food or limited-service segment of the industry as well. According to one generally accepted definition, full-service restaurants are restaurants that:

- Feature a dozen or more main-course items on the menu, and
- Cook to order

Full-service restaurants are generally categorised in terms of price, menu, or atmosphere.

Price: When the focus is on price, restaurants can be categorised as luxury, highpriced, mid-priced, or low-priced establishments.

Menu: Restaurants such as steak houses and seafood restaurants are full service restaurants defined in terms of menu. For example, Outback Steakhouse specialises in beef; Red Lobster features shrimp, crab, and lobster on its menu.

Atmosphere: Some restaurants are known primarily for their atmosphere that is, for their unique architecture, decor, and / or setting. Show business and sports motifs-currently very fashionable in the industry-provide themes for a growing number of popular restaurants. The Hard Rock Cafe chain, which started in London and now has restaurants in major cities around the world, features Elvis Presley, the Beatles, and other rock-star music memorabilia. Other categories.

Full-service restaurants can be categorised in other ways besides price, menu, or atmosphere. Family restaurants serve breakfast, lunch, and dinner, offering traditional menu items. Their pricing falls between casual dinner houses and quick-service restaurants. A major source of revenue for some family restaurants-such as Cracker Barrel—is an on-site gift shop. To compete against its market segment as well as other establishments, the fullservice restaurant prides itself on customer appreciation. To survive, full-service restaurants must have a loyal customer following. This is accomplished by offering unique menu choices and a creative atmosphere that will entice the customer not only to return, but also to inform his or her acquaintances of the establishment.

The biggest challenge for full-service operators is to attract customers, then maintain their loyalty. The 90s brought the theme restaurants. These include restaurants catering to music, movies, sports or environmental enthusiasts. Many theme establishments have the advertising and physical appearance to draw customers from all walks of life. Many are tourists who want an opportunity to view memorabilia and catch a glimpse of the creative interior that mirrors the establishment's theme.

Most full-service restaurants, especially theme establishments, will include logoed merchandise as a method of advertising. Customers will find T-shirts and a host of other items with a restaurant's logo on them. These items play an important role in earning customer loyalty and promoting the name of the establishment. Distributors have an advantage servicing the restaurant industry because they simply need to walk inside an establishment to get a hint of its décor and customer base, thus receiving a better idea as to what promotional products would be most appealing to the customers.

On the other end of the scale, limited-service restaurants cater to a much fasterpaced clientele. With corporate downsizing, employees are working longer hours and having meals ordered at the workplace. Longer hours and lack of time have transformed family mealtime into "home meal replacement." Fast-food restaurants and delis offer convenient alternatives to people on the go. The drive-up window has replaced the dining room in many limited-service establishments. A trend within the limited-service segment is the emergence of carryout services within grocery stores, retail stores, bookstores and gasoline convenience stores.

In US, the National Restaurant Association states that nearly 30 percent of all retail establishments are eating and drinking places. Both the retail and bookstore markets are incorporating food services as a marketing tool to keep customers in the stores longer. The grocery stores already have used food to entice its customers to stay and shop; however, many customers will purchase a carryout meal to avoid preparing a meal when they get home.

Gasoline convenience stores are growing tremendously because of the possibility for additional revenue from drivers traveling on a trip or returning home from work. Many are building in residential areas in order to be easily accessible to nearby residents. The limited-service segment opens many doors to food-on-the-go suppliers who are interested in testing unique products specifically designed for the customer on the move. With intense competition between limited-service establishments, owners must rely on creative ideas to separate themselves from the rest of the competition. For example, a product that fits in the automobile to serve as a reminder to visit a convenience store for gasoline and sandwiches is a marketing tool appropriate for people whose car has taken the place of the kitchen table.

With thousands of restaurants to choose from, distributors must understand the establishment, its clientele and the competition to offer promotional products that will make a lasting impact. Whether it is full- or limited-service establishments, there are differences in the needs of restaurants within these segments. What works for the Italian restaurant may not work for the Mexican restaurant down the street. Promotional products are heavily based on customer demand or the usefulness of the product for the market's customers.

Two full-service restaurants that have survived the times and made a lasting name for themselves both nationally and worldwide are Ithaca, New York-based Moosewood Restaurant and Driftwood, Texas-based The Salt Lick. Despite outside competition and slow seasons, both restaurants have retained customer loyalty by listening to the needs of its customers. With a combined 55 years in business, Moosewood Restaurant and The Salt Lick understand the importance of customer appreciation.

The Moosewood Restaurant is a vegetarian restaurant established in 1973 at a time when people were asking themselves if they could eat just vegetables. Situated in the same spot in Ithaca, New York, the restaurant has undergone several design changes over the years. Ned Asta, a collective member for 20 years, says the restaurant's logo also has undergone several changes. What is interesting about the successes of the Moosewood Restaurant and The Salt Lick is the creative uses of cookbooks and barbecue sauce to promote the restaurant on a grand scale. While it may not have been apparent to the establishments at the time, the cookbooks and sauce were innovative promotional products that continue to generate revenue for the restaurants more than 20 years after their inception.

Limited-Service Restaurant

People often find themselves with several things to do and not enough time to do them. It is for this segment of the population that limited-service restaurants were created. Whether it is a fast-food chain, coffeehouse or stop-and-go, the limitedservice establishment is providing customers with a demanding convenience. In US, the National Restaurant Association indicates that one out of five takeout food consumers is a daily user. Those customers represent half of all takeout occasions.

Major growth in quick-service restaurants continues to come from hamburger chains as well as chicken, sandwich, and Mexican-food chains. Much of the growth is outside the United States. The type or number of menu items alone does. not determine the winners. A commitment to good service and providing nutritional menu choices has taken center stage. McDonald's now guarantees hot food; fast, friendly service; and double-check drive-thru accuracy. A survey of 27 restaurant chains-including 19 quick-service chains-with 50,000 outlets found that at least three-quarters of them offered menu choices for health-conscious consumers.

Examples included low-fat milk, skinless chicken, and reduced or low-calorie salad dressing. Nine out of ten chains said they used vegetable fats instead of animal fats for frying. While a limited-service establishment may not have all the personal touches of a full-service restaurant, there is a loyalty among limited-service customers that promotional products can reach. With intense competition emerging between limitedservice establishments, it is becoming increasingly important to maintain a loyal customer base. An important method of accomplishing that is incorporating promotional products into the customers' orders.

For fast-food restaurants such as McDonald's and Burger King, children have enjoyed kid's meals that include plastic toys depicting the establishment's mascots. Coffeehouses have used creative ideas such as cooking a muffin in a logoed coffee mug that the customer keeps for refills during repeat visits. Other limited-service establishments include logoed T-shirts, matchbooks, coasters, magnets and buttons. Many of these items are complimentary to the customer as a reminder of the establishment.

The limited-service market has many opportunities for promotional products. The National Restaurant Association notes that in an average month 78 percent of U.S. households use some form of carryout or delivery. It is obvious that the limitedservice market has a large audience that can be reached via promotional products. For example, ast-food restaurants have been offering logoed glasses and toys to customers for many years. Promotional products are an inexpensive medium that limited-service establishments can utilise to promote their name and logo to the public.

The full-service market is custom-oriented; therefore, it is essential that distributors create a promotion that leaves a sense of appreciation in the customer. Full-service establishments want and need customers to return and a well-crafted promotional product could be the difference between a high turnover or a loyal customer base. The limited-service market works in a similar manner. Although limited service establishments need customers, the focus is to create name and logo recognition to a mass audience. With millions of people who enjoy hamburgers, limited-service operators must separate themselves from the rest of the competition that sells hamburgers. To accomplish this, promotional products with a relatively low cost and function can create long-term exposure to a large audience.

Food Service

Food service outlets in lodging operations range from gourmet restaurants to coffee shops and even quick-service outlets. Lodging food service sales are tremendous.

Transportation Market. Travellers eat at highway stops; on airplanes, ships, and trains; at airport terminals and train stations; and at other facilities in the transportation market-a market that enjoys about $3.7 billion in sales each year. Cruise lines put a great deal of emphasis on their food service. Industry surveys cite the food served shipboard as one of the top reasons for taking a cruise and selecting a specific line. Royal Caribbean International's 142,000-ton Voyager of the Seas carries 3,114 passengers and a crew of 1,181; fully 30 percent of the crew works in the kitchen. Royal Caribbean has won numerous international awards for its food.

Food service in airports and train terminals is often provided by restaurants – frequently limited-menu restaurants-and contract food companies such as ARAMARK that bid for the opportunity to sell food in the terminals. United Airlines maintains its own in-flight kitchens; other airlines buy their meals from Ogden

Entertainment Services (a division of ARAMARK), Sky Chef, or Dobbs International Services. Many airlines today are trying to differentiate themselves, at least on routes they share with several competing airlines, by serving more distinctive food in business and first-class sections, using fresh food instead of frozen items when possible.

Even the selection of wines available on board has been greatly upgraded in some instances. Although airline passenger traffic is strong, growth in food and drink sales has reached a plateau, in part because food service on many flights has been cut back due to the growing popularity of no-frills air carriers such as Southwest and Midway.

Recreational Market. The recreational market includes food service facilities located at sports arenas, stadiums, racetracks, movie theaters, bowling alleys, amusement parks, municipal convention centers, and other attractions. All together, this is an $11.7 billion market. In many cases, recreational-market food service facilities are concessions run by contract food companies. The largest contract food companies in the recreational market include Fine Host, Volume Services America, Ogden Entertainment Services, and ARAMARK.

Business and Industry Market. The business and industry market consists of nonfood service businesses that offer on-site food service to their employees. Most businesses that provide employee meals use contract food companies such as Sodexho and ARAMARK. At Pacific Bell in San Ramon, California, ARAMARK offers food service to 8,500 employees. A number of food stations serve such fare as Asian and Mexican dishes, sandwiches, salads, pizza, pasta, desserts, and specialty drinks called "smoothies."

Educational Market. One of the biggest changes in college food service programmes has been the gradual shift from mandated meal plans to a la carte operations. Due in part to this shift, many college food service operators have become revenue producers instead of revenue consumers for their colleges. Another change in college food service programmes has come about because an increasing number of nontraditional students are going to college today. Therefore, dining directors have had to change their food service programmes to accommodate preferences that are somewhat different from those of the typical 18-year-old.

Health Care Market. The health care market consists of three principal segments: hospitals and other medical centers, nursing homes, and retirement communities (including congregate food sites-community-sponsored meal centers for senior citizens). Many experts believe that there is enormous potential for food service management companies in the health care market. This can be attributed to a combination of factorsrapidly changing life-styles, an aging population, skyrocketing medical costs, restricted federal funds, and a lack of family support systems.

Most health care facilities run their own food service departments, some of which can be quite extensive. Many hospitals operate vending machines, visitor coffee shops, employee cafeterias, special dining facilities for doctors, day-care food programmes for employees' children, regular patient food programmes, and special patient food programmes that can include gourmet meals (with accompanying wines) served in patient rooms.

Retail Market. Two major trends in food service have surfaced in recent years. The first is the increasing tendency of Americans to eat food prepared outside of the home, as evidenced by the dramatic growth in restaurant food sales. The second trend, which is developing even more rapidly, is the growth in the take-out and delivery segment of the market. It is clear that

Americans are cooking less. It is also clear that there is a growing inclination to buy food prepared outside the home and bring it home to consume it. This last development is in line with marketing trends in other areas such as home electronics and furniture, where research has shown that, at an increasing rate, people use their homes as recreational and entertainment centers.

A good part of retail business take-out sales comes at the expense of traditional restaurants and quick-service outlets. This is due, among other reasons, to increased marketing by convenience stores and supermarkets of their prepared take-out foods. Supermarkets are increasing the size and scope of their take-out food operations. Some industry observers expect the average supermarket to increase in size from its present 30,000-50,000 square feet to 200,000 square feet (2,790-4,650 square meters to 18,600 square meters). Much of that space will be devoted to precooked take-out dishes and sitdown food service areas.

Many supermarkets already offer take-out salad bars in addition to their traditional deli sections. Using ovens in their bakeries, many of today's supermarkets are preparing a complete line of food products for their small in-store restaurants and cafeterias. Supermarket research shows that supermarket produce is perceived to be fresher than that sold in most restaurants. Some supermarkets are taking advantage of this perception by selling a wide range of freshly prepared salad and vegetable dishes.

Some have hired chefs to work in open kitchens so that customers can actually see that dishes are prepared with fresh-not frozen-ingredients. Another supermarket food service trend is the growth of food courts. Supermarket chains are installing food courts (similar to those found in shopping malls) in hopes of winning back some of the food dollars they have lost to restaurants.

Corrections Food Service. Correctional institutions-state and federal prisons and local jails constitute another segment of the food service industry. Correctional institutions often have a hard time attracting and retaining food service staff because they cannot offer much professional career growth. However, the unique challenge they do offer can be attractive to some people. A prison must offer a cyclical menu that is not overly repetitive and has the flexibility to meet special religious and medical dietary needs, while still offering a bit of creativity in both preparation and presentation.

Theft is another problem encountered by prison food service systems. Stringent controls must be used. Food costs are a further constraint on operations. Correctional institutions often have limited budgets for food service; economies of scale can thus make a substantial difference in the type and variety of food that can be offered to inmates. Because they enjoy economies of scale, contract food companies are now successfully competing in this area.

Military Food Service. Military food service is a very specialised area. Nevertheless, it deserves mention because of its diversity in terms of geography, type of facility, and size. Jobs in military food service range from space shuttle food preparation to aircraft carrier or nuclear submarine mess operations to Army, Navy, Air Force, Marine, and Coast Guard officers' club management at bases all over the world. Both civilian and military personnel are employed by many of these facilities.

Contractors. Contract food management companies are the major operators of noncommercial food service. Two of the largest are ARAMARK and Sodexho Contract food management companies are hired to operate restaurants and other food service outlets in convention centers, sports arenas, tourist attractions, colleges and schools, office buildings, manufacturing plant, and health care facilities. Contractors meet the need of businesses and other clients who want to provide food service to patrons and! or employees, yet do not want to get involved in an activity (preparing and serving food) that is outside their expertise.

Contract food management companies offer numerous careers in restaurant management. Many contractors recruit on college campuses. As increasing numbers of consumers want to either dine out or take prepared food home, the number of food-service operations has skyrocketed from 155,000 about 25 years ago to nearly 800,000 today. But there's still room in the market for your food-service business. Shifting demographics and changing lifestyles are driving the surge in food-service businesses. Busy consumers don't have the time or inclination to cook. They want the flavor of fresh bread without the hassle of baking. They want tasty, nutritious meals without dishes to wash.

In fact, the rise in popularity of to-go operations underscores some clear trends in the food-service industry. More and more singles, working parents and elderly people are demanding greater convenience in buying their meals and are turning to operations that provide that convenience. Though the future looks bright for the food-service industry overall, there are no guarantees in this business. Even the most successful operators will tell you this isn't a "get rich quick" industry. It's more like a "work hard and make a living" industry.

A hard reality is that many restaurants fail during their first year in business, frequently due to a lack of planning. Does this mean your food-service business must be an extremely complex operation? Not at all-in fact, the more streamlined you can make it, the better your chances for success.

Games in Hotels

Lotteries

European settlers brought the idea of lotteries to the New

World. While the Spanish lottery served as an example for many lotteries in Southern and Central America, lotteries in the North were an immediate outgrowth of English lotteries. In fact, tickets of the English state lotteries were sold in the colonies. New York authorised its first public lottery in 1746 to finance fortification of the city. This first lottery was not overly successful. The drawing had to be postponed due to sluggish sales, and even then the treasury ended up buying the remaining tickets.

Nevertheless, there was a second lottery at the end of the same year, this time to raise money for founding a college. The first lottery-related act after the revolution was aimed at suppressing private lotteries. It iterated the penalties of the law of 1774 but pardoned all offenses that had been committed after 1776. In 1790, a first lottery was authorised to repair the city hall of New York which was intended as the seat of Congress. Five years later, a lottery was held to benefit the poor, and, in 1797, one was authorised to improve certain roads.

The beginning of the 19th century saw a wave of public lotteries: a series of lotteries to improve navigation of the Hudson river, four lotteries for the encouragement of literature, the Black River lottery for building a road along this river, a lottery to finance construction of the state capitol, and a series of lotteries for the endowment of Union College. Organising lotteries had become big business.

Managers were required to give bonds to guarantee subsequent payment of prizes but also received commissions ranging from 10 to 15 percent of the amount raised. They no longer sold tickets personally but tended to sell them in bulk to lottery offices. Those lottery offices were a lucrative business. They not only sold tickets at a considerable margin but also offered lottery insurance and let out tickets. Letting out of tickets was possible because drawings lasted for several days, so one could rent a ticket by the day at a fraction of the cost of buying it.

Much more important was lottery insurance, which was basically side betting on whether official tickets would obtain a prize or turn out blank. An act was passed in 1807 against lottery insurance and amended in 1809 to cover private lotteries as well. The year 1810 saw the first failure of a lottery manager, which resulted in the state paying prizes at a loss of over 40,000 dollars. Despite these first mishaps there were new lotteries.

To promote medical science, a lottery was authorised to provide money for the purchase of a formerly private botanic garden. Further lotteries were authorised for improving navigation of the Hudson, as well as for educational purposes and road building. With the rising number and volume of lotteries, opposition to them grew. A new law against private lotteries and lottery insurance was passed in 1813.

Tribal Gaming

Gaming has been a part of the United States from the colonial era up through today. Lotteries were critical to funding the Revolutionary War, and the colonisation of America, and even helped fund the beginning of venerable institutions like Harvard University and Princeton. Indian gaming, originally part of tribal ceremonies or celebrations, existed long before Europeans came to America. However, as Europeans began settling America, they gradually took away every means of self-sufficiency American Indians had: destroying agrarian societies, killing the buffalo and forcing American Indians onto remote, desolate reservations. Today, gaming is often the only viable source of employment and governmental revenues available to tribes.

Today, gaming has replaced the buffalo as the mechanism used by American Indian people for survival. The proceeds from gaming are used by Indian Nations for subsistence, cultural preservation, and to replenish impoverished economies. Indian gaming has been a major catalyst for community growth and economic development, generating revenues for tribes like no federal stimulus effort ever has before. After decades of poverty and high unemployment on often geographically remote reservations, Indian people now see gaming as an integral part of tribal economies and the means to achieve self-sufficiency.

But maintaining the sovereign right to conduct tribal gaming operations hasn't gone unchallenged, and opposition from state and federal governments and privately held gaming interests still grows. Before the establishment of casinos, gambling games were conducted on the streets, in homes, or in private clubs. (The word "casino" comes from the Italian "casa", which means house.) The amount that could be won was limited to the funds of the individual players. By the 17th century however, gambling had become formalised, with special venues that offered players the opportunity to bet against the "house", which would act as banker, paying out all winnings and retaining losing bets. This gave players the advantage of potentially winning more money than they bet.

Edouard Benazet, who employed Parisian craftsmen to design the stylish rooms, opened one of the oldest casinos in Europe, at Baden Baden in Germany, in 1748. Despite several closures in its history, the Baden Baden casino still operates today. The casino at Spa, a Belgian resort town noted for its mineral baths, was built by the Prince Bishop of the province of Liege in 1763.

In 1857, Prince Charles III of Monaco decided to introduce gambling to his Mediterranean principality to boost its finances. Under the auspices of art lover Francoise Blanc and his son Camille, no expense was spared on the "belle epoque building" which was created by a number of architects, among them Charles Garnier, designer of the Paris Opera House. In the early 20th century Monte Carlo Casino quickly became a fashionable destination for the rich and famous of the day, including the director of the "Ballet Russe" in Paris, Sergei Diaghalev, Britain's King Edward VII, and the Italian tenor Enrico Caruso.

Some of the first casinos in American were established during the early 1800s in New Orleans, along the Mississippi River. Although, at that time, there were no casinos on the riverboats themselves, informal gambling was a popular way for travelers to pass the journey. Professional gamblers, called "sharps", would target wealthy passengers and relieve them of their money. Gambling moved westward with the expansion of the railroads and flourished during the time of the California gold rush and the Nevada silver era.

Las Vegas in Nevada owes its success to the mobster Benjamin "Bugsy" Siegel who organised gaming and bookmaking operations for The Mob (the Mafia). Due to a crackdown on gambling in the eastern USA, Siegel moved west in the 1940s. During the Great Depression gambling had been legalised in Nevada to increase revenue for the state, but what existed in Las Vegas at that time were a few decidedly down-market casinos that were frequented by the locals.

Siegel planned to open a luxurious hotel where the rich and famous could gamble and, after a failed attempt to take over an existing casino, he decided to build his own. Once Siegel had managed to convince The Mob to invest in his idea, building started, but costs escalated from initial estimates of $1.2 million to over $6 million, because everyone, including Siegel, was stealing money from the project. It is rumored that the palm trees were sold to the casino several times over and that Siegel's girlfriend, Virginia Hill, was accumulation money in a Swiss bank account.

The Mob soon discovered Siegel's skimming and ordered him to be killed, but decided to give him a reprieve until after the opening. The Flamingo Hotel and Casino finally opened on 26 December 1946. A huge party was organised, with many of the film stars of the day in attendance. The hotel was not finished, so the guests had nowhere to sleep. They parties for two days and then went home.

The Flamingo was a flop and Bugsy Siegel was eventually killed by The Mob in 1947, but his dream of making Las Vegas into a gambling canter survived. As other businessmen realised that Las Vegas had potential as a resort, investment flowed into the town. The Desert Inn Casino opened in 1950, followed by the Sands Casino in 1952, with the Dunes, and the Riviera opening in 1955.

Despite gambling being illegal, casinos continued to operate elsewhere in the USA thanks to widespread corruption in the police and government. One of the most luxurious "illegal" casinos was Chicago's Big House which operated between 1929 and 1950. Run by associates of gangster Al Capone, it was elegantly furnished, with mahogany gaming tables, oriental rugs and a free taxi service to shuttle players to and from Chicago's southside. The club was also the headquarters of a countrywide bookmaking operation.

During the 1950s virtually all the casinos in Las Vegas were controlled by The Mob. A US senate investigation into criminal activity in the casino industry found that skimming (retaining a portion of the profits) was rife, resulting in tax evasion on stakes and profits. When legislation allowing corporations to own Las Vegas casinos came into being in 1965, entrepreneur and multimillionaire Howard Hughes was the first to take advantage of this change in law, buying the Desert Inn and several other casinos, as well as plots of land in the city. When MGM, Hilton and Holiday Inn followed suit, the finances of the mob proved to be no match for the might of the major corporations, and gradually the casino industry was cleaned up.

Studies have shown that today's casino players are typically graduates in white-collar jobs with a higher than average income, who gamble to win money. A survey carried out by Roper Starch Worldwide Inc. of New York found that, for three out of four casino visitors, their prime motive is to win, while 57 per cent go for entertainment and recreation. Australians are the western world's biggest gamblers, spending over $2,000 a year per head of population. A close second are Americans at $1,800 per head of population.

Casinos operate around the world, mainly in tourist areas including Las Vegas, Australia's Gold Coast, and resorts in the Mediterranean and Caribbean. Gaming is mostly state controlled and is an important contributor to national and local revenues, although percentages vary from country to country. Gaming is a huge industry in the USA, where it is legal in 24 states. There has been a casino building boom in recent years, particularly in Nevada. Gambling was legalised in Atlantic City, New Jersey, in 1978, to revitalise the rundown seaside resort.

In 1987, after a legal battle, the US Supreme Court finally recognised the right of native Americans to operate gaming establishments on their reservations. Since 1989, over 300 new gaming operations have been established on Indian reservations. The largest casino in the world, Foxwoods Resort in Connecticut, is owned and operated by the Mashantucket Tribe and attracts over 16 million visitors annually. It comprises two hotels and five separate casinos. Foxwoods has 140,000m2 (1,5 million sq ft) of floor space, of which 28,000m² (300,000 sq ft) is devoted to gaming.

Las Vegas reigns supreme as the "casino capital" of the world, attracting 30 million visitors annually to over 50 casinos. When Wilbur Clark opened the Desert Inn on 24 April 1950, he ceremonially threw away the keys, announcing there would never be a reason to lock the door again. The tradition continues today, with most Las Vegas casinos opening 24 hours, seven days a week. The minimum age for gambling in Nevada is 21 years.

The 1960s saw the legalisation in the UK. Bringing the gaming industry within the law led to the implementation of strict controls to regulate payouts and how the games operate. The Gaming Board of Great Britain ensures the fair running of casinos and scrutinises casino personnel and operators. Of the UK's 116 casinos, 21 are located in London, with the remainder in major cities and tourist areas. Almost all countries in continental Europe have casinos. France has governmentregulated casinos in over 170 towns and cities.

Spain legalised casinos in the late 1970s and also allows slot machines in bars and arcades. In the Netherlands, a government company, Holland Casinos, was established to operate the casinos, which now exist in ten locations. Greece has nine casinos, which are privately-run government-allocated franchises. Belgium's eight casinos remain illegal but are tolerated by the government, which imposes taxation on them. In the 1970s casinos were legalised in Australia. They are run by private operators under franchises granted by the government. Fourteen casinos now operate in the major cities and Gold Coast resorts, contributing a $2 billion annually to state revenues.

Canada began opening government-owned casinos in the early 1990s and now has a number of resort casinos that attract tourists, as well as some smaller provincial casinos catering for the local population. Although South Africa introduced casino gaming during the apartheid era, confining it to the so-called "independent homelands", the demise of apartheid meant that the country had to face up to the reality of legalising gaming operations that were formerly not considered to be within the boundaries of the state. Casino gaming was recognised in 1994 and a rationalisation process, under the Gambling Board, has ensured that lucrative gaming licenses are equitable distributed throughout all nine provinces.

In many countries, gambling has gone in and out of favor depending on the prevailing moral, social and religious climate. Most objections to gambling are based on social and religious issues. However despite numerous attempts throughout history to outlaw gaming, it has still thrived. Banning gaming simply results in the establishments of illegal casinos. Gaming-related social problems are as old as gaming itself. In Roman times, gaming was restricted to one week of the year, during the Saturnalia festival (equivalent to the Christmas and New Year holidays). However this did not deter Roman players, who continued to gamble in private houses and clubs.

Even when fines (equivalent to four times the stakes) were introduced for players caught gambling, the Romans managed to evade the law by using engraved discs, called "roundels", instead of money. Almost as soon as playing cards were introduced to Europe, they were opposed. In Paris, legislation prohibiting playing cards was passed in 1377, and in Italy, playing cards and dice were burned. In the USA, many attempts were made to prevent gambling. Early Puritan settlers initially banned the possession of gaming equipment, but relented, allowing games for recreational purposes.

Later legislation was ineffective as it banned specific games. Players simply changed the names or invented new games. By 1910 gambling was made illegal throughout the USA, but due to widespread corruption among law enforcement officers, this law had little effect. In the 54 years since the first legal wager was made in sparsely populated Las Vegas in 1931, the gaming industry has evolved into one of the most dynamic and economically powerful forces in present-day American business.

With some form of gaming now legal in 48 of the 50 states and the now-dominant view that gaming is an enjoyable and morally acceptable form of entertainment, the gaming business is currently a $500 billion venture responsible for hundreds of thousands of jobs and billions of dollars in tax revenues and capital investment. It provides a strong economic impact that has repeatedly proven to be a financial boost for governments and the citizens these governments serve.

Buoyed by the success of gaming in Nevada and the tax-free status Nevada residents enjoy, gaming first expanded to Atlantic City in 1978. Before casino gaming was introduced in Atlantic City, the area had all but been abandoned by tourists, leading to a decay in both its social and physical stature. While casinos in Atlantic City have been criticised for failing short of completely revitalising the area, the simple fact remains that without casinos Atlantic City would not have 41,000 gaming industry jobs, would not have an annual direct tax impact of $600 million, would not have $5 billion in new capital investment related to gaming and would not have 10 times more annual tourist visits than in the years preceding gaming's introduction.

As day-to-day costs began to outstrip tax revenues during the early-to-mid-1 980s and as unemployment rates soared and retail sales dropped, state and local governments began seeking other forms of revenue and economic development. This created the birth of the riverboat gaming industry—and the 'face of the entertainment business in the United States would forever be changed. Beginning with Iowa in 1989 and continuing with Mississippi, Illinois, Louisiana, Missouri and Indiana, states heeded the voters' wishes and began legalising riverboat gaming, which in turn brought a new form of entertainmentto millions of people far away from the major gaming centers of Nevada and Atlantic City.

Land-based casinos in Colorado and South Dakota and Native American gaming ventures in many other states also contributed to the growing availability of what had been perceived as taboo decades earlier. If you combined all of the commercial gaming activities in the country and created one entity, it would account for $39.9 billion in revenue in 1994, a figure that would rank 12th among all companies on the Forbes Sales 500 list based on gross revenue being equivalent to sales in non-gambling accounting. This figure, for example, ranks ahead of Kmart's $34.3 billion but below Chrysler's $52.2 billion. In terms of aggregate sales, the Forbes Sales 500 increased by a healthy 8 percent in 1994, but gaming did even better, increasing 15 percent over the previous year.

So what do all these numbers prove? In simple terms, they show what a force gaming has become in relation to the national economy as a whole. With more than 90 gaming companies traded publicly, the national impact of gaming is felt on Wall Street and in small towns throughout the country. The numbers also indicate this country's growing demand for entertainment, an appetite that is directly related to a 6 percent rise in personal income from 1993 to 1994. Proportionally, more and more discretionary income is spent on various forms of entertainment, which includes sporting events, concerts, theme parks, movies and, of course, gaming.

Gaming is certainly not a cure-all for every state facing a budget shortfall, but under the right circumstances, gaming can produce remarkable economic benefits that create longterm stability and improve the overall quality of life. For examples on how to implement casino gaming to produce an undisputed level of success, look no further than Vicksburg, Mississippi, Joliet, Illinois, and Council Bluffs, Iowa.

Riverboat Gambling

Today, riverboat gambling is a different affair. For instance, the finer 19th-century riverboats had appointments like stained glass windows, chandeliers, and carved, gilded filigree woodwork. In contrast, modern riverboats may appear as quaint on the outside as their predecessors, but the interiors are heavily modernised with sports bars, glitzy Vegas-style decorations, and buffets. Another big difference is that nowadays the games are run by the house, so gamers play against a corporation.

In the old riverboats, the management didn't get involved in the gambling. It wasn't even allowed in some of the boats, but the staff would often turn a blind eye if no other passengers complained. Dishonest incidents amongst the players occurred, but the reputation of the professional gambler for cheating may be overstated. Punishment for such a travesty could be severe, including whipping and being dropped ashore at the nearest opportunity. Also, the management couldn't necessarily restrain the other passengers from meting out their own punishments.

Therefore, the professional gamblers depended on personal skill more than on hidden cards or tricks with mirrors. Games on the old riverboats were limited to cards. Now, you can play such games as slots, video poker, keno, craps, roulette, baccarat, and blackjack. Riverboat experiences come in many forms. Most gambling riverboats are based on the Mississippi River or one of its tributaries. It's possible to cruise in a boat whose paddles are still powered by steam engines; other boats are permanently moored.

In Missouri, you can find a "boat in a moat," which refers to riverboats that float in dug-out pools that are fed with water from the Missouri River. They are essentially as land-locked as rubberduckies in a tub. The Emerald Queen, a riverboat in Washington State, isn't even in a river. It sits in the Puget Sound, which is part of the Pacific Ocean.

In Nevada, there are at least two riverboats that have been removed from a water environment altogether. They sit-if you'll pardon the simile-like fish out of water. The Mississippi originates in Lake Itasca in northern Minnesota, then flows generally south for 2,470 miles to the Gulf of Mexico. It serves as a border for 10 states. This spread allows ample geographic area to find a riverboat, but it also means that the experience on each may be different, according to the laws of the state in which a boat is located.

Until recently, for instance, the Casino Queen, a riverboat in East St. Louis, Illinois was required by law to engage in river cruises unless restricted by weather or river conditions. Consequently, every two hours, the boat would chug upriver for an hour-long voyage. Recently this requirement was lifted, and it remains moored, open 23 hours a day. Across the river in Missouri, the President Casino also stays permanently moored. It's housed in the Admiral, an art-deco style riverboat that was used to host cruises earlier in this century. Known for being plush and luxurious, it is noticeably nicer than some boats across the river.

Since the Mississippi bisects the country, riverboat experiences are possible from within many Midwestern states. The boats are especially fun to check out during road trips or when staying in a Midwest city. Gaming riverboats currently operate in Illinois, Indiana, Iowa, Louisiana, Mississippi, Missouri, Nevada, and Washington. It's worth mentioning that riverboats can be experienced without gaming. The Delta Queen Steamboat Company in New Orleans operates three- to 14-night cruises on their steam-powered paddlewheelers. The Mississippi Queen is outfitted like a cruise liner, including a swimming pool, while the American Queen is outfitted nostalgically, with antiques and old-style grandeur (800-543-7637). The casino market falls into three categories:

- first, there is the 'grind' market, which includes local players who go to the nearest casino or gaming venue;
- secondly, there is the 'tourist' market, which takes in both domestic and international tourists who make a visit to a casino as part of a package that includes other features and trips; and
- thirdly, there is the 'premium' market, which is composed of the big playerssometimes called 'high rollers'-who can be either local or international. The casino sector in is extremely competitive in the. Premium market. These high rollers can wager more than US$5 million over just a few' days, and casinos endeavour to attract these players by offering free first-class air travel (or sometimes travel in a private Lear jet), limousines, and accommodation.

Club Management

A club is an association of persons with some common objective, usually jointly supported and meeting periodically. People join clubs to enjoy the company of friends in comfortable surroundings. The face of clubs has drastically changed over the last 100 years, and as we enter the 21st century, we can see continuous changes throughout the industry. But to truly understand the present, we must first look at the past. The first recorded clubs date back to ancient times, when people started gathering at the Roman baths. These establishments, run by managers, became places where select groups of people went with their peers to discuss social issues.

The coffee houses in 17th century London brought about the beginnings of the modern club. The clubs were actually special rooms in taverns which operated on an invitation-only basis. Over the next 200 years, clubs evolved through various forms, fulfilling diverse purposes, becoming what are known as "gentlemen's clubs." Dining clubs were a popular feature in Greek society.

As the United States entered the 20th century, clubs found that they had to cater to members with much more leisure time. Once considered an integral part of the social fabric of the upper class, the club has become a center for the American family and its recreational activities. Thus began the club as we know it today. The club industry is still evolving, conforming to today's social trends and population demands. Clubs have been around for hundreds of years, but most clubs in existence today are patterned after those of the British from the seventeenth and eighteenth centuries.

The Royal and Ancient Golf Club of St. Andrews, Scotland, founded in 1758 and said to be the birthplace of golf, is the forerunner of the modern country club. Today's city clubs are similarly related to English social clubs, where members meet over drinks and dinner in local taverns.

Services at Clubs

The unique nature of clubs and their membership status raises the service requirements and expectations of guests. Clubs, by their very nature and definition are selective.

Members want to feel like the service they receive is different, a step above that available to others. This raises the demands on all those who work for clubs, but especially for the general manager, who must meet a host of sometimes divergent goals.

The first priority of a club manager is member satisfaction. A club manager must be diplomatic, provide exemplary service, prepare the budget, and oversee the entire operation. Most club managers are not recent graduates; instead, they often come from the ranks of hotel management and are at a later stage in their careers. The job of assistant manager is usually an entry-level position for a college graduate with a degree in hospitality management.

An assistant manager might be in charge of food and beverage operations, supervising the purchase and service of food and beverages in the dining room and lounges. In this case the assistant manager would work closely with the chef, who is in charge of the kitchen, or the purchaser, who is in charge of the expenditure of club funds. Other areas of responsibility for the assistant manager include the athletic facilities, as well as the security and maintenance of the club-house itself. A large club might have more than one assistant manager to oversee specific areas of the club. For those interested in club management serves as the professional association for club managers.

Club membership has increased steadily over the last 20 years and will continue to do so. Due to this growth, the concept of the club has changed remarkably. Throughout the history of clubs, we have seen dramatic changes in the services and amenities offered to members. As managers, the future no longer lies solely in country clubs. There is now a wider scope of clubs including athletic, city, military, swimming, tennis, university, riding and yacht clubs with additional opportunities for advancement. To provide a better understanding of the services provided and the manager's role in a particular type of club, a description of the two most common types of clubs country and city is listed below.

In addition to controlling daily operations, a manager may be required to have a familiarity with antiques and the scholarly arts and should possess knowledge of wine. Because of the club's character and location, a city club manager can generally expect the heaviest use of club facilities in the afternoon hours during the business week. Countless jobs exist in the club industry and are described in the job descriptions for the private club industry.

Club managers' duties vary based on experience, size and location of the club and also the number of employees that one supervises. For example, in a small club that employs fewer than 20 people, the manager must be a "jack-of-all-trades," heading various departments and supervising employees. At a larger club operation with hundreds or even thousands of members, the club manager may act as a supervisory head, who is the main contact for the department heads and the liaison between the board members and the staff.

Financial Management

Golf clubs, in particular the larger clubs, are for all intents and purposes business enterprises (even though they are non-profit) and they should be run in a business-like manner. It is crucial that the finances of the clubs be well run. Every member of the club should have an interest in the finances and if those finances are poorly run it will soon become evident; The experience of clubs where finances are poorly managed generally results in a degrading of club life and disharmony.

Financial matters should not be left to the club accountant, treasurer, manager or finance committee etc. Thus :- The whole matter in the longevity and continuity of the club revolves around serving the membership. The entire general committee must be involved. The committee, under the principles of corporate governance, cannot shed its responsibility. It can delegate its authority, but not remove it's responsibility.

Service Management

Service is defined as work done for others. In the hospitality industry we need to ensure that the work for others far exceeds their expectations. The key is anticipating, rewarding and exceeding guest expectations. In the view of a senior hospitality professional it may be radical to say, that the hotel industry has it backwards when it tries to service the desires of luxury guests retrospectively. You must be out in front of the guest, anticipating his needs and then meeting and even exceeding them and meeting needs that the guest didn't even know he had.

Nature of the Product

The intangibility of service makes seeing hospitality as an industry a little difficult for many people. Often when people think of industries, they picture large manufacturing complexes with towering smokestacks and noisy production lines. These industries produce tangible products that usually can be handled, stored for future use, and uniformly produced. Service, on the other hand, is an intangible product. Respect shown to a guest cannot be held in the hands; pulling out a chair for a guest cannot be stored for future use; and acceptable practices in one culture may be considered rude in another, rendering uniformity in service impractical.

Some business related to hospitality also produce tangible products, such as special kitchen equipment used in commercial restaurants. But for most hospitality businesses, the main business is the creation of memorable experiences through furnishing services. Their shared mission is to provide services while also making a profit. Restaurants and hotels have a two-fold purpose: to satisfy the physical and psychological expectations of guests. They accomplish this through providing a good product (the meal or the room) and a good service (delivering the meal or room appropriately).

Delivery

Delivery of an intangible product naturally leaves room for conflicting perceptions of its quality. Not only might people within the industry disagree on some theoretical points, but customers and employees may also view the service delivery from quite different perspectives. A once-in-a-lifetime experience for the guest is often a routine occurrence for the employee. The guest is investing time, money, and emotions in the hope of receiving a pleasurable experience. All these are lost if the service fails to meet that expectation.

The employee, however, can merely resolve to do better with the next guest. Service does not run on a continuum from good to poor. Such a scale is impossible because the variables involved in determining good or poor service—guest expectations and the firm's image—are not fixed. Even the concept of value or relative worth is based upon guest perception. It is fair to say, however, that most guests want quality service at a fair price.

Guests perceive good service on the basis of their own expectations of the hospitality staff. Similarly, value based on the customers' expectations in relation to how much they spend for the service and how much they would spend for a similar service elsewhere. Certainly, people do not expect the same services from a low-priced hotel as they do from a high-priced hotel. However, what they do expect are the same or better services at the hotel or restaurant where they are guests (and at the same or better prices) than at the competition.

Good service is often equated with the number of amenities, the degree of personal attention/interaction, or the speed of service delivery. While these factors are related to service, identifying them with service quality is misleading. Service, and service quality, are contextually defined by the guest's expectations as well as the organisation's image. Good service at a McDonald's is entirely different from good service at Wolfgang Puck's—yet both can provide quality service.

Service Encounter

The period of time in which a customer directly interacts with a service is known as the service encounter. That interaction may take place with either personnel or the physical facilities and other visible elements. If the hospitality establishment's advertising leads a guest to expect valet parking, the presence or absence of such service affect's the guest's perception of the firm. In human interactions, both guests and employees bring to the encounter certain expectations and personality traits.

Guests measure the quality of service by comparing the services received with what they expected to receive, given the type of establishment offering the service. Five general elements comprise the scale by which service may be judged:

(1) tangibles,

(2) reliability,

(3) responsiveness,

(4) assurance, and

(5) empathy.

Since a majority of these are an assessment of human interaction, how an employee performs during a service encounter contributes heavily to the perception of quality service. Most employee-guest interactions that significantly influence the guest's perception of satisfactory or dissatisfactory service fall under one of three general categories:

1. Employee response to service delivery system failure.
2. Employee response to customer needs and requests.
3. Unprompted and unsolicited employee actions.

Service does not need to be "spectacular" to be considered good. In some settings, good service is almost unnoticeable, because everything goes along according to the guest's expectations. Generally, it is only when the service falls outside the limits of the guest's expectations that it is deemed satisfactory or unsatisfactory.

Services Products and Operations

Operations management deals with the production and delivery of service products. In this regard, it focuses on the day to day operations, improving the service operations in the medium term, and developing a framework for future operations. However, operations management is a line function where the management has to deal with day to day issues of providing quality and customer satisfaction as well as meeting the operational and financial targets of the company.

For the efficient and effective production and delivery of services requires planning as well as successful implementation of strategies. In the manufacturing sector, it's about the efficient and effective production of tangible goods that are normally studied under 'Industrial Engineering'. But in the service sector such as tourism and hotel or banks, the production function does not involve any production of tangible goods.

Nevertheless, services are considered virtual product, and as in the manufacturing sector, service products need to be produced and delivered to customer as efficiently and effectively as possible. In the production of goods and services, one of the critical issues is the efficient and effective allocation of resources. Such resources are raw materials, capital, human resources as well as machinery and equipment.

In addition, space and facilities (also considered as resources) are also required for the production function. Efficient and effective allocation of these resources for the production function becomes the ultimate objective of Operations Management function in general. In the service sector, the focus of operations management is mainly on managing customer expectations and experience.

Service products are either collection of service activities or a combination of services activities and some form of tangible goods that are offered in the market place for a price. Even most of the manufactured goods that are considered purely tangible can have some elements of intangible services attached to it. Services operation is different from the production of goods in many ways. This is because, services as products differ from the manufactured products and goods. In order to understand these differences, here first examine the nature and characteristics of service products. Three major characteristics any services are as follows:

- Services are intangible→Intangibility
- Services are heterogeneous→Heterogeneity
- Services are perishable→Perishability

The first important difference between goods and services is that the latter is intangible or virtual. This means, the service products cannot be seen or felt as in the case of goods. Service product is rather an experience. Some services such as teaching or treating a patient by a doctor are at the extreme end of the product range. They are called pure services where human interaction is high. But some service product such as a flight in an airline, provide some tangible components to the service element. The aircraft, seat, flight ticket etc. are such tangible components. It must be born in mind that every service product has some form of tangible component.

The second most important characteristic of a service product is heterogeneity. Being heterogeneous means, the delivery of a service product, even if it is similar in nature, is different from each other. For example, the experience of reserving a hotel room to checking in and staying in the hotel is different every time we purchase hotel product.

Moreover, because of this nature, it is also difficult to store the service products for future consumption. Service is thus a perishable product and it cannot be stored for future sale or use. Moreover, the consumer cannot claim any ownership as in the case of a manufactured good such as a car.

The fourth and one of the most important characteristics of services is the simultaneous production & consumption of service products. This means, the production and consumption take place at the same time. When the service products are produced and delivered (either by the employees or employees & technology), it is almost immediately consumed by the customer. Sometimes, the customer participates in the production and delivery process while consuming.

Hotel and Tourism Services

Travel & Tourism, including hospitality is the fastest growing service sector today. Some would include all these sectors under one umbrella of tourism and classify the tourism sector into travel, hotel, and restaurant or catering services. Some service products have tangible components that are highly visible. Tourism sector products such as airline seat, hotel rooms, or restaurant meals are such service products.

When we mean a service product, a customer should be able buy such products in the market. In this sense, an accommodation facility such as a hotel is not a product but a hotel room is a product. Similarly, an airline is not a product but the flight ticket is a product. In most cases, service products are also sold as packages. For example, a tour package is a holiday product, which consists of a flight ticket, hotel room and dinner etc. In this case, the operations management becomes rather complex where more than one service provider perform several tasks to provide the holiday package. This is the case of a tour operator, who buys various tourism products from different providers and packages them to be sold for the potential tourists.

This course will focus mainly on the operation of hotels where the key service products are rooms and bed, food and beverage services, and other services such as conference products. The different service operation centers are called Strategic Service Units (SSU). However, in a hotel, the primary service center is the rooms operations. Tourism is not only the largest growth sector among the service sector businesses but also most challenging. Competition is very high and the customer expectation is also increasingly demanding. Guest satisfaction accompanied by demand for quality service products and efficiency and effectiveness in resource allocation during service operations becomes the norm of this business.

The service concept should identify and describe the 'core service' and the 'supplementary services'. The term service concept often refers to the idea of defining a 'service product'. Service product may have some service components as well as tangible elements, which the customer purchases. However, the idea of 'service concept' is often said to consist of something more on top of describing 'service product'. The service product is the output of the concept that integrate other elements such as the service blueprint and service system, service process and service technology as well service delivery.

The whole idea of the 'product' can be well differentiated from a mass produced 'hotel product' offered by large-scale factory-like chain hotels. Therefore the product idea comes from the concept and, in order to produce and deliver such a product, managers would need to design and develop a satisfactory service blueprint and service system matched by reliable service technology and service process.

Therefore the terminology of service concept incorporates several aspects of the service operation, including what is in the mind of the customer shaped up by experience and expectation. In this sense, service concept should also help define an effective marketing communication strategy for the service business. Moreover, service concept is also considered as a strategic tool from which other service elements such as service blueprint, service process, and service technology are said to emerge.

Service Technology

The way a service sector establishment produces and delivers service products is called service technology. This does not necessarily mean that the process should include machines and equipment. Service technology is a technical term, which describes the process of service production and delivery as well consumption. It is a process of transferring the inputs into outputs.

The concept of service technology differs from one establishment to another even in the same sector. But service technology can remain the same if the concept of service production and delivery is same. For example, the operation concept of McDonolds is considered to be the same everywhere. Therefore, the service technology employed by the fast food chain can be considered the same. In other words, the operating plan and the operating process are the same everywhere. So is the case of many international hotel chains. However, the size of the operation, although maybe similar in concept, may require the operators to change the service technology in some cases.

Here, the type of service product offered, the equipment and materials used to produce the service, the design and décor of the facility, and even the customer profile are all considered same. Therefore, the employee profile and the training given as well as the training methods used are also considered to be the same when the service concept is same. This makes replication of service easier where the service products are more or less homogeneous. Such a process helps the service companies to standardise their service production process as well as the service products sold.

Service blueprint focuses on the foolproof design of the service process. In general, a blueprint contains Product-service Specifications and it is simply a picture of a service system. It begins with the development of a service system for every service operation and every service units or SSU. In order to design a service process, every service activity should be identified and documented. Further, every service system can be divided into a number of sub systems. For example, in the Room Division System, here have four major sub systems: front office, housekeeping, laundry & linen, and lobby or concierge system.

When developing a system for the front office function, have to identify all the key activities involved in the department. For example, reservation, registration (check in), room allocation and transfer to room record-keeping and accounting, checking out or settlement (payments) are major activities of the department.

Designing a service product is a complex process where the designers have to consider a number of variables affecting the production and delivery process of the service. Like in the manufacturing sector, concurrent or simultaneous engineering may be needed to apply.

The application of Japanese 'product design and development' methods such as Quality Function Deployment (QFD- where customers voice is integrated to the product designing) and Robust Designing (designed to work even in unexpected circumstances) may also find useful. Poke Yokes is another important development dealing with 'fail safe' or foolproof designing that was adopted from the Japanese.

A foolproof design can be developed, for example, for the Rooms Divisions Department based on the analysis of historical performance and future expectations. The following factors may be considered, for example, when designing a service system for this function:

- Type of guests served
- Number of guests arriving in a given time & frequency of arrival
- Number of staff employed & level of training and skills of the staffs
- Facility size, layout & design
- Level of guest expectation
- Management objectives related to quality, efficiency

Taking into consideration these factors, the manager, now, can identify clearly all the activities involved in every step of delivering the service. A clear service blueprint would help management identify the activities and processes, isolate the fail points (where things can go wrong), establish the time frame, and determine the amount of resources (including personnel) needed to perform the job.

The service blueprint should also have control points & type of control to be exercised during the service delivery process. Guest expectation & satisfaction and management objectives & targets are major control elements by which a manager can assess the performance. A successful and proven service concept should incorporate sound service technology and a clear service blueprint. The last aspect of service design and blueprint is the issue of value analysis where alternative designs are analysed and evaluated for the value that would generate to the customer. Such an analysis would also take into consideration of the 'cost versus benefit' aspect to the service provider.

Service Delivery Systems

All service delivery systems involve more than one component. A service system consists of a number of components systems & procedures linked with each other so that a service product or service output can be delivered to the customers according to certain specifications. Service Delivery System is not really different form a service system but it is often referred to those components of the service system that interact with the customer. The component systems or sub-systems of a service operation are not very much different from service sector to sector although the service activities may be different.

As a system, service delivery system consists of more than one sub-system. Depending on the nature of service provided, the number of sub-systems can vary. The key elements are the provider and the consumer. Normally in a service situation, here have a service provider who produces and delivers the service product. But a service cannot be provided if there is no consumer or customer.

In this case, however, both the provider and the consumer are human elements (or components) of the service delivery system. In addition to the human component, there are other key elements to consider. The five major components of the service deliver system are as follows:

- The Human component
- The Technology component
- The Material component
- The Facility component
- The Process component

Hotels and Service Delivery

Hotel is a unique but a common accommodation facility. For many, it is place to stay overnight a few days. But for some, it is home away from home. Therefore, the diversity of services that a hotel provides to its guests makes its operation rather complex. The fundamental product that a hotel offers is a room and a bed. This call the "Core product" or "primary product". In all hotels, the major source of business or revenue is the room sales. As a rule of thumb, this may accounts for over 70 % of the Total Revenue.

However, a typical hotel has more than one revenue center in addition to the Room Division department. Within the hotel product, therefore, the core product remains to be the 'Accommodation Product', which of course, consists of tangible and intangible elements of various products and services. Here, the room and bed elements are referred to as 'core service' and the secondary services such as reservation, reception, check-in, check-out, billing etc. are supplementary services.

Operations Analysis

Operations analysis should help managers develop plans

for future by forecasting future outcomes and developing operational budgets. In order to assess the quality of service delivery and service performance as well to plan and develop future strategies, managers should be acquainted with the nature and types of service operations and acquire the necessary skills and methodologies of analysis. Operations analysis involves researching and collecting pertinent data related to the operations and conducting several quantitative and qualitative analyses in order to evaluate the performance.

Operational planning derives from Capacity (Aggregate) Planning (AP). AP involves determining the resource capacity that the firm will need to meet its demand. The role of AP is to convert the strategic types of marketing plans or demand forecast associated with long range planning into overall capacity requirements. The aggregate capacity requirement will later serve as a basis for short-term resource and capacity allocations. Operational planning therefore involves setting operational targets and formulating methods or strategies to achieve those targets.

Of course, those targets may have more than one dimension such as the quantity or amount to achieve (number of guest to be served on a daily basis), completion time (standard check-in time for hotel guests), budget (weekly percentage food cost), or amount of resource (money) allocation etc. Also, operations planning may include a medium term agenda such as improving the quality of service or achieving a profit target quarterly.

The two most important processes in operations planning are forecasting the demand for output (such as the number patients to be treated or the number of room-nights to be sold daily or weekly/monthly or yearly basis) and estimating the cost of operations (budgeting) on a weekly/monthly or yearly basis. One last issue of any operations analysis is to measure and evaluate the performance. It is the measurement of service performance. There are several measures and criteria that we can use to assess the performance of a service operation. This may include both internal measures as well as external factors.

Forecasting Demand

Forecast mean forecasting demand. The demand for tourism and hospitality 'service products'. An accurate demand forecast provides estimates of 'service products' to be sold by the company in the future as bounded by the demand for services and potential capacity of the organisation. The number of units (of service products) that the hotel expects to sell such as room-nights should also be based on an estimated average unit price (average room price) so that an estimate for the annual revenue can be projected. The forecast of revenue is important because it helps to make marketing and management decisions as well as to budget the operational expenses.

Forecasting involves the process of estimating the future events or outcomes as accurately as possible using rational and deductive methods. Although intuitive methods are also used by some, most often it fails to produce dependable estimates. Therefore, managers often employ historical data in order to establish a trend. Sophisticated mathematical models are now available where several dependent variables can be used as in econometric models to forecast future events. Nevertheless, accuracy in forecasting remains one of the most important but difficult tasks to accomplish.

There are number of forecasting methods available today but choosing a methods depends on several factors such as resource availability, accuracy needed, data availability etc. However, all methods can be classified into four categories as 'judgment', 'counting', 'time series', or 'causal'. Judgmental method uses manager's intuition and experience etc. Counting refers to counting the number of units such as the physical inventory of rooms available.

A probability sample is counting of a portion of the entire 'population' in order to estimate some characteristics of the whole population. Statistical determinants such as the mean or averages, standard deviations, correlation coefficient etc are some of the characteristics that we can use to analyse and examine a probability sample so that accuracy of forecast can be established. Time Series are quantitative methods such as the Regression methods that can be used to predict the future based on the historic data of events such as volume of sales or number of units sold. However, any new variable or factors that might influence in the future could not be accounted for.

Operating Budgeting

As in forecasting the future outputs, managers also need to estimate the cost of operations. This is often done for a specific operating period such as a month, quarter or semi-annual period or for the year. In some cases, the operating budget may include the cost of certain fixed cost items such as rent and managers salary. Otherwise, the operating budget often accounts for the cost of good and services sold and the cost of labour.

Operating budgeting is normally a bottom-up process where the line managers prepare the budget at least 4 four-five months in advance when the budgeting cycles starts and send for approval to the top management. In some establishments, it can still be a top-down process where the top management plans the expenditure limits and make operating policies for the line managers. Operating budget does not include capital expenses such as the cost of purchase of assets, which is often characterised by zero-based budgeting (i.e. starting from the scratch).

Variance Analysis

In variance analysis, here monitor and record any variations from the 'planned targets' or performance standards. This can be the difference between actual volume of sales or revenue and the forecast sales and revenue, and the actual cost of operation versus the budget. Variations are measured both in absolute numbers such as room-nights sold and revenue in dollars or in percentages. In the analysis of operational expenses, budgeted figures become the standards against which the actual performance can be evaluated.

Variance analyses are normally carried out periodically (monthly, semi-annually etc.) and for key product/market segments in the case of sales and revenue and major cost items such as labour cost or food cost in the case of expenses. Performance and Yield analyses are extension of variance analysis where other complicated tools such as Portfolio Analysis can be used to assess and evaluate the actual performance and the causes of variations. Yield often represents outputs in terms of revenue and profit where as the performance can also be measured by several other criteria such as customer satisfaction and quality of service delivery etc.

Strategic Service Units

The strategic service units are considered extremely important for the successful operation of the hotel. In most cases, such service units should generate significant amount of revenue to be considered as a SSU. However, in some cases, a service unit such as the recreation unit may qualify to be a SSU although it does not generate any revenue. In the case hotel provided here, the strategic service units are:

- Rooms Division Department
- Lepoque restaurant

- Bee-bar
- Convention & catering unit
- Topocabana bar & lounge
- Room Service

The recreation services unit because it does not generate any revenue. Moreover, other revenue centers such as telephone and dry cleaning services are also excluded because the size of the revenue generated is not significant enough to have any impact on the hotel's operating profit.

Service Quality and Delivery

The term quality in service products is rather difficult to visualise or to measure because of the nature of intangibility. This section intends to provide the students with an insight of what constitutes quality in services and service delivery with a particular reference to the hospitality operation. The term quality cannot be defined or understood without the customer in the equation.

Quality derives from the state of customer satisfaction. It is a measure of how well an organisation meets the customer needs. Simply said, all customers have some degree of expectation when they buy a product or service from a provider or company. Customer expectation derives from the level of customer's understanding and knowledge of the product, and the expected value or satisfaction as perceived by the customer. The greater the experience and product-service knowledge the customer has, the greater is the expectation becomes.

In a competitive environment where there are more sellers in the market, an experienced customer would have a number of alternatives to choose from based on the expectation and perceived value. The issue of price therefore becomes linked to the value and quality of products and services bought. Operations management focuses on the aspects of production and service delivery. This is when the customer experiences the services at first hand. It therefore has a vital role to play in the overall issues of quality management.

In the case of a hotel, for example, the service providers and the facilities can be made user friendly to the guests. The guests can be elderly people, children, or even disabled people. The guest can also be a foreigner who does not speak the same language of the host country. Moreover, the guest can experience a number of problems related to room maintenance, status of room or cleanliness, and the quality of guest services such as information or accuracy in accounting and billing. All these are operations related quality issues.

The security and safety of guests during stay within the hotel and in the city while a resident at the hotel are also important. Proven and successful systems to guarantee security and safety to guests during the stay can provide quality to the overall package. Similarly, pertinent and timely information about the dangers such as terrorist bombing or insecure and risky neighborhood to keep out are other forms of product service quality that the hotel management can provide to the guests.

Finally, how guest complaints are handled and resolved, existence of guest relations and effective communication programmes, and efforts to boost and retain the hotel's reputation are other quality management issues that requires the help of other departments such as marketing.

Quality Management

Today, managing quality is as important as managing the company finances. Quality management is rather a science than an art. Quality Engineering and Quality Control are two key aspects of quality management. Quality engineering focuses on the production or delivery functions where quality control process establishes that the products and services are provided according to the pre-determined standards.

The term Quality Assurance refers to the entire system of establishing policies, setting standards, and developing procedures and guidelines by companies or organisation for the purpose of achieving quality. Therefore, Quality Management involves the planning, organisation, direction, and control of all quality assurance activities. Since quality provides value and satisfaction to customer and cost-effectiveness to the manufacturer or service provider, it also means performance and profitability.

Quality in Service Organisations

Adoption and implementation of quality assurance programmes in the service organisations is rather a new phenomenon. Since services are intangible and heterogeneous in characteristics, it is difficult to implement quality management programmes.

However, service companies have successfully carried out quality programmes by making the service product more tangible by reducing the human element and standardising their product delivery process. Application of technology and continuous training of employees as well as use of scientific methods in the production and in delivery have tremendously contributed to achieve this objective.

The dimensions of quality in the service organisations are different from manufacturing organisations. Time taken to deliver, timeliness of the service, completeness of the service, courtesy of the provider, consistency of service, accessibility and convenience of the service location, accuracy and responsiveness of the provider are some of the dimensions we can apply to evaluate the quality of services. The purpose of quality management is mainly driven by two objectives: customer satisfaction and profitability or benefits for the service organisation.

In essence, customer expectations before the purchase should coincide with customer satisfaction after consumption. But satisfying the customer is not the only organisational objective. If it is a for-profit organisation such as a commercial company, profit optimisation also becomes a major objective. However, non-for-profit organisations try to accomplish their objectives at the least cost, which is again a major objective. The following can be said as the major organisational benefits to be achieved by quality management:

- To guarantee customer satisfaction, and thereby repeat business in commercial organisation such as hotels
- To achieve cost-effectiveness in the long run through standardisation of service delivery as well as reduction of cost of error
- To optimise profit through perceived quality versus price attributes or to minimise the cost through efficiency.

Total Quality Management

Total quality management is a philosophy that drives not only from customer satisfaction but also efficiency and effectiveness in every management function of the organisation. Organisations that are committed to total quality work to achieve quality in every aspects of the operation in the company: from production planning to marketing and customer satisfaction.

The productivity of the organisation and the overall performance of the organisation, as measured by a number of key standards can be expected to improve the overall quality by adopting and implementing total quality approach to service operations. This means, the organisation stands to achieve efficiency and effectiveness in all strategic service units as well as in meeting the customer expectations. One major problem, however, would be employee productivity, which is not only difficult to measure or quantify but also difficult to achieve in many service organisations.

The key determinants of service quality are a) product-service design and service blueprint and b) service technology and service delivery. Service design drives from the service concept, which incorporates the various services to be carried out in a logical fashion. Service blueprint is the map to help identify the various activities involved in the service delivery process. The service blueprint also includes the fail points for control purposes. Service technology describes the process of transferring resources to produce the desired service output as well as the various components of systems involved in the service delivery.

Quality Process

The quality process refers to the entire process of managing quality. It normally consists of three elements: quality assurance, quality control and total quality management. Quality assurance is the organisation's commitment to guarantee quality. Such a guarantee may derive from company mission and broader goals as well as from clear policies. Existence of specific standards and procedures, quality determinants described above, and implementation of quality programmes, including resource allocation are all proof of organisation's commitment to quality.

Quality assurance

- Establish appropriate policies for operations and service delivery.

- Determine the required level of 'quality' in the design of product-services as well as the customer service delivery.
- Establish foolproof or fail-proof systems and methods to make sure the required level of quality is assured throughout the service delivery process.
- Make sure that required resources, equipment, and trained staff are in place.

Once the quality programmes are in place, the organisations should monitor and control the success of such programmes. The quality control process assesses the effectiveness of quality programmes by monitoring the implementation process during service delivery and the quality of service output based on certain pre-determined standards and objectives.

Total quality management (TQM) is the process of providing quality throughout the organisation as explained above under total quality approach. Total quality cannot be guaranteed unless the various departments involved the organisation commit to deliver quality. For example, in a hotel, the ultimate guest satisfaction depends on how successful is the front office operations as well as those of housekeeping department and maintenance services. Not to mention the behind the scene activities or staff functions such as sales and marketing, recruitment and training or the quality of laundry services.

6

Tourism and Travel Organisations

The travel and tourism industry is an interrelated amalgamation of those businesses and agencies that totally or in part provide the means of transport, goods, services, and other facilities for travel outside of the home community for any purpose not related to day-to-day activity. The various reasons for why people travel can be placed into five broad categories:

1. *Recreation.* Recreation includes leisure and activities related to sports, entertainment, and rest. Beach vacations, ski vacations, and adventure travel such as white-water rafting all fall into this category. Destinations such as the Caribbean, Disney World, and national parks benefit largely from recreational travel.
2. *Culture.* People travel for cultural reasons as well-a desire to learn about things and places that interest them. These interests can be historical, ethnic, educational, or they can relate to-the arts or religion.
3. *Business.* Business travel is a significant portion of all travel. This category includes individual business travelers as well as travelers attending meetings and ccnventions. The trend now is to combine business and recreational travel-thus business meetings and conventions are held at resort hotels, theme parks, and even on cruise ships, and spouses and even children often come along.

4. *Visiting Friends and Relatives (VFR).* Research has shown that much travel involves visiting friends and relatives. This is difficult to measure, however, and has little economic impact compared to recreational, cultural, or business travel.
5. *Health.* Many persons travel to visit diagnostic centers and receive treatment at clinics, hospitals, or spas such as the Mayo Clinic in Rochester, Minnesota, or the Canyon Ranch in Tucson, Arizona. This type of travel, too, has relatively little economic impact.

The U.S. Travel Data Center has done a good deal of research to determine what types of Americans travel and how many of them there are. According to the center, 150 million Americans take one or more trips away from home every year. Some groups, as we have pointed out, have a higher tendency to travel. Demographic segmentation is widely used in almost all industries as demographics are easily measured and classified. This is segmentation based on income, race, age, nationality, religion, gender, education, etc.

Psychographic segments are based on attitudes, interests and opinions (AIO), selfconcepts and lifestyle behaviors. Usage segmentation is a broad term that applies to the purpose for which something is used, the frequency or regularity of usage, size of purchase (or expenditure), timing or seasonal consideration, and more. Several types of market segmentation exist, with demographic and geographic segmentation being the most commonly used. As marketing knowledge has advanced and competition has increased, however, the need for a more precise segmentation tool has grown. Psychographics, often referred to as lifestyle, is just the tool.

Psychographics has been around for more than 30 years, but is still one of the least understood concepts in marketing research. It seems that every scholar has his or her own definition of exactly what constitutes psychographics. Some define it simply as values or lifestyles while others have more elaborate definitions. Their definition claims that psychographics "seeks to describe the human characteristics of consumers that may have bearing on their response to products, packaging, advertising and public relations efforts. Such variables may span a spectrum from self-concept and lifestyle to attitudes, interests and opinions, as well as perceptions of product attributes"

Psychographics are used to determine lifestyle characteristics and traits that can be correlated into targeted marketing programs. Psychographics and lifestyle are often used interchangeably, but psychographics is actually the way that lifestyle is made operationally useful to marketing managers. Psychographics appraises a consumer's activities, interests, opinions, and values and correlates them with a consumer's demographics.

Psychographics allow for a more complete picture of an individual, making it easier to understand how to market products to them. One can not begin to explain psychographics without first defining the manner in which psychographic research is conducted. Psychographic research is quantitative research that attempts to place consumers based on psychological, as opposed to strictly demographic dimensions.

Just as internal and external environment factors affect the hospitality industry, internal and external psychological factors affect the guests and clients of the hospitality industry, and thus the industry as well. Research that attempt to classify people's internal motives and behavior is called psychographic research. Hospitality promoters use psychographic research data to decide which market segments to target and what kinds of amenities to offer at a location. All psychological motives can be classified as either basic or secondary.

Basic motives influence everyone and include unlearned needs such as thirst, hunger, sex, fear, and avoidance of pain. Secondary motives are learned needs and include achievement, desire for power, and other specialised needs. Secondary motives usually vary from person to person. People's basic needs from a lodging facility are a good night's rest in a comfortable and safe room. Beyond that, lodging facilities appeal to secondary motives by offering luxury suites that symbolise achievement or esteem.

All foodservice establishments fulfill the basic needs for nourishment. Secondary motives are fulfilled by celebrating special moments—birthdays, wedding anniversaries, bon voyages—in social settings provided by restaurants and hotel banquet rooms. In all areas of hospitality, people expect to be safe from harm. Highly publicised attacks on tourists in Florida in 1993 influenced whether some people chose to visit the state. The desire to avoid pain influences some people to byepass sites where outbreaks of disease have occurred or where political conflicts might erupt in violence.

In psychographic research, the push/pull theory explains the combination of push and pull forces in human motivation. According to the push/pull theory, internal factors lead or "push" people to travel, while external forces "pull" them to certain destinations.

Positive destination images, enhance the pull effect. But negative destination images may trigger the basic human motives of avoidance of pain or fear. These motives may cause some people to byepass that destination, choosing another that they perceive as safer. Other people may prefer their homes to places away regardless of image or time or money available for eating out or travel. They may fear flying or suffer motion sickness. Or they may not be comfortable dealing with change or new experiences.

The tourist psychographic profile is an important tool for marketers. Knowing what kind of person would be attracted to a particular place helps marketers develop and place advertising to attract the right personality types. For example, placing an ad for Yosemite National park (a typical U.S. psychocentric destination) in a magazine featuring mountain climbing in Nepal (a typical U.S. allocentric destination) probably would have little effect. The readers of the magazine would likely be looking for excitement in exotic locales. The ad probably would fare better in a history magazine, whose readers might be looking for a psychocentric locale for their vacation.

Marketers combine information from psychographic and demographic studies to find out what services will attract specific market segments. For example, knowing what factors motivate senior citizens to use hospitality services helps operators tailor their services to attract this growing market. Because of their freedom to travel year-round and their increasing numbers and purchasing power, seniors will continue to be an important marketing segment of the industry. Some businesses, such as Choice Hotels, have already set up programs to target this expanding market.

Many travel and hospitality companies have programs aimed at senior citizens. Holiday Inn and other establishments offer a discount for members of the American Association of Retired Persons (AARP). Some restaurants offer special menus for seniors, usually smaller portion meals and lower-calorie menu items. Some respond with modestly priced, all-you-can-eat buffets, a feature especially attractive to this group. Psychographics helps marketers understand consumer behavior. Consumers behave unpredictably. "They demonstrate loyalties to brands (or not), blindly follow trends (or not), and buy according to their convictions and aspirations (or not).

Individuals are innovators in some product categories, but not in others. What they say they do and what they really do are seldom the same". Psychographics is one way to clarify the behaviors consumers exhibit. Psychographics, like all other segmentation tools, also helps minimise risks. On the other hand, psychographics also has several limitations associated with it. Psychographic research is complex and often confusing. It can also be very costly.

Completing psychographic research usually costs upwards of $50,000. Critics also claim that the categories psychographic research places consumers in overlaps so much that it does not differentiate among consumers. Psychographic research can also be lengthy and narrow, or unable to be projected onto an entire population. Even with these limitations, however, psychographics have been used successfully innumerable times.The government of Bermuda conducted psychographic research in the United States to determine who would be most interested in going to Bermuda on vacation. In a sample of persons who were potential vacationers, three groups emerged:

- The price and sights group. These people were interested in seeing the most things for the least amount of money. They wanted tours that covered ten countries in nine days at a bargain price. The best cruises were the cheapest ones that visited the most ports, and a good hotel was one that offered budgetpriced accommodations within walking distance of everything they might want to see.
- The sun and surf group. These people sought a vacation where they could lie on a beach and get a golden tan. Value was important, but even more important was finding a destination where there was good weather, guaranteed sunshine, and a beautiful beach where they could soak up the sun and swim in clear waters.

– The quality group. The quality of the vacation experience was of paramount importance to this group. Members of this group felt they had worked hard for a vacation and now it was their turn to relax and be taken care of. This group valued destinations and accommodations that were first-class or deluxe. Service was very important-they wanted and expected lots of pampering and were willing to pay a fair price for it. They also wanted gourmet dining and sophisticated entertainment.

Travel Agencies

A travel agency is a business that sells travel related products and services to end-user customers on behalf of third party travel suppliers, such as airlines, hotels and cruise lines. Customers of travel agencies include tourists and business travellers. Some agencies also serve as general service agents for foreign travel companies in different countries.

Travel agencies have been organised mostly since the development of commercial aviation from the 1920s, although Thomas Cook was a notable early, pre-flight pioneer in 1841. The Portuguese company Viagens Abreu is the oldest travel organisation, founded in 1840. Some operate with a chain of stores and others are one store operations. A few of the larger travel agencies sell their own products. Agencies without their own product are arguably more impartial and more likely to offer something to suit the traveller; they are known as independent agencies. there are three different types of agencies: these are Multiples, Miniples and independent agencies.

Most travel agencies do not sell airline tickets only; their services vary, and many of them sell more cruise ship packages than airline tickets. Most travel agencies also arrange car rental deals for their customers, and many concentrate on arranging charter or group trips to different destinations. For this, they deal with regular airlines, but many times, they also hire charter airlines. Many travel agencies exclusively represent a small group of supplier airlines, cruise and car hire companies and, often, the logos of the supplier companies are displayed on the windows of the agency's office.

Travel agencies also market and sell train and hotel products. Generally, their goal is to try to fit an ideal schedule onto the requirements of each specific customer. The phrase travel agency has changed meaning since the emergence of companies like Thomson or Thomas Cook, who are now considered to be tour operators rather than travel agents. The difference is that tour operators manufacture and sell their own holidays whereas independent travel agents sell holidays from all the tour operators without limiting the range they offer to just their own product.

The best travel agents deal honestly with a wide range of customers. In the UK a group of just such travel agents formed a consortium which became known as Worldchoice. Each agency was independently owned, bonded members of ABTA and Worldchoice was the vehicle for both commercial negotiations with the tour operators and also a forum for best practise.

The travel agents are there to act on your behalf to see that restitution is made if you have a problem with a particular part of your travel experience. ASTA, for example, is the only travel association aggressively fighting to improve the travel experience, and air transportation in particular, for all consumers, not just those with access to the Internet.

Travel agents, unlike instructions on a Web page, are experts in understanding and deciphering the myriad of travel information and codes out there. It's what they've been trained to do and they do it every day. They provide convenient one-stop shopping.

Travel agents are your neighbors, not the impersonal voice thousand of miles away. They know what you want and what you value in your travel experience. They have a vested interest in making sure you have the best travel experience possible.

Travel agents are there to make sure you get where you want to go, when you want to go and for the best price. They have intimate knowledge of the destinations they sell and are able to select the most appropriate travel arrangements to meet their clients needs.

Instead of checking a long list of travel Web pages, which only provide rates and fares for the companies that have contracted with them, why not go straight to the source? A travel agent has all the information at their fingertips, saving you a few hours in front of a computer screen.

Travel agents work for their clients (you-the consumer), not for a travel supplier. It makes sense that a happy customer will be a repeat customer. Travel agents are out to find the consumer the best rate available. Agents are there to save you money as well as time.

Everyone is different and each of us travels his or her own road to success, but over the years we have noticed a number of qualities that make for success in the travel agency business. Here then are some observations about just a few qualities that successful agents bring to the table when they start out.

If you are not already a agent, the very fact that you are reading this web site suggests that you like to arm yourself with all the information available before making a decision. We regularly hear from agents who signed up with the first agency that caught their eye. Now they regret it and wonder if we can point them in the right direction.

We explain to them (hopefully with a certain amount of patience) that we cannot make decisions for them.

The thing many beginners (especially those with no real experience of being in business for themselves) fail to understand is that the sellers of business opportunities are just that - sellers. Just as the car dealer won't volunteer that the car you have your eye on sits at the bottom of the "Consumer Reports" safety rankings, the ads for a host agency offer won't volunteer the downsides of their offer or reveal that a better deal is being offered by someone else.

Please understand, we are not saying these people are being dishonest. They are simply putting the best face on what they have to offer. That's simply what sellers do. When you start selling travel, you'll do it too. We sure that if you are considering starting a travel agency you have visited at least several sites offering such business opportunities and we are also sure you understand what we are talking about. Becoming a travel agent is easy. The problem is knowing what kind of travel agent to become.

There are probably as many ways of being a travel agent as there are travel agents. No one does it exactly the same. This is where a lot of people make costly mistakes. Because they don't know the full range of options available to them, they pick the first one that comes along. Or they look at two or three options and pick the wrong one. There are two basic types of agents.

— Referral agents.

— Booking and selling agents.

Within each category there are a lot of different ways to go about it but, for now, let's consider these two basic types one at a time.

Referral Agents

Referral agents, as the name implies, do not actually book

or sell travel products. Instead, they simply refer people to a travel agency. That travel agency's "inside agents" do all the work of closing the sale and making the booking. In exchange for steering the customer to the agency, the referral agent receives a percentage of the commission that the travel agency gets from the supplier (the cruise line, the airline, the hotel, or whatever). The referral agent also typically books his or her personal travel through the agency and receives a commission on that as well (a sort of "rebate" or "discount" in effect).

As a referral agent, you don't have to know a great deal about the mechanics of the travel industry. You don't have to know all the airline codes, or what's the best hotel in Hawaii, or the difference between Category C and Category D on a cruise ship. Your job is to communicate the fun and excitement of travel and get people to call the toll-free number of your agency. So far, there's nothing new or controversial about this.

It's been going on for decades in the travel industry, where referral agents have traditionally be known as "bird dogs." But in recent years, some travel agencies have made the use of referral agents the core of their business model and the practice has been getting a lot more attention. And attracting some controversy. Referral agencies issue their referral agents a photo ID that the agent can use to receive some travel industry discounts and courtesies from some suppliers. This annoys some people in the travel industry but, the practice is perfectly legal. The agencies that accredit travel agencies have not taken any action against the travel agencies issuing these cards, nor have any travel suppliers.

The federal government specifically declined to take any action, saying this was simply an alternative way of marketing travel. The fact of the matter is, the referral agencies sell an awful lot of travel and who wants to argue with success?

Booking and Selling Agents

A lot of people, however, are attracted to the idea of becoming travel agents because they love getting involved in all the details of planning wonderful trips, across the country or around the world. Or perhaps they have developed some expertise in a particular destination or type of vacation or mode of travel and they are looking for a way to turn what they love into a source of income.

Travel agents like this clearly do a lot more than the referral agent. They work with their clients to determine what kind of travel experience the client is looking for. Then they research the available options, speaking directly with the travel supplier. Then they present the options to their client, help the client make a decision, and make the booking arrangements with the supplier. In exchange for doing all this work, they receive a much higher percentage of the commission than the referral agent. In fact, they might get it all!

The term "booking and selling agent" is something we are using here just to make clear the distinction between referral agents and all other travel agents. As far as the travel industry is concerned, an agent who does all the booking and selling is a travel agent pure and simple. If you are interested in becoming a referral agent, you will find information about that option elsewhere on this web site. For now, however, let's concentrate on how to become a full-fledged booking and selling agent.

Being a travel agent means representing and marketing travel products that are created by someone else. You are not going to start your own airline, or go out and buy a cruise ship, or build a chain of all-inclusive resorts. That's why you so often hear travel agents referred to as "outside sales representatives." "Outside" because you do not work in the office of the company whose products you represent.

Whether you deal directly with a travel supplier or through a middleman, it's important to remember that you are not an employee, either of the host agency or the ultimate travel supplier. Because you are not an employee, you do not receive a salary or any of the benefits (medical, dental, vacations, etc.) that go along with being an employee. You make your money ("get paid") through commissions on what you sell. You negotiate your commission level with either the host agency or the travel supplier. Sell a lot, make a lot. Sell a little, make a little.

Although you are independent and on your own, you are never alone as a travel agent. You must constantly work with others to provide service to your clients. Virtually every travel agent must form a relationship with a host agency. And your success hinges on your understanding of this relationship. There are many ways to connect with a host agency. You can do it for free, or you can pay a fee. You may have to sell yourself to an agency. Or several agencies may compete in offering you the "best deal" to sign up with them.

Regardless of how it happens, once you've hooked up with a host agency, a commitment has been made. If money has changed hands then a certain "investment" has been made. Even though it is possible to work with more than one host agency at the same time, it is far more convenient to work with just one, so a certain sense of loyalty tends to develop. It can be a hassle to switch host agencies, so inertia sets in.

Perhaps for these reasons, many travel agents start to think that they work for this host agency. They may know, intellectually, that this is not the case. But they behave as if it is. Because the host agency has a certain way of doing things, they start to think that this is the only way of doing things. Again, on an intellectual level, they may know this is not the case, but they behave as if it is.

They are thinking like employees. They gradually start thinking that their destiny, their success, is wrapped up with the destiny of the host agency. This is a mistake, but an easily corrected one. However, it is not the biggest mistake beginners make. No, the biggest mistake newcomers to the travel agent profession make—especially those who have had no prior experience running their own business—is that they think they are customers of the host agency. This is especially true if they paid a fee to get set up as an outside agent with that agency.

You and the host agency are two separate and independent business entities that have freely entered into a purely business relationship, because each party has independently decided that there's something in it for them. In the business-to-consumer model there is an unspoken assumption that the business is smarter and more powerful and that the customer is less knowledgeable and less powerful. Therefore, the reasoning goes, the customer's interests must be protected. In the business-to-business model there is an unspoken assumption that the parties involved are equally capable.

Travel Organisations

On April 20, 1931, the American Society of Travel Agents (ASTA) was formed in New York City, to defend the rights of US travel agents over the power of the growing commercial airline systems of the day. Now headquartered in Alexandria, Virginia, ASTA still represents travel agencies and agents. The international body for registering travel agents is the International Air Transport Association (IATA), although most travel agents are registered through national bodies such as the Australian Federation of Travel Agents.

ASFA, The Association of Special Fares Agents, Airline Consolidators, Bucketshops and Discount Travel Agents is the mother source for finding cheap fares online.

ASFA was founded in 1985 as a platform for discount travel specialists, consolidators and bucketshops from all over the world. ASFA agents are registered and bonded according to the laws of the countries and states that they are operating in.

Many agencies feared their services would no longer be needed when many airlines and other travel companies began to sell directly to passengers over the Internet. They were afraid they would be victims of what management science experts call disintermediation. Another worry was over the fact that airlines have been cutting back the commissions paid to travel agents on each tickets sold; the airlines feel that they are perfectly capable of dealing directly with their own passengers and do not need travel agents as much as in the past to fill seats.

Since 1995, many travel agents have exited the industry, and relatively few young people have entered the field due to a collapse in salaries. However, others have abandoned the "brick and mortar" agency for a home-based business to reduce overhead, and those who remain have managed to survive by promoting other travel products like cruise lines and train excursions, or by promoting their ability to aggressively research and assemble complex travel packages on a moment's notice (essentially acting as a very advanced concierge).

Many travel agencies have developed an internet presence by posting a website, with detailed travel information. Full travel booking sites are often complex, and require the assistance of outside travel consolidators. These companies such as Sabre and others can provide up to the minute, detailed data on tens of thousands of hotel vacancies. Some of the popular online travel sites allow visitors to compare hotel and flight rates with multiple companies. They often allow visitors to sort the travel packages by amenities, price, and or proximity to a city or landmark.

Modern Trends

Travel agents work hard on behalf of the consumer. The role of a travel agent is to make the process of going on a trip—whether for work or pleasure—be a stressfree and memorable experience. Travel agents spend time not only booking tickets and searching for affordable prices, but also personalising their services for individual clients. The job of a travel agent has grown and adapted to reflect the changes within the travel industry, and to reflect the difference in the way people think about travel.

Travel agents recognise that consumers today have done their homework and are more knowledgeable about what they want. Clients who turn to a travel agent desire an in-depth, personal approach and want the advice and expertise of a professional. This is why a travel agent:

- Distills product information;
- Investigates and supplies competitive information;
- Stays abreast of the most current and timely promotions;
- Analyses the current promotions;
- Clarifies the fine print, such as cancellation penalties and restrictions;
- Makes recommendations on travel-related options;
- Simplifies the research and subsequent transaction;
- Enhances the trip with value-added benefits and amenities;
- Uses their clout to obtain the best possible arrangements in seemingly impossible situations; and
- Gets problems resolved.

The Internet has helped transform the travel industry. It helps educate the consumer by providing vast amounts of information about destinations and different travel options. Both consumers and travel professionals have benefited from the Internet, which makes the possibility of travel to exotic places more imaginable. It has helped consumers see in full color and, in some cases, real time, where they would like to visit. The Internet gives travelers the ability to do comparative shopping for attractive deals or packages. It also has helped many travel agencies, hotels, resorts and other travel-related suppliers flourish by bringing in business through Web sites.

The Internet has become such an integral part of the travel agency business that 98 percent of travel agencies currently subscribe to a consumer on-line service or an Internet access provider in order to help them better serve their clients. Gathering information increasingly involves the use of the Internet. Almost 95 percent of agents have conducted online research. Nearly 83 percent of travel agencies report they have booked directly on supplier's Web sites without using their GDS or calling the supplier in question.

The Internet can be a powerful tool. It can increase the scope and reach of a consumer's efforts and allow a person to check hundreds of options or research destinations in depth. But to make the Internet work effectively, a person has to understand where to look and what questions to ask, otherwise hours can be wasted surfing the Web and ultimately produce unsatisfactory results. This is where a travel agent can make a world of difference.

A professional travel agent is trained to guide a client through the entire process of planning a trip, whether for business or for leisure. Travel agents take classes, participate in seminars, become destination specialists and join professional associations, in order to ensure they make each client's travel experience as personalised, convenient and memorable as possible. When planning a business trip or family vacation, the Internet can be a valuable resource, but it cannot replace the expertise and guidance of a travel agent.

Also, during travel crises, the Internet can't replace a human being who will persist to help a client. Travel agents, meanwhile, can offer a myriad of intermediate options. There are some things technology cannot replicate, and personal touch is one of them. The Internet is a valuable resource, but it cannot replace the expertise, guidance and personal service of a travel agent. At a time when travelers are stressed out with hectic schedules, travel agents have all of the information at their fingertips, saving valuable hours of surfing on the Web.

Agents also can offer insider tips generally based on personal experience. The leisure travel industry has changed from being an option of the upper class to one open to all segments of society—in fact, travel has become an everyday part of life whether for a meeting across the country or a last minute trip to a nearby city. Over time it has become price driven. Many people today base a large part of their travel buying decisions on cost and convenience of travel. People are booking closer in to their travel dates. Thanks to dramatic discounting across the industry, consumers have been conditioned to wait until the last minute before booking in hopes of securing a deeply discounted package deal.

Consumers value the services and unbiased expertise offered by professional agents who represent an impartial source of information for travelers. Travel agents have and will survive in the new marketplace, because consumers know the value they provide. While there has been contraction and consolidation of brick-and-mortar travel agencies, the number of travel agents has remained fairly steady. Some travel agencies have grown and improved their businesses through new business practices. For example, many travel agencies have focused on providing an increased value to their customers by becoming experts or specialists in certain types of travel or specific destinations. Some agencies have implemented new services that add value to client transactions, such as tracking of frequent flyer accounts or discounted upgrades.

Web Technology for Travel Agents

Both the travel and tourism industry and Web based electronic commerce are changing rapidly. The global gross output of travel and tourism was estimated at US$3.4 trillion and is expected to double by 2005. The World Wide Web (WWW) is also growing at a rapid rate. Latest estimates of Internet users range around the 120 million mark. Organisations are becoming increasingly aware of the business potential of engaging in electronic commerce over the WWW. The WWW supports electronic commerce in four major tasks.

- Attracting new customers via marketing and advertising.
- Serving existing customers via customer service and support functions.
- Developing new markets and distribution channels for existing products.
- Developing new information based products.

Information Technology

The travel industry is an intensive user of information technology (IT) for reservation, accounting and inventory management functions. Raymond and Bergeron refer to the types of systems used by travel agents as:

i) global distribution systems (GDS) such as Galileo, Sabre and Amadeus which are used for reservations, information search, client management and reporting.

ii) organisational information systems (OIS) which are used for accounting, reporting, record management and billing.

IT has helped in reducing costs and improving service to customers. Travel and tourism is an industry sector that is highly dependent on up-to-date, accurate information. There are potential problems associated with travel agents having multiple software systems that are not interconnected. For example, data may become difficult to transfer from one system to another. It is proposed by Raymond and Bergeron that travel agents should choose the GDS as the basic system infrastructure, rather than the OIS, since it provides the most critical information to the business.

When selecting a GDS they should look for user-friendly systems having the potential to interconnect with their OIS. However, their study did not consider the WWW, and how it could be integrated with the GDS and OIS. The Internet has tremendous potential for creating business opportunities for travel agents. There are various aspects of electronic commerce that can be exploited by travel agents. Some of these are listed below.

1) Using the Internet to build customer relationships—by having customers interact directly with the web site;
2) Gathering information from customers and potential customers to create customer profiles which can be used in marketing and product development;
3) Information partnerships—cooperation between organisations to provide a better service to the customer;
4) Transactions—reservations and bookins;
5) Specialised information provision according to the profile of the user;

6) Information and products that can be down-loaded by the user.

The opportunities provided by the WWW, coupled with business process re-engineering, have the potential to radically change the nature of the travel industry. Airline companies have already started to market their products directly to the consumer via the WWW, in some cases allowing bids to be made for spare seats.

Some believe that as many as 20% of travel agents will go out of business within the next three to four years, due to the growth of large on-line travel agents, and the customers' ability to transact directly with airlines, hotels and the larger tour operators. Given the potential of the WWW in travel agencies, it is proposed that they should take an enterprise wide approach in their utilisation of Web technology focussing on the potential of business process re-engineering. Although traditional retail travel agents are facing greater competition through on-line travel agents, the WWW provides an alternative to using the travel wholesaler.

The agent, if he or she wishes to do so, is now able to source travel and accommodation information, amongst other things, via the WWW. Customers of the travel agents also have the potential to interact with the agency in a more flexible way by accessing their web site at a time of their choice. Reinders and Baker suggest there are few, if any obstacles, to extending the electronic market in travel and tourism products. The technical communications infrastructure from customers' homes provides an electronic market place.

However, according to a survey by Reinders and Baker one element of confusion for consumers is the alternative platforms for electronic commerce, such as interactive television. They conclude that many consumers will wait and see which will be the market leader before making a decision on technology platform. Travel agents are typically classified as small businesses. In Western Australia, two thirds of small businesses use a computer in their day-to-day operations and thirty percent of these are connected to the Internet.

In a survey conducted by the Institute for Small Business research the uses of the Internet were: email 81%, accessing information 79%, and marketing 32%. Research by Dutta, Kwan and Segev, found that many small businesses had an Internet presence, but few took full advantage of the various forms of electronic commerce. For example, few organisations customised information according to the type of user, performed online tracking of customer behaviour, and provided online forums for customers. It seems as though even many of those that have implemented Web technology are not making the most of it.

The influences on executive decisions related to technology adoption in small businesses have been studied by Harrison, Mykytun, Riemenschneider. They found that an executive's decision to adopt IT to help his/her firm compete is a function of attitude (perceived positive and negative consequences for the firm), subjective norm (social expectations), and perceived control (resources to overcome obstacles). Additional variables such as firm and individual executive characteristics had no unique effect on adoption decisions.

Although there is general concensus that senior management support is important in IT adoption and implementation in small businesses, a study found that it may not be as critical as external IS expertise. While top management support is essential for IS effectiveness, high quality external IS expertise, in the form of consultants and vendors, is even more critical for small businesses operating in an environment of resource poverty.

Web Diffusion

The research into the diffusion of Web technologies within organisations is still in its early stages. Jarvenpaa and Ives put forward five propositions as a result of their studies of Web diffusion in two organisations in the USA. The five propositions are described below.

1) The introduction of Web technology is likely to occur with only peripheral involvement of the information technology function.
2) The introduction of Web technology is likely to occur with minimal if any involvement by top management.
3) The introduction of Web technology is likely to be accomplished by an ad-hoc, cross-functional group that has no formal organisational responsibility.
4) A performance crisis can be used to stimulate the introduction of Web technologies to an organisation, but it is not essential for this change to occur.
5) The introduction of Web technologies to an organisation can be triggered or supported by staged events, some of which could be deliberately manufactured.

Business Process Re-engineering (BPR)

Business Process Re-engineering (BPR) looks at enterprise processes, those that cut across business units. The information systems built for specific functions or units have often become out-dated because new processes transcend what was often seen as a compartmentalised set of functions. BPR is about identifying, and modelling business processes and changing existing systems to support those processes. There are many facets to re-engineering, although one trend is towards using newer technologies to support new ways of working. The need for business process redesign comes about because of the following:

- rapidly changing technologies;
- shorter product life-cycles;
- increased competitive pressures and the increased demand for quality products and services;
- inefficient use of organisational resources due to organisational change, or lack of change.

For travel agents, the changing technology and increased pressures and demand for quality service would appear especially apposite. Despite the potential of BPR, there are some that are rather wary about it as an organisational strategy. Martinson and Revenaugh for example, are of the opinion that whilst BPR has been an important concept in the nineties it has been commonly associated with negative connotations such as corporate downsizing and inflated consultancy fees. They go on to say that BPR has commonly been associated with slashing staff numbers, and while this may be a short-term fix, they suggest it is not a long-term strategy for success.

World Wide Web

Following are some issues related to travel agents and their use of the WWW.

1) The take-up rates of Web technology in travel agencies.
2) A model of Web technology diffusion is tested on the travel agencies used in the survey.
3) The type of strategy that the agents used for the decisions relating to the adoption of the WWW.

A recent study identified the major obstacles and perceptions that have prevented some agents from tapping into web-based electronic commerce. The various forms of web based electronic commerce that agents use are also examined. Since the travel industry and web technology are changing rapidly, the emphasis has been put on the strategy of technology adoption in the study. In this context there are a number of additional questions that are worthwhile examining. These areas or questions relate to broader issues such as: "Do small businesses plan their technology adoption?" and "Is re-engineering unlikely to be carried out in small organisations?"

The research was based upon useable responses from seventy-one travel agents in the Perth Metropolitan area in Western Australia. The questionnaires were completed by the senior managers or owner managers. Although over 50 per cent use electronic mail, almost 60 per cent do not use the WWW to search for information or provide a Web site for their customers and have no immediate plans to do so. Those that use the WWW typically use it to retrieve information on hotels, locations, fare and timetable. Few perform transactions at other sites such as bookings or payments. Those agents that have a Web site use the site primarily to provide information to the customers or potential customers.

Although some agents have established formal and informal links to other sites, their sites rarely allow customers to perform bookings and other transactions, down load brochures and gather information about customers. In this respect a restricted set of electronic commerce features are implemented. As many as 44% of agents in the survey have never considered using the WWW. Only 8 per cent classed their approach as an enterprise wide examination of the business processes. The other 48 per cent took either a modular approach or have done very little planning at all.

The lack of planning is confirmed by the absence of strategic plans which incorporate the WWW and the lack of cost benefit analyses on the benefits of the WWW. It appears that there is a significant number that are unconvinced by the benefits that can be derived by using the WWW. In nearly all cases the driving force behind the adoption of the WWW was the owner manager of the travel agency. Only one agency took on new staff to deal with the transition of working with the WWW.

Lack of adequate training was the most frequently stated problem in relation to using the WWW. Others included perceived operating costs, integration of WWW with other applications and a need for the re-engineering of business processes in total conducted any sort of feasibility study including a cost benefit analysis on the potential benefits of web technology.

Process innovation and redesign involves making radical changes to process methods and tasks. Very few of the agents viewed the adoption of the WWW as a radical amount of change. This can be seen by the small percentage that actually performed enterprise wide planning.

Only 8 per cent of agents actually took this perspective. They chose to view the potential adoption of the Web technology as an ad-on to their existing systems rather than something that required a radical re-think of the organisational processes.

Time was never given as one of the obstacles to implementing the Web technology. Indeed, it appeared that travel agents viewed the adoption of the technology as something that was relatively quick to perform since they did not adequately take into account the time for planning and developing a strategy.

For all those that have investigated the adoption of the WWW (whether or not they decided to proceed with it) the initial idea came from top management. Risk was not put forward as a major deterrent or obstacle for the adoption of web technology.

Clearly, the key enabler for re-engineering is information technology based.

Only two percent of agencies employed extra staff as part of the process of Web adoption. None of the agencies gave any additional incentives to staff, such as extra pay, in cases where the WWW was being used. Very few of those that used the WWW had undergone a systematic training programme on how to use it effectively.

Very few travel agents do a form of planning that could be considered to be BPR, even though as suggested earlier in the paper, the context has all the ingredients that would make BPR a very plausible option. In some cases the shift to using the WWW is done in a bottom-up fashion by the travel agency. That is, the PC is purchased, the Internet service provider is decided upon, the browser is chosen. This is done independently of any planning that may, and more usually may not, happen in the organisation. It is little wonder that those that do use the WWW realise only a small part of the electronic commerce possibilities that are available.

In a sense, the introduction of WWW facilities into travel agents has many parallels to the widespread introduction of microcomputers in business (small and large) in the early eighties. It was often done without proper planning and resulted in under use, and subsequent poor rates of return on the investment. Suppliers of travel and tourism related products and services, such as Atlas Travel Technologies (ATT) and Galileo, are set to launch Internet booking engines that travel agent subscribers can add to their Web sites, enabling consumers to make on-line bookings and have them queued to the agent.

These types of facilities are an option to the travel agent to help them take a greater portion of on-line business. The problem is that they are tied again to a supplier, which would typically restrict the options available. The other major problem is that customers with Internet access will soon have more choice in booking their flights, hotels, and packages directly with the vendors, thereby by-passing the travel agents.

Reinders and Baker provide some optimism for agencies with staff who can navigate better through the electronic market place and find better deals on flights and hotels for example, than the do-it-yourself netsurfer. They believe this type of agency will still attract customers. This may be so, but their monopoly is coming to an end.

Electronic Markets

The travel industry, one of the largest and fastest growing industries in the world, appears particularly interesting in terms of the possibilities offered by electronic commerce. It is one of the industries where business is conducted successfully on the Internet already today, and where the importance of electronic commerce is likely to grow. It is also expected that the travel industry will be one of the first industries to be transformed by technology and to experience Internet disintermediation as Internet-based purchase and sales models arise.

Theoretically, the presumed suitability of the travel industry for electronic commerce can be explained by the qualities of the travel services and the tourist product. The tourist product is highly information-intensive, offering potential for value-adding informational services. As an almost totally informational service, all transactions and arrangements can be made online. The only nonvirtualisable part is the actual travel, the physical passenger traffic. According to Byerley and Ewers, the tourism sector appears to have a very large potential as a generator of usage of networks and value-added services.

Typically, the products need to be viewed and booked at a distance and the products are natural candidates for multimedia descriptions. Electronic markets are not a new phenomenon in the travel and tourism industry. It has been possible for travel agencies to book flights and hotel rooms online since the mid-1970s through the so called computerised reservation systems (CRS), also known as global distribution systems (GDS). Using the global CRSs, travel agencies can make reservations directly from their terminal with any airline and on all continents without having to go through coordination processes or contract negotiations.

The global CRSs, nearly all of which are airline-owned, provide the basic functions for the reservation process such as product presentation, reservation, fare quote and ticketing and additional services. Traditionally, CRSs have had at least two major practical limitations:

First, small and medium-sized tourism enterprises remain under-represented in most CRSs, effectively (SMTEs) endangering their competitiveness and market share. Considering the fact that the vast majority of tourism enterprises around the globe can be classified as SMTEs, this limitation of the CRSs put not only the SMTEs at issue at a disadvantage, but also the prospective tourists, whose choice of service providers is more restricted as a result. In addition, the fact that many SMTEs are not connected to CRSs has had a negative effect on the rapidity of the booking process.

Second, the customers themselves have not had direct access to these proprietary computerised reservation systems, meaning that the travel industry currently relies on an outdated distribution network, essentially relying on third-parties, and hence is faced with a need to change. As a result of the opportunities offered by the Internet, a great number of suppliers can, and will, be connected over a common—and open—computer network. The Internet serves as the medium providing online access to travel industry actors at destinations worldwide. Through this network consumer access to CRSs or similar systems, for instance independent, proprietary systems developed by travel agencies in cooperation with IT companies, is now possible.

An almost unlimited amount of tourist service providers—including small ones—can be reached directly or through travel agencies online, meaning that the tourists are offered a considerably greater choice of suppliers. A possible implication is that we will be moving from what was primarily straightforward reservation systems to consumer-friendly networks including trip planning, video clips and virtual tours, maps, weather forecasts, chat rooms, and personal services, as well as direct payment facilities in addition to the direct booking opportunities. As the consumer is directly connected to a real-time system, the tour operators, airlines, hotels and the prospective tourists all can benefit from the greater opportunities to make last minute reservations.

In the travel and tourism industry, as in most other industries these days, the impact of electronic commerce is an issue of great interest and concern for industry players as well as researchers. Although most of the different electronic age scenarios that have been put forward contain some elements that intuitively may appear realistic, it seems to be the case that the scenarios suggesting an industry reformation of some kind, especially the threatened intermediaries hypothesis, have attracted by far the greatest attention by business representatives as well as researchers.

The logic of the threatened intermediaries hypothesis is that the firm's value system is in an ongoing state of flux in part due to advancements in information technology. IT, and especially the direct business-toconsumer communication possibilities offered by the Internet, allows manufacturers to internalise activities that have been traditionally performed by intermediaries which, as has been shown by Benjamin and Wigand, add significant costs to the value chain. Hence, intermediaries may be by-passed in the distribution chain, resulting in a redistribution of profits along the value system, which may benefit both manufacturers and consumers.

Besides such obvious advantages of electronic commerce as greater convenience and a wider selection of items and information, the consumer may also experience price reductions as a direct result of the the redistribution of profits resulting from the disintermediation effect and more suppliers being able to compete in an electronically open marketplace. The threatened intermediaries hypothesis was presented by Malone et al., who used the term 'electronic brokerage effect' for the phenomenon. Their forecasts were based on a conceptual analysis rather than on empirical studies, but according to the authors, a dramatic example of the shift toward electronic markets had already occurred in the airline industry by the time the study was made.

The case for the elimination of intermediaries as a result of electronic commerce is based on questionable assumptions, concluding that more, rather than fewer intermediaries will be involved in electronic markets. Their assumptions are backed up by the results of an exploratory study by Bailey and Bakos, suggesting that the need for intermediaries is not likely to be eliminated in the near future, although some of the traditional roles of intermediaries may become less important as a results of advances in IT.

Bakos argue that electronic marketplaces will more than compensate for this disintermediation by promoting the growth of new types of electronic intermediaries. Likewise, Girishankar argues that Internet-based selling is creating a breed of virtual intermediaries and new versions of traditional middlemen and product distribution channels. Chircu and Kauffman go a step further to propose an 'IDR cycle', a recurring pattern of intermediation, disintermediation and reintermediation, arguing that traditional non-technological middlemen will be able to reintermediate in the long run as EC-able intermediaries.

Traditionally, the travel distribution chain has been heavily dependent on intermediaries, i.e. travel agencies, whose business concept is to tie travelers and tourist service providers, mainly airlines and hotels, together. Tourists, especially from an international point of view, have varying holiday preferences and, hence, a demand for a great choice of resorts and service providers, highlighting the importance of establishing extensive distribution networks of different tourism industry actors.

As we speak of a disintermediation effect in the travel industry, it should be noted that the discussions on the precarious existence of the travel agencies by no means are new or exclusively connected to the emergence of the Internet. As a matter of fact, the travel agency has been pointed out as the one actor in the travel distribution chain under severe pressure for quite a long time.

Recently, the issue of disintermediation has been brought up again as a result of the fact that electronic markets are emerging on the Internet, a global medium through which the prospective travelers can manage all their arrangements by themselves as direct online bookings or through e-intermediaries. However, visions on different methods for consumer self-bookings through IT developments—and their possible disintermediational implications—have been presented in the travel and tourism literature long before the commercial possibilities offered by the Internet became widely known.

With the commercial potentials offered by the Internet today being a matter of common knowledge, many statements on the trying conditions facing travel agencies in the electronic age have been made in academic works, the popular press, at organisational levels, and by travel industry representatives, denoting that their threat of being squeezed out of business is real. The concerns do not necessarily always originate from a direct disintermediation threat, but from the indirect effects of by-pass opportunities offered on electronic markets, namely (i) the necessity to refocus and reinvent as new roles emerge for travel agencies as a result of the changing business models ; and (ii) heavy commission cuts.

Most larger airlines have already lowered the commission rates to travel agencies as a result of high distribution costs and the potential for launching their own reservation services on the Internet. In online bookings, the commissions are particularly tiny, and will probably continue to be cut since the work involved is less demanding. However, a common and intuitively reasonable view is that travel agencies themselves can gain some control over the design and implementation of IT and act creatively on the opportunities e-commerce can give them.

Competitiveness in today's tourist economy is increasingly determined by the ability to develop and assimilate innovative ways to respond to the dynamic environment and its new paradigms in the production process of valueadding tourist services. It should be noted that the threat of being by-passed in the travel distribution chain in some works has been extended to concern not only travel agents, but tour operators as well. However, the retail travel agent must be carefully distinguished from the tour operator, as the retail travel agent is just a retailer, while the tour operator is without doubt a manufacturer of a particular travel product. The inclusive tour offered by the tour operator is not something the individual customer himself can put together by contacting online travel sites. It is a tourist product in itself.

Consumer Problems

Determining how the Internet will transform markets

begins with an understanding of how consumers accomplish their interests—i.e. consumer behavior. Although the threat of disintermediation may be real as a result of the customer opportunities offered by ecommerce, intuitively there seem to be, however, several potential hindrances to a mass-market adoption of direct consumer-to-producer electronic shopping solutions. This goes not only for the travel industry, but also for most—if not all—other industries as well.

Potential consumer barriers to e-commerce arise from several issues, but here our aim is merely to look into different industry- and product-specific problems and practical limitations associated with electronic travel bookings by individual customers. Well-known barriers to e-commerce such as cost of entry, and security and privacy issues are excluded from this work.

A prerequisite for a consumer making his own travel arrangements on the Web is that he has some degree of proficiency with the Internet. Consequently, a lack of knowledge or experience with the Internet can constitute a serious barrier to consumer-to-business electronic commerce not only in the travel industry, but in any industry sector. Beside, or in addition to the limitations of the user, technical problems or systems limitations, as well as the poor usability of the service providers' Web sites (the term usability including, as has been suggested by Rajani and Rosenberg, aspects as color, sound, navigation and placement) may obstruct Internet bookings.

The first non-technical problem is about finding the right service providers, i.e. locating the Web sites offering the services needed. A typical problem regarding the Internet has been the immense supply of information, and the subsequent difficulty of finding the information you are looking for—at least to find it quickly enough. Accessing the many sources of information requires knowledge (to know where the servers are located), time and perseverance, as it is often not possible to book travel directly on-line and certainly not possible to buy the separate parts of a trip through the same supplier.

Having found the right service providers, the issue of availability remains. In most cases, there will be some available flight to the destination, but not necessarily the cheapest alternative or by the desired airline. Naturally, the same goes for the accommodation reservations. In a situation like this, is it possible to find cheaper and more suitable flights through other travel sites connected to another, competing CRS (or an equivalent system)? As we speak of the problem of finding service providers and the availability issue, one should bear in mind that the greatest customer convenience is achieved when all the reservations and gathering of travel information can be made from the one and the same source.

Another related problem concerns the rich supply of service providers, and the uncertainty that can result in, especially if the consumer's knowledge and experiences of the travel industry leave a great deal to be desired. How is the potential traveler to know if the service providers found are the most inexpensive and reliable? Although price comparisons can be made among the service providers, they cannot be made for service providers whose sites the customer has not found.

For many travelers the price of the journey may be the primary priority. However, getting the lowest possible fare is likely to be very hard—if not impossible—if you don't have some basic knowledge about the pricing principles of the travel industry and follow the strategies your travel agent uses to get you a low fare. The basic guidelines include : Stay over on a Saturday night; avoid traveling on Mondays, Fridays or holidays; purchase your ticket more than 21 days in advance; use the same carrier for all legs of your journey; depart mid-morning or late evening.

Not only is knowing the low-price booking strategies necessary for making a non-expensive and well-planned booking. A journey consists of many problematic elements that an inexperienced traveler may not consider. For instance, what is the minimum time needed to pass in transit at different international airports? Travel is a complicated industry with a lot of rules, meaning that many people want to interface with humans. Consumer online reservation systems (where the consumer himself is responsible for planning the trip and making the arrangements) may prove to be impractical for all but the most sophisticated users due to regulatory obstacles, currency fluctuations, and the complexity of international flights and CRS systems.

As many tourists—at least today—lack the possibility, knowledge, or courage to shop electronically, it seems reasonable to assume that they want familiar, reliable travel agencies, who, according to Wilson, still offer knowledge and intuition that cannot be found in an online service, to administer their travels. This also holds for travel arrangements made over the Internet. In addition, it has been pointed out that the price offered by online travel sites is often considerably higher than the price offered by the travel agencies, partly owing to the fact that the customer's knowledge of the pricing principles in the tourism industry usually is very limited.

Although the potential for making price comparisons often has been mentioned as a great consumer benefit of electronic commerce, it is no doubt a time demanding task. Naturally, this goes only for travel sites offering online bookings, since identical price inquiries easily can be sent to several Web-based travel agencies. As a result of any, some, or all of these potential problems, the whole process of making travel arrangements on one's own can be extremely time consuming.

7

Tourism Economy

In the course of the globalisation of economies and societies, tourism is showing many indicators of development leaps and distortions: continuing growth in tourist flows as a source of environmental damage, new destinations and markets, with resulting increase in competition, risk of overcapacity, particularly in the key tourist areas of air traffic and accommodation, polarisation and increased trend towards concentration among industry providers. There is also the expectation of growth in "manmade" travel and adventure environments worldwide and major expansion in tourist offers and infrastructures (mega-events, leisure parks, transport systems)—with uncertain economic, social and ecological prospects.

The growth rates predicted for tourism and its anticipated continuing expansion, with the associated potential for employment and macroeconomic welfare effects are, however, dependent on specific conditions, such as a growing world economy, low energy prices and a global decline in conflicts. The world economy is characterised by internationalisation and globalisation. So far, the dismantling of borders to production and trade has been concentrated on the group of developed countries in the OECD. This situation has been unaffected by the emergence of a number of Asian NICs.

Within the OECD, trade is highly regionalised. Besides the international trading and production networks, regional ones are also emerging. Regional integration processes of this kind will probably continue and develop into free trade zones of increasing size. However, the picture of future economic growth in many forecasts differs widely in the individual regions and groups of countries. Whereas growth in the industrialised nations will converge, only a few of the group of developing nations and NICs will make the jump to the next stage.

So far there is no indication that growth in the more developed nations will change significantly. This, together with the expectation that the group of developed nations will gain new members, adds weight to the hope of further growth in tourism. Which are the main characteristics of the tourism of today? First, its steady and continuous growth: 25 million international arrivals in 1950, 165 million in 1970, 693 million in 2001 and 1,5 billion forecast for the year 2020. Even if tourism growth appears to slow down in the very recent years, there is no evidence of saturation of demand, at least on the global level.

International tourism receipts show as well a sustained growth, with annual percentage increases higher than those of the World Real Gross Domestic Product. Globalisation is another feature of tourism: in 1950 the top fifteen destinations in the world accounted for 97 percent of foreign visitor arrivals; in 1970 it was 75 percent; in 1990, 67 percent and in 2001 it accounts for only 62 percent. Tourism is vulnerable to international crises and economic recession. The aftermath of the 11 September terrorist attacks combined with a global economic slowdown produced, for the first time in decades, a reduction of international tourists in 2001, compared with the previous year.

One year ago, WTO carried out an analysis based on two considerations: the vulnerability of tourism, a major sector of the economy, to the externalities of war and terrorism, on one hand, and on the other, its intrinsic resilience linked to the persistence of the demand for travel and leisure, which must have an outlet despite any obstacles. No matter what difficulties and risks consumers may perceive, they will still seek to travel, even if it means changing their destination or postponing their trip. This essential consideration is what allows us to remain reasonably optimistic.

The progress of the situation from the third quarter of 2001 and through the first nine months of 2002 has largely confirmed our analysis. Six observations can be made.

1. The crisis has been global. 2001 was marked by a loss of consumer confidence and by a feeling of apprehension with regard to travel, especially by air. This was the first crisis in 20 years and the deepest one in the history of international tourism. Revenues were harder hit than arrivals: in dollar terms, international tourism receipts declined by 2.6%, and amounted to 464 billion dollars. International tourist arrivals were down 0.6 per cent from 697 million in 2000 to 693 million in 2001.
2. In spite of it all, the collapse predicted by some did not take place. Indeed, it must be kept in mind that the reference year, 2000, the millennium year, was an exceptional one in all respects. There were an additional 45 million international arrivals that year (+6.9 per cent), whereas the decline from 2001 in absolute terms was just 4 million arrivals. Taking 2000 and 2001 together, puts growth in line with the average for the decade.
3. The different regions and destinations were affected to varying degrees. Four categories of destinations have particularly suffered: those that depend on the

U.S. generating market, the Unites States itself as a destination, long-haul destinations in general, and finally the Arab-Muslim world, which has been the victim of image problems and unfair generalizations. The Middle East, South Asia, North Africa, North America and the Caribbean were especially affected, while Europe and Sub-Saharan Africa held steady. East Asia and the Pacific maintained its growth.

4. The impact also varied widely according to market segment. In general, nearby leisure destinations have prospered due to widespread apprehension about travelling far from home; domestic tourism has also held its own; international tourism, generally speaking, has suffered less than long-distance air transport. Air travel, business tourism and conventions, luxury hotels, and cruises during the winter season were particularly affected, while social tourism, rural tourism, rail and road travel made gains.
5. Notable changes in consumer behaviour were observed.
6. The crisis has also accelerated structural changes on the supply side

Lingering uncertainty regarding the global economic situation has led multilateral organizations to revise forecasts they made in the first quarter. The analysis shows that the slowdown in household consumption is causing a decline in growth rates. There is a downturn in world production, affecting the main tourism generating countries and a lowered world GDP growth expectation by three-tenths of a percent from the forecast of 2.8% earlier in the year. According to US analysts, total production could slow down due to the effect of the stock market's decline on consumption and investment.

Analysis of the industry's current situation show that the state of the economy is exerting a large influence on the number of tourism trips and that the perception that the economy is not recovering as clearly as it was hoped presents a problem with regard to expectations of maintaining employment levels. The purchasing power of the national currency of the chosen destination is another variable with significant influence. The introduction of the euro is perceived in Europe as a positive factor (enhances transparencies, facilitates transactions and purchases and eliminates foreign exchange commissions). However these effects are not easy to see in the short term and some price hikes have been attributed to the introduction of the new currency.

Economic Importance

Tourism is one of the most important sectors in the economies of develping countries. Currently, tourism is the most important sector and major source of foreign exchange earnings in Thailand, Australia, and New Zealand. It is ranked second in Hong Kong, Malaysia and the Philippines, and ranked third in Singapore and Indonesia. For example, in New Zealand, the tourism industry employs more than 200,000 people, with projections of a 14% annual growth till the year 2000. In Hong Kong, tourism employs 12% of the workforce and contributes about 7% to the economy.

The tourism sector in Thailand supports over 1.5 million jobs and contributes 5% to the economy. Tourism is also gaining importance in China. By the year 2000, China expects to receive 55 million visitors with foreign exchange earnings of US$14 billion, which will contribute 5% to China's economy, making tourism one of the most significant components of the national economy. In Singapore, the healthy overall balance of payments is attributed to the huge surplus achieved by the tourism sector which contributes about 10% to the economy.

Despite Singapore's open economy, and its vulnerability to external shocks and import leakages, tourism has made a significant contribution to output, employment, and income. Based on 1988 input-output tables, Khan et al. estimated that tourism contributed 11.9% to Singapore's GDP (Gross Domestic Product) in 1992, while employment accounted for 13.4% of the labor force. The employment effect of a million dollars in tourist expenditures would create 25 new jobs. The results ts showed that every dollar of tourist expenditure would generate S$1.97 of output and S$1.05 in income.

The income multiplier for tourism was larger when compared to Hong Kong, Indonesia and Malaysia, while the tourism output multiplier was greater relative to other sectors of the Singapore economy. Comparisons with previous studies showed an increase in the contribution of tourism over time, a strong indication of the significance of tourism in the Singapore economy. The estimated economic impact of tourism is also significant in South Korea. According to Lee and Kwon, the total impact of tourism receipts of US$4.7 billion in 1993, generated US$11.7 of output, US$2.4 billion in income, and created 350,000 full time jobs.

The secondary impacts were also found to have a considerable effect on the economy. The findings suggested that tourism should be promoted as a strategic export industry. Tourism serves as an important means to increase economic growth, raise the quality of life, create employment, and improve the overall balance of payments by helping to offset deficits in other sectors. Many Asia Pacific countries show a net surplus in their tourism balance of payment account. Japan, Taiwan, and South Korea are major tourist generating countries in the region and this is reflected by the deficits in their respective travel balance of payments accounts.

Mak and White attributed the travel account deficits for these high income countries to a higher allocation of disposable income to leisure travel. The relaxation of travel restrictions in Taiwan also had a significant impact on its travel account, due to the large increase in outbound travel. On the other hand, China, Thailand, and Singapore are major receivers of tourists, enjoying a huge surplus. As a percentage of exports, tourism contributes more than 13/n to the economies of Australia, New Zealand, and Thailand, again reflecting its ranking as the top export. Its contribution to the GDP is significantly greater in Singapore (10%) and Hong Kong (7%).

Almost all Asian nations are committing substantial manpower and resources to attract more arrivals whose expenditures represent significant contributions to national income and foreign exchange earnings. For example, Singapore has unveiled a new tourism blueprint titled "Tourism 21" that is expected to turn the nation into a world class tourism business center and the tourism capital of the East. Plans call for increasing arrivals and receipts by 6.4% and 6.6% annually to 10 million and US$11.4 billion, respectively, by the year 2000. Even Indonesia and Malaysia have raised their commitments towards developing the tourism sector.

Indonesia plans to make tourism the nation's number one foreign exchange earner by the year 2004, when arrivals will hit 11 million and receipts reach US$15 billion from current levels of 4.3 million and US$5.4 billion, respectively. In the current Seventh Malaysia Plan, which ends in the year 2000, a number of strategies were formulated to turn tourism into a top revenue earner for the country. Millions of dollars will be allocated for tourism infrastructure in an effort to increase arrivals and receipts to 12.5 million and US$6.3 billion, respectively, by the end of this decade.

With increasing competition for the tourist dollar, the national tourism organizations of New Zealand, Thailand, Australia and Hong Kong, among others, have also allocated an increase in tourism funding to tap the emerging tourism markets that promise new income and employment opportunities. The rapid growth of the tourism industry is a reflection of the region's booming and diversified economies. Economic growth has ranged between an average of 6% to 9% in the last decade, in contrast to 3% to 4% growth achieved by the rest of the world.

Only the industrialized countries of Australia, Japan, and New Zealand show a lower rate of growth than the rest of the region. China, which has achieved double-digit growth over the last 5 years, is poised to become one of the world's largest economies and surpass Japan in the next decade. The region is expected to maintain its growth at a rate between 6% to 8% over the next decade. Strong economic growth in Asia is attributed to a focus on market reforms, export oriented industries, stable currencies, diversification of the economy, and massive injection of foreign capital.

Billions of dollars are being poured into the tourism infrastructure to accommodate a burgeoning Asian tourism industry. This has intensified trade, investment, and travel within the region and with the rest of the world. Asian governments have also sought to avoid extremes of inflation and unemployment, and are keeping budget deficits small or running surpluses. It is no wonder that the region has attracted much attention from the rest of the world regarding its success. The opening up of Indochina, Myanmar, and China to tourism, and given the increasing number of companies setting u p bases and new businesses in the region the volume of business travel will rise. This will provide ample marketing opportunities for travel-related businesses.

As a result of strong economic growth, disposable incomes have soared in Asian countries and along with it, the propensity to travel. Leisure consciousness has been enhanced with travel no longer seen as a luxury. In fact, it is now seen as an affordable commodity to be enjoyed by all who choose to engage in a variety of leisurely pursuits. Some Asians may see travel as a status symbol, while others see it as relief from the pressures of work. The introduction of a 5-day workweek in China will provide Chinese residents with more leisure time that will likely be devoted to travel.

A number of Asian countries have recorded significant growth in real per capita income over the last Syears with Singapore (7.3%), Thailand (6.8%), China (10.3%), Korea (6.7%), and Indonesia (7.1%) showing the highest growth. Rising incomes have created a middle class of sophisticated and affluent Asians who are better educated, have more disposable income, and who appreciate the value of leisure. Research by Mak and White has shown travel propensity and tourism spending to be positively correlated a ed with per capita income among the major Asia Pacific countries. This means that increases in income levels will enable a greater proportion of Asians to travel overseas.

Unlike previous generations, this generation of primarily young travelers are intent on enjoying the fruits of their labor. Although price conscious, they still demand high qualify products. Since Asians are more likely to travel in groups and families, more travel products and services, such as tour packages that incorporate activities, must be designed to cater to their needs. This may include travel to exotic places, soft-adventure travel, cruises, and sports related tours, among others. Disposable incomes will continue to rise, and thus fuel the demand for leisure travel. The trend among Asia Pacific countries is towards more frequent regional holidays to various destinations and resorts within the region.

Tourism Taxation

The tourism sector can be taxed either by taxing the businesses in the tourism sector or by taxing the tourists directly. Both methods may be implemented either via the general tax system of the economy or through special tourism taxes. The World Tourism Organisation has identified 40 different types of taxes applied to the tourism sector in both developed and developing countries. Of the 45 taxes, 30 are directly payable by the tourists and 15 are levied on tourism businesses. Airlines and airports, hotels and other accommodation, road transportation, food and beverages and provider of tourism services, these five broad sectors are involved in tourism taxation. The practicality of taxing each of these sectors is highlighted below.

Airlines and airports: In long haul destinations, international transport occupies a major part in the total cost of holiday packages and hence taxing this sector should, in principle, be lucrative. However, although this is an option for developed countries, this is beyond the reach of most developing countries because they normally do not own an airline company or if they do own one, it is often unprofitable. Revenue may, instead, be generated from airport-related taxes.

Hotels and other accommodation: This is normally the most important revenue generator of the tourism industry and is also easier to tax. However, the practicality of taxing the accommodation sector also varies between developed and developing countries and tends to be more problematic in the latter. The hotel sector is often highly subsidised or receives investment and tax incentives from the government in developing countries, with the aim of attracting foreign and domestic investment to the sector. The motivation is twofold, first to expand the sector as a part of a policy to expand the tourism industry and second, to protect the sector because it is a relatively unstable one due to its highly seasonal nature. The contradicting implication is that the easiest and major target for tourism taxation is most likely to be freed from taxation.

Taxis, food and beverages and tourism services: These sectors are relatively easy to tax in industrialised countries but form part of fragmented small business sectors and do not normally contribute a major proportion of tourism revenue. They include such sectors as entertainments, handicrafts, jewellery and other souvenirs. In most developing countries, these activities form part of the informal sector or of the hard-to-tax formal sector and it is difficult to raise much revenue from this source.

Environment and gambling: Ecotourism tax is a relatively new form of taxation that destinations such as the Balearics levy in an attempt to counter the environmental damage caused by mass tourism. Carbon tax and landfill tax are more general environmental taxes on the level of carbon emissions and wastes respectively, but are borne by tourists as well. Although gambling (in-shop and racing) is not legal in some countries mainly due to religious opposition, casinos are socially accepted in several countries.

Tourists are involved in gambling and casinos, and hence bear the tax associated with those activities. The tax can be levied on the suppliers rather than tourists as in the case of the UK where the betting tax that was initially levied on the gamblers is now levied on the gross profit of bookmakers. Since taxing tourism businesses is not always a lucrative way of raising tax revenue, much tax revenue from tourism is generated from consumption taxes and special tourism taxes applied directly to tourists' consumption. Consumption taxes take the form of general sales taxes or value added tax (VAT).

Sales tax/VAT is levied in almost all countries, regardless of the tourism taxation policies. Therefore, in the presence of this type of sales tax, tourists are being taxed without any deliberate tourism tax policy on the part of the government. In the spirit of optimal taxation, some countries discriminate between domestic and tourism consumption, such that the latter is taxed at a higher rate or an additional tourism tax is applied to tourists' consumption. However, this entails administration problems in enforcing and monitoring such taxes.

Special tourism taxes are generally levied directly on tourists and they can take several forms. Common forms include taxes on hotels and restaurants, passenger services, tourist transport, entry/exit taxes and hotel accommodation taxes. The last tax is the most common and, as the name suggests, hotel accommodation tax is simply a tax on the tourists' expenditure on accommodation. The rate levied usually depends on hotel class and the season. It is relatively easy to collect, although discrimination across hotel classes sometimes creates administrative problems.

Entry/exit taxes include those on airport departures, which are fixed amounts that have to be paid when leaving the country, on airport embarkation, which is paid on entering the country, and the visa fee. These taxes are usually levied at a flat rate and are relatively small in amount: for example, the airport departure tax has been within the range $1-6 in Singapore, Indonesia, Malaysia, Philippines, and Thailand, and was set at $10 in Malawi, Tanzania and Zambia.

Most of the arguments in favour of taxing the tourism sector are based on the fact that tourism products are consumed jointly with unpriced natural amenities and public goods. Unpriced natural amenities include the sun, sea and wildlife, while public goods can include security and health services. The question of public goods, their supply and their pricing, is relatively more important in tourism than in many other industries, in part, because of the needed role of the government in asset preservation and, in part, because of the greater role of the government in the normal routine when foreigners reside temporarily within its own borders.

Main reasons for tourism taxation can be considered under the following categories. Besides providing law and order, under which contracts can be enforced and property rights protected, so ensuring that the private sector is operating efficiently, one of the main roles of the government is to provide 'public goods'. The technical definition of public goods comprises the following: indivisibility, ie. commodities are not divisible into units that can be sold individually; non-excludability, ie. no one can be excluded from benefiting from the product; the free-rider problem, where it is difficult to charge users an appropriate fee.

Common examples of public goods include national defence and street lighting. The distinctive characteristics of public goods makes it difficult to provide them via the private sector because there is no price mechanism that controls the market. They can be provided only by the government, which uses its right to tax to generate the resources necessary to supply them.

Domestic taxpayers usually finance the provision of such goods. The influx of tourists imposes an extra cost on the government relating to the provision of items such as greater security and an improved environment. As non-residents, tourists do not pay to finance these extra costs. A tourist tax will, therefore, serve to redress the balance and impose the burden on those who are responsible for them. There are often user charges for some attractions, such as parks and safaris, but in other cases, such as street lighting and public security, enforcing payment is difficult. In such circumstances, taxing the may be the only way of 'charging' them for the public goods they consume.

Higher government revenue can increase welfare by such means as financing improvements in public services. Furthermore, it may help to reduce the burden of income taxation on domestic residents, and it may also be an alternative policy for countries that want to reduce their dependency on trade taxes while, at the same time, not imposing an additional burden on domestic residents. The WTO estimates that 'tourist countries' obtain around 10-25% of their tax revenue from the tourism sector.

In some small specialised tourism countries such as the Bahamas, over 50% of government revenue is generated from the tourism sector. the net tourism earnings in the Maldives accounted for 40% of government revenue. In Mauritius, about 12-15% of tax revenue is collected directly and indirectly from the tourism sector. The tourism sector is an unusual sector for revenue generation. Developing countries tend to undertax their tourism sector, failing to exploiting fully the economic rent emerging from the sector.

Such rent results from less than perfectly elastic demand for their tourism products, due to the differentiated nature of their natural amenities. The degree of inelasticity of demand depends, in part, on the degree of differentiation of the destination and affects the ability to tax. The greater the degree of differentiation of the destination, the more inelastic demand will be and, hence, the greater the scope for taxation. Tourism product differentiation generally occurs in terms of types and quality of attractions (endowments), types and quality of goods and services sold in the country, geographical location and distance.

Examples of attractions with very inelastic demand are the pyramids of Egypt, the Taj Mahal and the Grand Canyon. However, tourism is a composite product with multiple components, and each of the components can be taxed at a different rate. Researchers examined that the effect of a hotel room tax on non-lodging consumption and find that tourists 'respond to marginal increases in price of lodging partly by reducing some of their non-lodging expenditures and partly by reducing their savings and/or spending at home'.

Taxation on tourism may be exportable in the sense that tourists bear the major burden of the taxation. Tax incidence refers to the distribution of the tax burden between the buyers and the hoteliers whereas tax exporting refers to the extent to which the burden of the tax is distributed between the residents and the non-residents. If the hotel industry is an enclave with a high proportion of foreign investment, then the distinction between tax incidence and tax exporting is minor because the incidence of the tax on the supplier is actually exported. Under a partial equilibrium framework, the incidence of a hotel room tax depends on the relative sizes of the elasticities of demand and of supply.

Hotel room tax was more readily exported than similar taxes levied on meals, drinks and entertainment and the general sales tax. Hence the exportability of tourism taxes is liable to vary between different components of the tourism product. Many developing countries under balance of payments and foreign exchange pressure have targeted tourism as a means of development. In many cases, no proper management strategies have been formulated especially at the initial stage of the tourism development.

Natural resources have been degraded to the point where environmental sustainability is threatened. Regulating the inflow of tourists and taxation are the two most popular tools used, or considered, to remedy the problem. However, regulating the inflow of tourists may not be the ideal solution because it deliberately contracts the tourism sector and this may have negative repercussions on the economy. It should also be remembered that many countries are investing resources to expand the tourism sector, and therefore it would be contradictory to pursue these two policies simultaneously.

Moreover, it is believed that unconstrained growth (not limiting tourist arrivals) is usually beneficial in the sense that it increases the level of per capita income, thus providing more funds for maintaining the environment and sustaining growth. On the other hand, regulation through taxation not only provides the government with revenue (if designed properly) but also targets only the activities and individuals involved in the environmental degradation process and is, therefore, an efficient way to tackle the problem.

Furthermore, with higher revenues, more resources will be available to sustain the development of the industry. The tourism sector does not only rely on the natural amenities in the country but also on public goods. A strong regulatory framework, such as maintaining high health and food preparation standards, is also important in the success of the tourism sector. Taxation can generate the necessary resources to provide these requirements. Of course, the tourism industry has no inherent right to have the taxes it pays ploughed back into the industry. However, appropriate earmarking of tax revenue can help to sustain the tourism industry and also help to reduce and combat the associated degradation of the environment.

The taxation issues involved in controlling environment degradation and sustaining tourism are similar. The basic method is to use the Pigouvian tax, whereby the tax rate should correct for the divergence between the market price and the social marginal cost. Such taxes should be applied to all users, including both domestic residents and tourists, and should as far as possible be directed to the goods and services that generate the externalities so as to avoid inefficiencies. If resources are to be exploited only to the economically desirable limit, then the social marginal cost (hence tax rate) should be set sufficiently high to include not only the opportunity costs to local residents in terms of environmental damage and congestion costs, but also the maximum possible rent extractable.

On the other hand the price, hence the tax rate, should not be set so high as to hinder consumption of the product and tourist arrivals in the country. Congestion is an important facet of sustainability. High congestion, often caused by tourists themselves, reduces the quality of tourism services, which can lead to a reduction in arrivals, especially of high class and high spending tourists. The presence of crowds may detract from the enjoyment of tourists seeking solitude and privacy. Discomfort in crowds, long queues at popular places, traffic congestion and an untidy environment will not only affect the quality of tourism services but also the quality of life of domestic residents.

Tourism taxation may be used both to reduce the inflow of tourists and to compensate the local residents. However, many tourism activities are not priced, for example, sun, sea and sand, and if some are priced, the associated transaction costs relating to monitoring and enforcement are generally very high. Thus, they are supplied at a zero fee to all users and the problem of free riders is difficult to avoid. An entry/exit tax is an easy way of extracting economic rents from the tourism services the destination country is selling because it is often a tax included in the airfare, unnoticed by many travellers. Sometimes countries discriminate between domestic residents and tourists, so that only tourists pay the tax. However, an entry/exit tax has some disadvantages.

First, by capturing rents from tourists, an entry/exit tax does not provide any incentive for tourism to reduce their demand for the specific good that is causing the externalities, as should optimally be the case. The tax will reduce the number of tourist arrivals. Hence not only the demand of the externality generating commodity will fall but demand for other tourism services will also fall because of the complementary nature of tourism demand. The economic benefits normally attached to expanding the tourism sector may then be constrained.

Second, a uniform entry/exit tax does not offer first degree price discrimination in the sense that both low and high income tourists or short and long stay tourists pay the same amount of tax. This may discourage short stay tourists.

Third, since it is levied mainly on foreigners, or at a higher rate on foreigners, it may fail to take full account of the full contribution of residents to environmental degradation.

Taxes levied directly on the tourism sector are sometimes difficult to justify. The amount of tax collected may be small but the tax can still have a substantial negative impact on the tourism sector, with repercussions on the overall economy. This happens especially with taxes levied directly on tourists, such as visa fees. It is not only the high fees required; there is often unnecessary bureaucracy (indeed discrimination between tourists of different nationalities) that can greatly raise the compliance costs for the tax payer and act as a deterrent to visiting the country. This may contract tourist arrivals and affect other sectors related to the tourism sector.

For countries where tourism comprises a major part of the economy, this can adversely affect the employment level and the balance of payments resulting in an overall contraction of the level of economic activity of the economy. The fiscal effects are likely to differ from country to country and from time to time, for three main reasons.

First, the effects depend on the policy of the government. If the government wants to maximise revenue, the tax rates will tend to be high. On the other hand, if the government wants to promote the sector, tax rates can be very low. In some case the government goes further by providing subsidies, such as subsidies for airport and parking infrastructure, and investment incentives to businesses.

Second, the effects also depend on how important tourism is to the economy. Obviously, the higher the contribution of tourism in the economy, the higher will be the effects of tourism taxes on the government budget.

Thirdly, the number and types of linkages with other sectors in the economy and leakages from the economy that the tourism sector brings about are also important. As a general rule, linkages tend to increase government revenue and leakages lead to a reduction in revenue.

The amount of revenue that is obtained from tourism taxation depends, in part, upon the value of the price elasticity of demand for tourism. If the price elasticity of demand is high, the effect of an increase in tax may be to decrease revenue. In the case of tourist accommodation, researchers obtained, demand elasticities for accommodation that were significantly different from zero. They also reported a significant price elasticity of demand for the lodging industry based on a survey of the properties owned and managed by the American Hotel and Motel Association.

Taxation generates revenue but, as in the case of trade taxes, it invites retaliation by other countries if they feel that the other government is unfairly treating their citizens. For example, Kenya and Tanzania introduced visa charges for UK citizens in retaliation to the application of visa fees by the UK on their citizens. Retaliation is always a threat and in most cases the eventual outcome is lower welfare for both countries.

The country with a more inelastic demand for tourism will lose less but, compared with the case without retaliation, both countries lose. However, if a developing country imposes, say, an entry tax on tourists who are mainly from developed countries, then retaliation will tend to affect the developing country to a lesser extent. This is because the number of tourists from the developing country visiting the developed is fewer than the number of tourists from the developed countries who visit developing country.

Energy for Tourism Development

Every business has a balance sheet expense called 'energy'. For some, the amount is only a few percent of the total operating expense, but for many businesses—particularly in the tourism sector—it is a major item that heavily influences 'bottom line' profits. Yet, many businesses do not understand the way they use -and often pay for—energy, which is often inefficient and results in both waste and unnecessary expense. But the cost of energy is not just a business expense—its generation and use can also be a significant expense to the environment and to the community, although this cost is rarely paid.

For a tourism business that relies on the fossil fuels of coal oil and gas to run their operations, this environmental expense shows up as air and water pollution, toxic waste and climate change. Although tourism businesses and their customers may not pay these costs directly, they are all impacts that can have a direct effect on a tourism business by reducing the desirability of tourism destinations. The mounting environmental debt from fossil fuel energy use is cause for great concern, which is beginning to drive actions to reduce these environmental impacts. Further, as customers become more aware of these impacts, they increasingly demand action to reduce them through their purchases of cleaner goods and services.

In the tourism sector, this awareness is driving an expanding 'ecotourism' movement, but it is also having a general impact on the sector. Governments, business and individuals are responding through a wide range of actions, beginning with energy efficiency and continuing through investments in renewable energy. In this response, many tourism businesses are discovering that it is possible to reduce their energy expenses, increase profit and meet increasing customer expectations of environmental responsibility. Renewable forms of energy thus offer an exciting opportunity to the tourism sector.

Renewable Energy

Renewable energy is abundant, clean, and inexhaustible. It is also the most cost-effective energy source for a variety of applications, meeting between 15 and 20 percent of total world energy demand and 24 percent of the world's total electricity supply.Renewable energy in the form of traditional biomass fuels, such as wood and crop residues, represents about 14 percent of the world's total energy consumption-a larger share than coal (12 percent). However, the contribution of newer renewable energy technologies is increasing rapidly. Biomass, geothermal, solar, small-scale hydropower, and wind technologies have grown proportionally faster than any other electricity supply technology, and now supply about two percent of total global energy demand.

In just two decades, the wind energy industry has grown from a producer of small machines for remote power applications into a modern, multi-billion dollar industry supplying grid-connected power. At the beginning of the 21st century, more than 30,000 megawatts (MW) of wind turbines generate clean electricity in more than 30 countries. Consequently, the cost of wind-generated electricity has dropped seven-fold, which makes windpower competitive with most fossil fuel technologies in locations with a good wind resource.

Renewable energy is generally the cleanest option for producing energy, particularly to eliminate greenhouse gas emissions. But there are many other advantages for both individual tourism businesses and their regions or nations. These include:

Energy Security: RE can diversify the energy supply, thereby promoting energy security and price stability. Renewable energy technologies can be used in conjunction with national utility grids, local "mini-grid" systems or as 'stand-alone' systems. For some applications, RE can reduce dependence on imported fuels, an issue that is particularly important for the tourism sector in developing countries where petroleum imports can account for 50 to 60% of the trade deficit. The use of RE can help countries reduce their payments for oil imports and allow scarce hard currency resources to be used for national priorities.

RE can also enhance energy security by decentralising energy supplies with smaller, modular, and rapidly deployable projects that are particularly suited to the electrification of remote communities and businesses in developing countries. For isolated groups with small power requirements, connections to national utility grids are generally expensive and often not cost-effective. Renewable energy-based "mini-grids" or "standalone" systems are, in many cases, better options to provide electric power.

Economic Security: RE is often the most economical choice because of its scale. The modular nature of many RE systems means they can be built (and paid for) as the demand for energy grows, and embedded within the existing energy network, if there is one. By contrast, large, centralised energy systems take much longer to build and are normally designed to supply a future power demand that may not eventuate. Central power plants and transmission lines are also vulnerable to power interruptions. For the tourism sector, increasing the reliability of power supplies and minimising power outages can be a key element of customer satisfaction.

Environmental Security: For most tourism businesses, maintaining environmental quality is a prerequisite for continued business. RE can offer direct environmental benefits, particularly for developing countries, by improving air quality as a result of reduced airborne emissions of pollutants compared to traditional fossil fuels. This is particularly important in cities where carbon monoxide, nitrous oxides and hydrocarbons from petroleum-fuelled transport create ground level ozone and other forms of air pollution. Many of these centres are tourism hubs and transit destinations losing business from the environmental concerns of tourists.

The 1999 European Union 'Eurobarometer' survey showed that good air quality was a key criterion for selecting holiday destinations. Burning fossil fuels also emits carbon dioxide, the key greenhouse gas linked to global climate change. The resulting impacts from increased concentration of greenhouse gases includes altered rainfall patterns, floods and droughts, an increase in the frequency and intensity of storms, shifts in climate zones, and sea level rise—all of which can dramatically affect the tourism industry.

The areas most at risk—small islands, coastal zones, flatlands and wetlands—are primary tourism destinations. A shift in climatic zones and subsequent changes to fauna and flora may mean that many countries will loose their key tourism sites. Increased flood and storm events can also destroy basic infrastructure and increase the incidence of vector borne diseases such as malaria.

These impacts will continue to lower visitor numbers to the effected regions. Although tourism businesses may only be very small contributors to greenhouse gases in these areas and unable to affect the overall global emissions, their participation in efforts to reduce greenhouse gases should not be underestimated.

Indeed, it is these regions that can demonstrate the effectiveness of clean energy options to other areas of the world. Renewable energy systems can offer tourism businesses a positive community image that can be actively promoted to clients. This positive image can also be important to employees who can not only feel a sense of pride in the environmental leadership of their employer, but also benefit from a better working environment. Several studies have shown, for example, that buildings designed to heat and cool themselves using solar design are more comfortable and lower worker absenteeism.

Employment: Developing and expanding markets will create employment in areas related to the design, development, sale, application, manufacture, installation, and servicing of renewable energy-based systems. Although this may not be a direct benefit to tourism operators, it can be a useful element in government discussions that may benefit the tourism sector, such as creating policies to invest in renewable energy projects.

Other Benefits: Creating a strategy to employ energy efficiency and renewable energy can also produce other benefits if used as a basis for sustainable development. Taking a resource efficiency approach to water and sewage, for example, can multiply the benefits obtained through energy efficiency improvements. For example, using efficient shower roses can reduce water and energy use by up to 70 percent without sacrificing shower "comfort". The saved water alone can be used in other areas, while the lower hot water demand can enable the use of solar water heaters.

The major limitation in renewable energy systems lies in the intermittent and sitespecific nature of the energy source. Solar cells, for example, generate electricity only when light is available and wind generators operate only when there is sufficient wind. However, even though such resources are intermittent, they are often highly predictable. In terms of electricity, most modern grid systems can absorb up to twenty percent of their total capacity from intermittent generating sources such as wind.

Even this limitation can often be overcome with a mix of technologies. For example, wind energy and photovoltaic systems combined with another generating source such as hydropower can provide a much higher percentage of electricity in a grid system.

Crops harvested on a continuous basis can often fuel biomass energy systems and solar water heaters can store heated water in a tank for later use. RE systems can also be capital intensive as most of their cost is incurred when they are built. However, their zero or low fuel cost means the cost of energy over the life of the system (life-cycle cost) is often competitive with other energy options. Another key issue that can limit RE development is the need to establish trained support. Past experience has shown that many failures have resulted from lack of maintenance or inappropriate operation. RE technologies are also at different stages of development and therefore may have technical limitations.

There are different renewable energy technologies, but the most appropriate technology depends on both the available renewable energy resource and the particular application, such as providing electricity for lighting or heat for cooking. There are basically three types of renewable energy:

- Heat Energy
- Electrical Energy
- Transport Fuels

For many tourism businesses, the majority of energy demand—60-70 percent—is for hot water and space heating. About 20 percent of total demand is for electricity and the rest powers transport. Of course, these percentages can vary greatly, but they illustrate that heating applications are often the first place to look for opportunities to utilise renewable energy or energy efficiency.

Heat Energy

For the tourism sector, renewable energy technologies can provide thermal (heat) energy via solar, geothermal and biomass energy resources to heat buildings, provide hot water and cook food. Buildings and water can be heated using a number of renewable energy technologies. These include:

- Passive solar design;
- Solar thermal systems, (including domestic and commercial hot water systems and pool heating);
- Geothermal systems (including ground-source heat pumps);
- Biofuel systems.

Often, several technologies can be used together. A solar hot water system, for example, can be used together with a wood-fired boiler to heat water.

Electrical Energy

There are basically two applications for renewable energy electricity: as electricity fed into central power distribution facilities—also called the transmission grid or simply 'grid'—and electricity for remote areas where a grid is either weak or not available, such as small islands. In both cases, renewable energy can often (though not always) be used in conjunction with other generating options, such as diesel generators.

For businesses that would like to generate their own power, either in a standalone system or to feed into a power grid, the following section gives some guidance on different options.

Transport Energy

Renewable energy can be converted to liquid fuels to provide motive power. The most successful and most widely used technology is to convert crops such as sugar cane to ethanol that can be used directly or blended with petrol. The largest and most successful use of energy crops is the US program to produce ethanol from corn (4 billion litres in 1999) and the Brazilian industry to produce ethanol from sugar cane (14 billion litres in 1999). Crops and crop waste can also be used to create 'biodiesel' and biogas for use in transportation applications.

8

Travel Formality and Regulations

Tourism development in India has passed through many phases. At Government level the development of tourist facilities was taken up in a planned manner in 1956 coinciding with the Second Five Year Plan. The approach has evolved from isolated planning of single unit facilities in the Second and Third Five Year Plans. The Sixth Plan marked the beginning of a new era when tourism began to be considered a major instrument for social integration and economic development. But it was only after the 80's that tourism activity gained momentum. The Government took several significant steps.

A National Policy on tourism was announced in 1982. Later in 1988, the National Committee on Tourism formulated a comprehensive plan for achieving a sustainable growth in tourism. In July 1991, tourism was also declared as a priority sector for foreign investment. In 1992, a National Action Plan was prepared and in 1996 the National Strategy for Promotion of Tourism was drafted. The other major development that took place were the setting up of the India Tourism Development Corporation in 1966 to promote India as a tourist destination and the Tourism Finance Corporation in 1989 to finance tourism projects.

Altogether, 21 Government-run Hotel Management and Catering Technology Institutes and 14 Food Craft

Institutes were also established for imparting specialised training in hoteliering and catering. India is a country known for its lavish treatment to all visitors, no matter where they come from. Its visitor-friendly traditions, varied life styles and cultural heritage and colourful fairs and festivals held abiding attractions for the tourists. The other attractions include beautiful beaches, forests and wild life and landscapes for eco-tourism, snow, river and mountain peaks for adventure tourism, technological parks and science museums for science tourism; centres of pilgrimage for spiritual tourism; heritage trains and hotels for heritage tourism. Yoga, ayurveda and natural health resorts also attract tourists.

The Indian handicrafts particularly, jewellery, carpets, leather goods, ivory and brass work are the main shopping items of foreign tourists. The estimates available through surveys indicate that nearly forty per cent of the tourist expenditure on shopping is spent on such items. Domestic tourism is as old as the Indian society. According to available statistics, domestic tourism has grown substantially during the last one decade. It increased to 175 million in 1999 from just 83 million in 1991, thus registering a compound annual growth of 9.8 per cent. The growth of inbound tourism since Independence has been quite impressive. It was just around 17 thousand in 1951. From this level it rose to 2.48 million in 1999.

Tourism has emerged as an instrument of employment generation, poverty alleviation and sustainable human development. During 1998-99, employment generation through tourism was estimated at 14.79 million. Domestic tourist spending per year is around Rs. 24,000 crore and foreign exchange earnings from the tourism are estimated more than Rs.12,011 crore. Tourism receives have grown at a phenomenal rate of about 18 per cent since 1951. Thus Tourism has become the second largest net foreign exchange earner for the country.

In order to speed up the development of tourism in the country several thrust areas have been identified for accomplishment during the Ninth Five Year Plan. The important ones are development of infrastructure, products, trekking, winter sports, wildlife and beach resorts and streamlining of facilitation procedures at airports, human resource development and facilitating private sector participation in the growth of infrastructure. The basic strategy during the 9th Plan is to establish effective coordination with all the relevant agencies to as to achieve synergy in the development of tourism.

For the 9th Plan period (1997-2002), the Planning Commission has approved a Plan outlay of Rs. 793.75 crores for the Ministry of Tourism comprising Direct Budgetary Support of Rs. 485.75 crores and internal and external resources of Rs. 308.00 crores. Tourism development is a composite subject and does not necessarily mean the development of only the tourism facilities like hotels, restaurants, recreational activities etc.

In fact, creation of tourism infrastructure will be meaningful only if the areas has the minimum basic amenities and infrastructure like roads, water, electricity, sewerage and telecommunication facilities. This aspect has given importance in the Tourism 'Synergy' programme. The State Governments have been asked to prepare Master Plans for the development of tourism based on the same concept. The organisations involved in the development of tourism in India are the Ministry of Tourism and Culture with its 21 field offices within the country and 18 abroad, Indian Institute of Tourism and Travel Management, National Council for Hotel Management and Catering Technology, India Tourism Development Corporation, Indian Institute of Skiing and Mountaineering and the National Institute of Water Sports for HRD development in the area of Tourism.

Accommodation Facilities

Accommodation of quality is basic infrastructure for the development of Tourism. The Ministry of Tourism approves hotels from the point of view of their suitability for international tourists. Various incentives and benefits are linked to such approvals. As on September, 1999 there were 1229 hotels with 68032 rooms and on the approved list of Ministry of Tourism.

Some of the recent initiatives taken by the Government to boost tourism include grant of export house status to the tourism sector and incentives for promoting private investment in the form of Income Tax exemptions, interest subsidy and reduced import duty. The hotel and tourism-related industry has been declared a high priority industry for foreign investment which entails automatic approval of direct investment up to 51 per cent of foreign equity and allowing 100 per cent non-resident Indian investment and simplifying rules regarding the grant of approval to travel agents, tour operators and tourist transport operators.

ITDC

In 1996 a public sector corporation was set up under the Ministry to pioneer the development tourism infrastructure specially hotels in the country. The present network of ITDC comprises 26 Ashok Group Hotels, 6 Joint Venture Hotels, 5 Restaurants, 11 Ashok Travel and Transport units, 29 Duty Free Shops at 6 Airports and a Down-Town Duty Free Shop in Delhi. The Government is actively considering disinvestment of ITDC to ensure private participation.

The major constraint in the expansion of international tourist traffic to India is non-availability of adequate infrastructure including adequate air seat capacity, accessibility to tourist destinations, accommodation and trained manpower in sufficient number. Much has been achieved by way of increasing air seat capacity, increasing trains and railway connectivity to important tourist destinations, four-laning of roads connecting important tourist centres and increasing availability of accommodation by adding heritage hotels to the hotel industry and encouraging paying guest accommodation.

But much more remains to be done. Since tourism is a multi-dimensional activity, and basically a service industry, private sector and voluntary organisations become active partners in the endeavour to attain sustainable growth in tourism if India is to become a world player in the tourist industry

Tourism Policies

The impact assessment of the sectoral policies on the specified sector suffers from a serious methodological problem. Briefly, it may be argued that the development of a sector is not solely dependent on the factors within the sector: it is influenced by the general socio-economic environment, the political system and the overall policy framework. Thus the study integrates within itself the dynamic aspects of historical changes that are taking place at the macro-economic level. Similarly, Tourism Policy would not have evolved on its own without being influenced by the general tenor of macro-economic policy.

Tourism policy thus has a socio-political grounding as much as it has a macro-economic colouring. The 1980s witnessed the era of liberalisation initiated by the Congress Government at the Centre. The process of liberating the Indian economy from the shibboleths of 'license-permit Raj' culminated in the initiation of the structural adjustment programme in 1992. "Objectives, Thrusts and Macro-economic Dimensions of the Eighth Plan" endorsed by the National Development Council, clearly outlines the context within which the structural reforms were initiated: "The need to restructure our systems of economic management has become an imperative if India is to emerge as a vibrant and internationally competitive economy in the 90's.

Systems of control and regulation, developed for good reasons in the past have outlived their utility and some positively (sic) stand in the way of further progress. Such dysfunctional systems have to be overhauled in the light of emerging realities. "The process of structural adjustments has brought about far reaching changes in the Indian economy at a breath-taking pace. The impact of these changes over the tourism sector need to be studied in a dynamic context. Nevertheless, the above should not be taken as ignoring the fact that sectoral policy does have a direct and unambiguous impact over the concerned sector.

Tourism Policy, as a statement of intent by the Government, would form the reference point for action and criticism. Any initiative by Government in Tourism by way of legislation or direct investment is envisaged within the framework of Tourism Policy. The debates in Parliament had taken recourse to the received policy of the Union Government while making references to particular cases. The backdrop of a policy always serves as a guideline for further executive and legislative initiatives. It would be cynical to regard these policy statements as mere exercises in eloquence and additions to the already existing volumes of wishful thinking.

Furthermore, Policy statements by Government should be viewed in their evolutionary stance. It would be a negation of the democratic content of our political system to view a Policy statement as a static and rigid formulation, at a point in time, applicable for years to come. Thus, since 1982, various initiatives undertaken by the Government need to be perceived as additions or modifications to the received Policy. While it may be argued that these changes in the policy are only marginal and superficial from the viewpoint of equity and social justice, it would be an oversimplification to view the latest policy statement as nothing but the "nth" version of the Policy formulated in 1982.

Recognising the all-pervading inertia that looms large in matters governmental, one is often tempted to deny the scope for lobbying which makes possible the desired modifications in the policy corpus. In short, policy, as a body incorporating proactive intentions, is amenable to periodic reviews and possible modifications. The issues stressed in the preceding paragraphs provide the framework within which Tourism Policy needs to be considered. In brief, there is more to policy in tourism than is found in the Tourism Policy. Perhaps, the links within a macro-economic framework need no special mention.

The first ever Tourism Policy was announced by the Government of India in November 1982. It took ten long years for the Government to feel the need to come up with a possible improvement over this. Thus the National Action Plan for Tourism was announced in May 1992. Between these two policy statements, various legislative and executive measures were brought about. In particular, the report of the National Committee on Tourism, submitted in 1988 needs special mention. In addition, two five-year plans – the Seventh and the Eighth – provided the basic perspective framework for operational initiatives.

The Seventh Plan advocated a two-pronged thrust in the area of development of tourism, viz., to vigorously promote domestic tourism and to diversify overseas tourism in India. While laying stress on creation of beach resorts, conducting of conventions, conferences, winter sports and trekking, the overall intention was to diversify options available for foreign tourists. The Tourism Policy, 1982 was more an aggressive statement in marketing than a perspective plan for development. Its main thrust was aimed at presenting India to the foreigners as the ultimate holiday resort. With a view to reach this destination, the following measures were suggested by the Policy:

1. To take full advantage of the national heritage in arriving at a popular campaign for attracting tourists;
2. To promote tourist resorts and make India a destination of holiday resorts;
3. To grant the status of an export industry to tourism;
4. To adopt a selective approach to develop few tourist circuits; and,
5. To invite private sector participation into the sector.

The Planning Commission recognised tourism as an industry by June 1982. However, it took ten years to make most of the States to fall in line and accord the same status within their legislative framework. At the beginning of the Eighth Plan, 15 States and 3 Union Territories had declared tourism as an industry. Four States had declared hotels as an industry. The National Committee on Tourism was set up in July 1986 by the Planning Commission to prepare a perspective plan for the sector. Within the broad framework of the Seventh Plan, the Committee had to evolve a perspective plan for the coming years.

By September, 1987, the Central Government declared more concessions for the sector: these included tax exemption on foreign exchange earnings from tourism (a 50% reduction on rupee earnings and a 100% reduction on earnings in dollars), a drastic reduction in tariff on import of capital goods, and concessional finance at the rate of 1 to 5% per annum. The Tourism Development Finance Corporation was set up in 1987 with a corpus fund of Rs. 100 crores. Until then, the sector was financed on commercial lines by the Industrial Development Bank of India, Industrial Credit and Investment Corporation of India and other commercial banks.

The National Action Plan for Tourism, published in May 1992, and tabled in the Lok Sabha on 5 May 1992, charts 7 objectives as central concerns of the Ministry:

- socio-economic development of areas;
- increasing employment opportunities;
- developing domestic tourism for the budget category;
- preserving national heritage and environment;
- development of international tourism;
- diversification of the tourism product.,
- and, increase in India's share in world tourism (from the present 0.4% to 1% during next 5 years)

As per the Action Plan, foreign exchange earnings are estimated to increase from Rs.10,000 crores in 1992 to Rs.24,000 crores by 2000 AD. Simultaneously, the Plan aims at increasing employment in tourism to 28 million from the present 14 million. Hotel accommodation is to be increased from 44,400 rooms to 1,20,000 by 3 years. Other provisions in the Action Plan include a discontinuance of subsidies to star hotels, encouraging foreign investment in tourism and the setting up of a convention city for developing convention tourism.

The Action Plan envisages the development of Special Tourism Areas on lines of export processing zones. Special Central assistance is to be provided for the States to improve the infrastructural facilities at pilgrimage places. It proposes to set up a National Culinary Institute, and projects a liberalised framework for recognition of travel agents and tour operators. The Eighth Plan document makes a special mention that the future expansion of tourism should be achieved mainly by private sector participation.

The thrust areas as enumerated in the Plan include development of selected tourist places, diversification from cultural related tourism to holiday and leisure tourism, development of trekking, winter sports, wildlife and beach resort tourism, exploring new source markets, restoration of national heritage projects, launching of national image building, providing inexpensive accommodation in different tourist centres, improving service efficiency in public sector corporations and streamlining of facilitation procedures at airports.

The Eighth Plan aims at luring the high spending tourists from Europe and USA. It also envisages a 'master plan' to integrate area plans with development of tourism. This is envisaged to ensure employment opportunities for the local population. In April 1993, the Government announced further measures aimed at export promotion. The existing Export Promotion of Capital Goods Scheme (EPCG) was extended to tourism and related services. Against the existing 35%, the tourism sector would now pay an excise duty of 15% only on capital goods import, subject to an export obligation of 4 times the cargo, insurance and freight (CIF) value of imports. With an obligation period of five years, this came as a boon to the hotel industry. The cost of construction had also come down by 20%.

In addition to the above policy pronouncements by the Union Government, our planners had envisaged the possibilities of developing specific regions on a zonal plank. Special area programmes like the Hill Area Development Programme and the Western Ghats Development Programme form part of the overall national plan. The Eighth Plan document stipulates that the strategy in such designated special areas is to devise suitable location-specific solutions, so as to reverse the process of degradation of natural resources and ensure sustainable development. This approach perhaps needs to be integrated into the project of special tourism areas, now being made popular by the Government.

The federal principles enshrined in the Indian Constitution require that the tourism sector be treated as a State subject. As such, the Department of Tourism (under the Ministry of Civil Aviation and Tourism at the Centre) undertakes certain promotional and developmental activities with a view to enhance the sectoral potential. The Department has certain regulatory functions to perform involving the hotel industry, travel agencies and tourist operators. Over the years, there has been considerable erosion of powers so far as State Governments are concerned. The sustained campaign for privatisation in all the policy documents has left limited space of operation for the States.

The public sector is increasingly being perceived as an agent of inertia than of change and hence the pressure for a hands-off policy. On the other hand, the Union Government has been usurping the powers of the State with some pretext or the other. Promotion schemes, designed at the Centre, are transferred for implementation at the State level. The special Central Assistance, for example, granted for the development of infrastructure at the pilgrim centres, carries with it a pre-defined scheme and mode of execution. Furthermore, there are occasions when the Centre forces the State Governments to extend certain subsidies and concessions to the sector.

The terms of such concessions would have been fixed by the Centre and the States would have no choice but to fall in line. For example, during the State tourism minister's conference in December 1991, the States were urged to freeze water and electricity rates for 10 years. They were also asked to exempt certain hotels from local and state taxes for 10 years. Seventeen circuits and destinations were identified under the National Action Plan for development through Central assistance and investment by the States and the private sector. The centres were identified by the Centre and the States were asked to do the needful. There were also times when the federal division of power resulted in operational contradictions.

For instance, by 1989, many foreign hotel chains like Hilton, Hyatt, Penta and Kempinski had applied for licenses for investing in India. However, the revenue departments of the respective States failed to locate and allocate land for the construction of hotels. The scheme, thus, fell flat. Curiously, the Union Government was not hesitant to make use of Constitutional provisions when it suited its interests.

The Yunus Committee had suggested the creation of the Tourism Board on lines of the existing Railway Board. To begin with, the empowered committee of secretaries challenged the idea of creation of a Board. It was said that the Railway Board as an independent entity was created for historical reasons. It would be difficult for tourism to be looked after by a Board, because legally the sector would come under the Industrial (Development) Act. It was also found that such a Board would not be viable financially. In 1991, the think-tank on tourism created by Minister Madhavarao Scindia rejected the idea of a Board in toto. It was emphasised that the Board cannot be in charge of a sector that is basically under the jurisdiction of the States!

Federal Interventions

It is common knowledge that the resource-base of the States is very narrow, making them vulnerable at the negotiating table. However, States have the freedom to resist the Centre's strong- arm tactics, provided State assemblies stand-by the interests of the States. For instance, State legislatures may refuse to freeze water and electricity rates on grounds of revenue generation. In that event, the concerned Chief Minister or the Minister of Tourism may convey the intensity of resistance that he is confronted with, and thus refuse to comply with the Centre's diktats.

It is heartening to realise that the States have often exercised their power of self-determination and consequently refused to toe the line drawn by the Centre. This offers enough scope for possible interventions at the federal strata of our political system in matters of policy formulation.

Privatisation

According to the Approach Paper to the Seventh Plan, " there is a vast potential for development of tourism in the country. Tourism should be accorded the status of an industry. Private sector investment will have to be encouraged in developing tourism and public sector investments should be focused only on development of support infrastructure". Thus the seeds of private initiatives were sown during the Seventh Plan. The Government took the matter of privatising the tourism sector seriously by 1988. It was during the tenure of Mr. S.K. Mishra as Tourism Secretary that the talk of inviting private investment into the sector began.

The Government permitted foreign equity participation up to 5 1 %in tourism projects. Foreign charters were allowed to operate in the country for the first time. Foreign companies were allowed to repatriate their profits to the extent of 3%. The structural adjustment programme, initiated in June, 1992, paved the way for privatisation in almost all sectors of the economy. The Annual Plan (1992-93) document emphatically enunciated the Government's position vis-a-vis tourism: "The future growth of tourism will have to be achieved mainly through private initiative.

The State will contribute to tourism by planning broad strategy of development, provision of monetary and fiscal incentives to catalyse private sector investment." The process of privatisation brought in its wake big investments and private involvement at various levels. As an offshoot, environmental considerations were thrown to the winds and there were instances of large scale human rights violation. The self- correcting nature of policy made provisions for stricter controls in this regard. More seriously, privatisation meant alienation of the majority of our population and their deprivation. Employment generated in tourism is generally seasonal and ill paid.

The private sector- induced pockets of tourism had the potential of turning into centres of pollution, drug trafficking and prostitution. The Seventh Plan proposed that tourism be declared an industry. However, it took time for the States to implement this, even though they agreed in principle. The smokeless industry had the advantage of generating maximum value-added, because of low-cost inputs. The Tourism Policy Statement carried certain provisions in favour of the hotel industry. It stated that there should be provision for depreciation in the balance sheets of hotels. Being an export industry, hotels were to be given excise concessions.

The provisions of the Monopolies and Restrictive Trade Practices (MRTP) Act were relaxed for hotels, because any hotel with 300 or more rooms would have incurred an investment of Rs. 25 crores. The document also hinted at lower tariffs for power and water and regulations for easy import of equipment. As a follow-up, hotel and shipping were added to the list of 27 industries exempted from Section 22 A of the MRTP Act. The consequences of declaring tourism as an industry need to be studied in detail. It is not possible to capture its implications in an exploratory work like this. However, it is obvious that the private sector has primarily benefited to a great extent by this measure.

The arena of policy formulation should be self-evaluating and self-correcting. In the case of Tourism Policy, this has proved to be the plus point. As an illustration, the Policy statement of 1982 made no mention of infrastructure development. The successive governments at the Centre failed to create proper tourism infrastructure, thus resulting in loss of traffic. This lacuna was corrected in the National Action Plan. However, much of this change was due to intensive lobbying by such agencies like the Indian Association of Tour Operators (IATO), the Travel agents Association of India (TAAI) and the Indian Hotels and Restaurants Association (IHRA).

It is for the voluntary agencies and pro-people forces to exploit the avenue of lobbying at various levels. The environmental implications of tourism development did not form part of the 1982 Policy. The consequences are too obvious to be written about. However, the NAP, 1992 did carry specific provisions for environmental protection and harnessing. From Policy to Cartooning Policy statements may also lead to justifiable flights of fantasy.

Broadly, our successive policy pronouncements in the realm of tourism falls within the "liberalising" framework of the macro- economic policy environment. The Finance Bill, 1988, had assured 50% tax exemption on foreign exchange earnings in the sector, and a further 50% exemption if re-invested. In effect, it amounts to 100% tax concession. Luxury hotels enjoy exemptions of all kinds with a view to encourage tourism earnings. These tax exemptions coupled with provision of soft loans to the sector led to a boom in the tourism related private investment.

The Economic Survey 1991-92 aptly summarises the ultimate aim of such incentives for private sector participation: " The Government has tried to expand the economic space in which the people can exercise their initiative and ingenuity. It hopes to do more to expand their opportunities, to enhance their potential. But what shape the economy takes ultimately depends on what the people make of it. In that sense, the future is in their hands." We should not forget that tourism is an industry which emerges in the context of unresolved socio-economic structural issues, such as land distribution patterns or the take over of traditional occupations by modem mechanised capital.

Tourism happens to be a source of livelihood for millions in India and aggressive privatisation does not ensure social and economic safety nets. In the face of the unhindered entry of international capital and successive alienation, perhaps, it is difficult to agree that "the future is in our hands" Eco Tourism and Sustainable Development. The Draft Tourism Policy 1997 states that "in the context of economic liberalisation and globalisation being pursued by the country, the development policies of no sector can remain static."

The policy further states that "the emergence of tourism as an important instrument for sustainable human development including poverty alleviation, employment generation, environmental regeneration and advancement of women and other disadvantaged groups in the country" requires support to realise these goals. India's tourism resources have always been considered immense, in a tourism audit. The geographical features are diverse, colourful and varied. The coastline offers opportunities for developing the best beaches in the world. There are a wealth of eco-systems including bio-sphere reserves, mangroves, coral reefs, deserts, mountains and forests as well as an equally wide range of flora and fauna.

The Policy further states that "international tourists visiting interiors of the country for reasons of purity of the environment and nature contributes to the development of these areas particularly backward regions". Thus Tourism "should also become a reason for better preservation and protection of our natural resources, environment and ecology". The policy recognises that sustained growth of tourism can give rise to conflicts. To ensure that the growth of tourism takes place along desired lines, certain guidelines have been framed:

1. to remove the constraint of the information gap.
2. to create a tourist product that is desirable and supported by an integrated infrastructure.
3. to involve all agencies, public, private and government, in tourism development.
4. to create synergy between departments and agencies that have to deliver the composite tourist product.
5. to use both the circuit and scheme approach so that peoples participation through panchayats, local bodies, NGO's, and youth organisations will create a greater awareness of tourism. The Central Government can thus concentrate on larger investment oriented projects.
6. to create direct access for destinations off the beaten track.
7. to diversify the product with new options like beach tourism, forests, wild life, landscapes and adventure tourism, farm and health tourism.
8. to ensure that the development does not exceed sustainable levels.
9. to develop the seven north-eastern states, the Himalayan region and Islands for tourism.
10. to maintain a balance between the negative and positive impacts of tourism through planning restrictions and through education of the people for conservation and development.

The strategy for development should take into consideration the carrying capacity, local aspirations and benefits likely to accrue to the community. In particular specific policies and guidelines for eco-tourism development and adventure tourism are to be formulated, primarily through a regulatory framework.

The Draft Guidelines have been approved at a State Ministers Conference and have been circulated to various trade and industry bodies. The guidelines draw a distinction between mass or resort tourism and nature or eco tourism, as the kind of tourism that has a lower impact on the environment and requires less infrastructural development. The Ministry hopes that the environment conscious international tourist will be made aware that India is taking steps to protect its ecology and environment.

Apart from the do's and don'ts, the guidelines are governed by a tourism management plan, the key elements of which are the protection of natural resources and a positive involvement of local communities, along with an optimum number of environmentally conscious visitors. The principles of management are scientific planning, effective control and continuous monitoring, development of physical infrastructure, zoning and a Management plan for public use of natural sites. The management plan should establish standards for resort development, style and location of structures, waste disposal, treatment of sewage, control of litter, use of public spaces and fragile areas.

The operational guidelines rely on sensitisation of all the role players and this programme is based on a self-regulated environmental code. Area specific rather than universal development plans keeping in mind the unique character of the location and its economic and social environment are important. This would help the State Government to coordinate with the industry in managing visitors and their activities. NGO's working on socio-economic programmes in forest and remote areas could have a closer coordination with tourism service operators to transfer economic benefits, particularly the handicraft production and marketing sector.

The guidelines are only a beginning, and it is hoped that with increasing awareness of the visitor the industry will regulate its practices. There is an emphasis on the needs and perceptions of the international tourist running through the discussion on the guide lines although the data from the National Parks makes it evident that the domestic tourists outnumber international visitors, although they do not pay the same amount as the foreign visitor either in entry fees or for board and lodging and transport facilities.

They do however demand a much higher per capita use of resources like water, fuel for heating and cooking and transport. They also make the same intensive use of time and try to maximize their stay by the number of animals and birds they can view in the 24-hour period. It is interesting to note that no democratic participation has been called for in the policy formulation process, and all the amendments to the policy have come from trade associations and government think tanks. The tourism Advisory Committee also consists of eminent persons and community representation has been ignored.

The elite nature of the policy makers is well represented in the quotations given above from the policy document. The policy clearly recognises the debate on the tourism issue which has surfaced wherever tourism development, particularly in the case of tourism projects relating to the "gifts of nature" like beaches, rivers, mountains and forests, have already been developed. However, mere recognition of the hostility of people to tourism development is not enough to change the nature of tourism development or the resistance to tourism or what many have termed a poor tourism culture.

Perhaps to understand this in a better perspective, we should look at the issue of sustainable development in a critical way. Perhaps we can question the impact of sustainable development on the environment and sift through the jargon of development planners, international agencies, and environmental activists to see how sustainable development can be achieved without all the contradictions that are apparent as in the case of the tourism sector. Sustainable development is change that can be sustained or continued for the time period concerned.

Development we can say with some confidence is a process of directed change, but any process embodies both the objectives and the means of achieving the stated objectives. Can we set sustainable objectives (as growth in sustained consumption of) for resources that now are recognised to have ultimate limits or what we may call non-renewable resources or what we may call the balance between the use and conservation of such resources? The concept of sustainability originated in the context of renewable resources like forests and fisheries and was subsequently adopted by the environmental movement.

In most cases it is understood to mean "the existence of the ecological conditions necessary to support human life at a specific level of well being through future generations." However, in addition to ecological conditions there are social conditions that influence ecological sustainability in a nature-people interaction. The social connotations have been described by Barbier who has defined social sustainability as "the ability to maintain desired social values, traditions, institutions, cultures or other social characteristics."

The term sustainability came into usage in 1980 when the IUCN presented the World Conservation Strategy where sustainable development was linked to conservation of living resources. However, the fundamental goals have often been lost sight of because of operational goals (e.g. food, water, shelter, health are fundamental goals to be realised through self reliance, cost effectiveness, appropriate technology, people centred-ness etc.) Consequently, the WCED made its definition brief: Social Development is development that meets the needs of the present without compromising the ability of future generations to meet their own needs. They did not make any assumptions on the direction in which changes in demand would take place. (E.g. equity, social justice, self-determination, or cultural diversity).

India's tourism policy follows the mainstream SD thinking by adopting all the critical objectives: revive growth change the quality of growth meet essential needs for jobs, food, energy, water and sanitation ensure sustainable levels of population conserve and enhance the resource base reorient technology and management risk merge environment and economics in decision making reorient international economic relations make development more participatory. These objectives are responsible for building a very broad consensus on the issue of sustainable development, yet the debate at the operational level continues.

Most participants in the debate now accept that many human activities are reducing the long-term ability of the natural environment to provide goods and services, which will eventually affect human health and well being. Many also accept that poverty is devastating the lives of millions in the Third World since there is no consensus between what is environmentally necessary and what is economically and developmentally feasible. The level of inter-dependence between the two insights is yet to be incorporated in the concept of Social Development. Some problem areas are: Environmental degradation, already affecting millions in the Third World, is likely to reduce human well being across the globe. Who is responsible for this rapid degeneration? Is it the poor or the rich? The poor have no option but to exploit resources for short-term survival.

If we take the example of forests and their resources, which have been traditionally outside the market system and in the sphere of tribal or indigenous peoples rights, they are today seen as exploiters of the forests as against tourists, with all their demand for infrastructure and superstructure, who are seen to be conservationists. The inter-linked nature of the problem of sustainability is such that the impact of degradation will be quicker on the poor than on the rich. Can Sustainable Development be the metafix it claims to be in reconciling increasing industrial, agricultural and resource use productivity with environmental needs.

The weakness of the Social Development argument lies in the techno-economic approach to solutions with regard to common property resource management, through know how transfers, resource pricing, subsidy policies and building management capabilities. Deeper processes such as land reforms, industrial demands on raw materials, over consumption, changing legal and political structures are either ignored or looked at in a cursory manner. For instance how can we claim a consensus between those who are concerned for the survival of future generations with those who are concerned with the survival of wild life, or human health and subsistence?

We will also fail to understand why, even when there is a broad consensus, projects on the ground result in conflicts. Suggested refinements could be:

– a distinction between ecological and social sustainability and in the process an identification of the inter-linkages

- a distinction between renewable and non-renewable resources, between environmental processes crucial to human life and crucial to other forms of life dependent on the resources.
- a distinction between the techno-economic aspects of social sustainability (infrastructure, services, government) with political and cultural sustainability.
- a distinction between equitable development and local participation, and decentralisation, what many have called NGOisation of sustainable development.

This is because no rigorous testing of local participation leading to social equity or to sustainable resource use have been reported. Case studies reflect personal, organisational or political preferences. Tourism is one of the activities which has caused concern because of the effects of increasing human traffic on fragile environments. Countries which are looking towards Tourism as a means of economic growth, like India, have limited resources and cultural restraints and they have the greatest need to pay heed to the possible negative impacts of tourism. The environmental impact of tourism is a basic issue, whether we are looking at a developed or an underdeveloped area, region or country.

The costs of tourism for a country like India include extensive investment in fixed assets with a low rate of return for infrastructure, transportation, accommodation, cultural institutions, exhibition centres, and park facilities. To this maybe added the social and cultural costs like additional demands on infrastructure like land, water, health services; the creation of new jobs for displaced people; the cost of positive community relationships; the disparity between the lifestyle of visitors and those who serve them; the possible friction between local residents and new users of valued local resources; the perception of local residents of the spending of scarce capital resources on what they consider low priority areas like tourism; cultural cost of alterations in local ceremonial or traditional values; loss of privacy for local communities as tourists come to gape at their living conditions and rituals.

Tourism also causes increasing congestion and pollution as thousands of visitors flock to parks and sanctuaries in motorised vehicles; there are changes in accessibility, landscape and the ecological balance between man and nature; there is the cost, both monetary and human, of creating conservation zones (core/buffer) with unforeseen or undesirable side effects; which have been observed in the ecotourism movement. The benefit of revenue from tourism does not always redress these problems but goes towards the cost of administering the project. The tourism industry is generally self-centred and not given to educational, cultural or exchange programmes on a philanthropic basis.

The natural environment, with the best will in the world, cannot escape damage with the volume of visitors. As more and more tourists, both domestic and international seek the exotic and remote destinations around the world, the likelihood of the environment suffering as a result become greater. Forests can suffer from trampling, fires, tree felling for facilities and waste. Wildlife, despite the protection in national parks, has suffered a loss of habitat, hunting and poaching, viewing and photographing, leading to an interruption of feeding and breeding patterns or hunting for food undisturbed. These are the prized moments for the viewer.

The trade in wild life trophies or tourist souvenirs is the more deliberately destructive aspect of such tourism. The building of tourist lodges in materials that are not integrated with the environment and the pressure they put on the land and water bodies is also wilfully destructive. Management techniques that include being less user friendly or control of numbers by closing access or by multiplying the number of attractions and areas or charging higher admission fees are generally not popular with the tourist or the tour operator and are also difficult to implement because of high administrative costs.

The Government of Kerala has taken a policy decision to develop tourism. The tourism programme has grown very rapidly, as the figures for tourist arrivals in the state indicate. The growth has covered both inbound and outbound international tourism as well as the arrival of domestic tourists to Kerala. The Department of Tourism at the State level has also taken up Central Government projects and following from the National Action Plan, Kerala was the first state to identify a special tourism area, Bekal, to be developed with foreign investment into a big mass tourism project, to help India achieve its 5 million arrivals and access higher returns in foreign exchange.

None of these developments have involved discussion and debate at the state or local level. These have been administrative decisions, and when the secretary, tourism was questioned on the undemocratic manner in which tourism decisions were taken, he saw the issue of tourism as beyond the comprehension of local people. On the other hand, foreign experts were invited to suggest how and what kind of tourism should be developed in Kerala, which had had very little exposure since the Kovalam Beach Resort never realised the potential of international arrivals, being overshadowed by Goa.

Today, the tourism policy of the government visualises many new products and new players in the sphere of tourism. These include new beach resorts, hill and wildlife as the basis for adventure tourism, special tourism areas for intensive development, backwater cruising and festivals that package the culture and craft of Kerala for the benefit of the tourist. Every district now has a privately sponsored tourism festival, which often contravenes the Coastal Zone Regulation as it promotes tourism awareness. The second aspect of the tourism policy is the dependence on the private sector to develop the infrastructure and the superstructure for tourism and its related activity.

Today, the Kerala Government, Tatas and the Casino Group are the major players in tourism development and they have an understanding of tourism that does not look beyond the commercial aspect of tourism development. There is also the desire to invite foreign investment for large-scale development to increase the number of arrivals from abroad to enhance foreign exchange earnings. An intervention-in policy making by office bearers of local self government bodies who can function in the interest of local people is essential. This can be effective only when they have an enlightened awareness on the developmental options that the government offers to the people of the state.

When EQUATIONS began to acquaint itself with the Bekal development plan, it was surprising for us to learn that not a single panchayat opposed tourism development because the thrust of the government's propaganda was that tourism generated income and employment. Several studies relating to tourism development in Kerala indicate that the socio-cultural impacts of tourism have been very negative, particularly, relating to the issue of drugs and prostitution.

Tourism projects have also displaced local people and affected their traditional occupations. The environmental impacts of tourism have also been negative particularly in the coastal zone and in the hills. Tourism needs regulation rather than promotion. Not only regulation, but the issue of tourism needs to be debated so that there are people-centered objectives rather than growth-centered objectives. Unless the people of Kerala arrive at some consensus on the kind of tourism they want to develop to achieve economic objectives, the control of outsiders, multinationals, international agencies and the monopoly houses in India will not end.

One area that needs to be focussed on is the issue of gender and tourism. Women panchayat members, being leaders of their communities, have the added task of familiarising themselves with the gender issues that emerge in the developmental debate, since most planners are male and most models are male dominated. India is a gendered society, which means that human relations in economic, social and cultural life, as well as in the political framework are determined and rnediated by gendered perceptions.

To clarify further, gender does not mean only the difference between men and women biologically but on their human relations being based on the status of women in society and therefore the perceptions of their social role and function. Tourism and the industry that supports it, as well as the administration that encourages its development, growth and expansion, is an interpersonal activity which is influenced by and in turn influences local and global gender perceptions. There is a list of global perceptions that have been researched, to develop a gender framework, for analysing developmental activity particularly tourism.

1. *Tourism as a part of modern consumerism*: Consumerism embodies social practices as well as signifies social change. As leisure time and wealth increase, tourism consumption also increases. As expansion reaches the remotest corners of the world, the marketing and consumption models between guests and hosts have indicated several possibilities for gender analysis. Power, control and equality in tourism are articulated through race, class and gender in the practice of tourism.

Men and women through interconnected economic, political, cultural, social and environmental dimension., are involved in different ways in the construction and consumption of tourism. It is the recognition of these differing realities that shape tourism marketing, tourist motivation, and resident action. This process may be called the creation of stereotypes. For example, in all Asian societies where traditional society is intersecting with global economic systems, we have seen that the major public role of women in the tourism industry is in sex tourism. The faster the process of liberalisation and globalisation, the greater the spread of sex tourism.

2. *Tourism as an aid to development*: Women activists have always seen the statistical approach to tourism as apolitical. If tourism is seen as an activity that depends on leisure time and disposable income, then the enabling conditions are hierarchical and influenced by class and global economic strengths. In tourism advertising women are seen as passive, available and dependent. Women are thus sexual and exotic markers in the tourism brochure. Destinations reinforce this stereotype not only of the resident community as a whole (poor and ready to serve) but also of the women as inferior or as objects of gratification or as playthings.

3. *Tourism and Division of Labour*: Tourism, like other activities, perpetuates the international and domestic division of labour. This means that there are gendered employment activities (cooking, cleaning, serving, handicraft etc.) as well as control of waged work. There is also no computation of unpaid labour by women. The question that tourism raises is that women do not have leisure from certain types of work, and this compulsory, unpaid labour is extended to their working life as well as economic opportunity.

Tourism encourages classifications like women's work.

4. *Tourism development and its influence on changing value systems*: Tourism is an essentially modern activity that promotes 'tradition' as a unique and authentic product. In this process of commodification, not only is it important to define the other, but to define the gendered other. These changes are reflected in identification with tourist behaviour, changes in family systems age and sex hierarchies in the struggle for economic power as well as changes in the social and political status of different sexes in different classes and different production systems.
5. *Tourism and environment*: What is our relationship to the environment, how do we use these resources, how can we regulate the consumption driven nature of tourism and how can traditional practices be documented and compared with the approach of providers of tourism services, is now being looked at. For example, it is suggested that as agriculture becomes less productive, tourism (rural, farm, beach or resort) ecomes a va ua e a ternative ecause it a ows a combination of domestic responsibilities of women, with tourism work, which is seen as an income source that can support small scale farming and thus conserve the countryside. Such an approach suggests that there is a need to change women's relationship with nature, the environment and their place in the ecological system.

CIVIL AVIATION POLICY

Mission

To maintain a competitive civil aviation environment which ensures safety and security in accordance with international standards, promotes efficient, cost-effective and orderly growth of air transport and contributes to social and economic development of the country.

Strategic Objectives

The objectives of this policy are the creation and continued facilitation of a competitive and service-oriented civil aviation environment in which:

i. the interests of the users of civil aviation are the guiding force behind all decisions, systems and arrangements,

ii. safe, efficient, reliable and widespread quality air transport services are provided at reasonable prices,

iii. there exists a well-defined regulatory framework catering to changing needs and circumstances,

iv. all players and stakeholders are assured of a level playing field;

v. private participation is encouraged and opportunities created for investors to realize adequate returns on their investments;

vi. recognizing that aviation today is an important element of infrastructure, rapid upgradation of airport infrastructure to world class with priority to the busiest airports and those handling international flights;

vii. recognizing that transportation of air cargo is vital to the economic growth of the country, creation and development of specific infrastructure for air transportation of cargo and express cargo is encouraged,

viii. "airline operations and acquisition of aircraft" is conferred "infrastructure" status for overall growth of civil aviation sector in the country

ix. domestic and international aviation in the country are encouraged to grow at par with world aviation industry;

x. inter-linkages with other modes of transport are encouraged and stimulated;

xi. trade, tourism and overall economic activity and growth is encouraged;

xii. international cooperation in aviation and development in tune with international trends and best practices, consistent with airspace sovereignty is promoted;

xiii. indigenous development of aircraft, components and aviation products is encouraged,

xiv. Security of civil aviation operations is ensured through appropriate systems, policies, and practices, and

xv. Effective systems are put in place for timely crisis and disaster management, including investigation of incidents/accidents.

Consultation with Users

1. The success of any policy depends upon the benefits it gives to the various users. A constant interaction with and amongst all categories of users is paramount for successful implementation of and constant improvement in the policy. There is an urgent need for an institutional arrangement at different levels for such interaction.

2. Therefore, Facilitation Committees consisting of representatives of various users of civil aviation sector i.e. government, passengers, tour and travel operators, aircraft-operators, airport-operators, exporters and importers, cargo handling agents, aerosports, Flying Clubs, etc. will be set up at national, regional and local levels to ensure that the interests of ultimate users are

best safeguarded. There will be regular monitoring and feedback between the Facilitation Committees of national regional and local levels. There will be mandatory prior consultation with these Facilitation Committees before amendments in policy/ rules / regulations are undertaken.

3. Highest priority will be accorded to the passengers/ users and suitable mechanisms will be set up for this purpose, including publication of Citizens' Charters and effective action for, and monitoring of, grievance redressal.

Regulatory Framework

1. In the context of a multiplicity of airlines, airport operators (including private sector), and the possibility of oligopolistic practices, there is need for an autonomous regulatory authority which could work as a watchdog, as well as a facilitator for the sector, prescribe and enforce minimum standards for all agencies, settle disputes with regard to abuse of monopoly and ensure level playing field for all agencies. Therefore, a statutory autonomous Civil Aviation Authority (CAA) will be constituted. The basic objectives of setting up of the Authority will be to ensure aviation safety, security and effective regulation of air transport in the country in the liberalised environment.

2. The functions of the CAA will be as under:

   i. set the standards for various agencies and personnel of civil aviation sector;

   ii. issue license to these agencies and personnel;

   iii. regulate tariff;

   iv. ensure that these agencies and personnel continuously fulfil the standards;

v. take appropriate preventive/corrective/punitive action against the agencies and personnel for violations of set standards;

vi. ensure that there are no unfair trade practices and market dominance through encouragement of entry and fostering of competition in accordance with Competition Policy of the Government;

vii. ensure level playing field for all agencies and

viii. study and analyse the trends in international and domestic civil aviation, project likely future scenario and publish periodical reports.

3.

i. The agencies mentioned above include airport, airport-operators, passenger aircraft operators, cargo aircraft operators, helicopters, private aircraft operators, flying clubs, aero-sports clubs, security agency, training institute, air-travel operators or any other agency having role in civil aviation sector.

ii. The personnel mentioned above include pilots, flight engineers, navigators, cabin crew, flight despatchers, aircraft maintenance engineers/ technicians, air traffic controllers and personnel engaged in the maintenance of communication, navigation, surveillance/ air traffic management systems and other ground aids.

4. Civil Aviation Authority will conduct safety and security audit including flight inspections of the concerned agencies to ensure that they are meeting the prescribed standards.

5. Civil Aviation Authority will be required to publish Annual Report on the Air Safety and Security Environment in the country.

6. Civil Aviation Authority will also be required to make available information regarding passenger and cargo traffic including regular analysis in an appropriate consolidated format on a commercial basis.
7. A comprehensive Indian Aviation Law will be framed to replace the existing Acts relating to aviation and security which will be in tune with the present day civil aviation scenario, and would also put the proposed CAA in place.

Private Sector Participation

1. Private sector participation will be a major thrust area in the civil aviation sector for promoting investment, improving quality and efficiency and increasing competition.
2. Competitive regulatory framework with minimal controls will be created to encourage entry and operation of private airlines/ airports.
3. Private sector investment in the construction/ upgradations/ operation of new as well as existing airports including cargo related infrastructure will be encouraged.
4. Rationalization of various charges and price of ATF/ AVGas will be undertaken to render operation of smaller aircraft viable so as to encourage major investment in feeder and regional air services by the private sector.
5. Training Institutes for pilots, flight engineers, maintenance personnel, air-traffic controller, security will be encouraged in private sector.
6. Private sector investment in non-aeronautical activities like shopping complex, golf course, entertainment park, aero-sports etc. near airports will be encouraged to increase revenue, improve viability of airports and

to promote tourism. CAA will ensure that this is not at the cost of primary aeronautical functions, and is consistent with the security requirements.

7. Government will gradually reduce its equity in PSUs in the sector.
8. Government will encourage employee participation through issue of shares and ESOP.

Airport Infrastructure

1. The Government will aim at ensuring aaequate world class airport infrastructure capacity in accordance with demand, ensuring maximum utilization of available capacities and efficiently managing the airport infrastructure by increasing involvement of private sector.
2. Greenfield airport will be permitted by the Government where
   (i) the existing airport is unable to meet the projected requirement of traffic or
   (ii) a new focal point of traffic emerges with sufficient viability and
   (iii) the new location is normally not within an aerial distance of 150 kilometers of an existing airport
3. Encouragement will be given to development/ construction in private sector of small airstrips/ helipads /heliports, which are smaller and cheaper to construct. These will be particularly suitable in remote hilly or island areas, large business, city centers, factory locations and at other important nodal points. This will also facilitate increase in small aircraft operations
4. Private sector participation
   (i) Private sector will be free to undertake

(a) construction and operation of new airports/ airstrips/ helipads/heliports including cargo complexes, express cargo terminals, cargo satellite cities and cargo handling facilities

(b) upgradation and operation of existing airports/ airstrips/helipads/heliports in consultation with the existing operator including cargo complexes, Express cargo terminals, cargo satellite cities and cargo handling facilities

(ii) Foreign equity participation will be permitted up to 74 % with automatic approval and 100 % with special permission of government

(iii) Private sector participation will include participation of state government, urban local bodies, private companies, individuals and joint ventures on Build-Own-Operate (BOO) basis or any other pattern of ownership and management depending on the circumstances.

(iv) Restructuring of major airports of Airports Authority of India will be undertaken through long-term lease to private investors for efficient management, improvement of standards of services/ facilities and attracting private investment

(v) At privately managed airports, air traffic control (ATC) and aviation security will continue to be provided by the Airports Authority of India (AAI) and customs and immigration facilities by respective Government departments.

(vi) The equipment needed for any service would normally be provided by the agency responsible for the service and an equitable system would be established for sharing of revenue between different agencies. Keeping in view their respective investments and responsibilities.

5. All airports /airstrips /helipads /heliports used for scheduled air-transport services will be licensed by Civil Aviation Authority.
6. Airport/ airstrip/ heliport/ helipad operators will follow ICAO guidelines for levying airport/ airstrip/ heliport/ helipad charges based on cost recovery principle. The CAA would put in a place a regulatory mechanism to prevent abuse of monopolistic nature of such infrastructure.
7. An objective and well-defined transparent mechanism for allocation of slots at airports will be ensued at all times.
8. CAA will ensure fair play between different airport/ airstrip/ heliport/ helipad operators and user agencies so that no airport/ airstrip/ heliport/ helipad operator is accused of discriminating against any particular airline or any other user. Similarly, Government will ensure that no airport-operator is discriminated against with regard to allotment as point of call, if there is demand for air services from such airport.
9. More international gateways shall be provided. It would be ensured that there is at least one international airport in every region of the country in order to give a boost to trade and tourism and adequate capacity in all the routes.
10. Major thrust will be given for increasing the share of commercial revenue from non-aeronautical sources by giving total freedom to airport/ airstrip/ heliport/ helipad operators in the matter of raising non-aeronautical revenue
11. New Ground Handling regulations with following broad particulars envisage :
    (i) At airports managed by AAI, new private investors have been allowed by AAI to undertake

ground handling besides national carriers and self-handling by carriers which will increase competition resulting in improvement in services and reduction in costs.

(ii) At private airports, at least limited competition will be mandatory.

12. A rationalized dynamic system for airport charges for AAI airports will be introduced for

(i) optimum utilization of airport by using peak and off-peak time charges,

(ii) increasing revenue of airport operators

(iii) promoting airports in far-flung regions by having varying airport charges from airport to airport depending upon the facilities available at the airport.

(iv) promoting use of small aircraft

13. A new Directorate of Lands shall be established in AAI and land use guidelines will be formulated for utilizing vacant land.

(i) Vacant land at airports will be evaluated for construction of aviation related activities (e.g. cargo complexes, aircraft maintenance facilities, etc)

(ii) For optimal exploitation of airport land for civil aviation purposes, private-sector/ State Government participation would be welcome.

(iii) Land at such airports where there is no likelihood of future use for civil aviation purposes will be utilized for other commercial purposes like gold courses, tennis, etc. either by AAI itself or in joint venture.

(iv) Effective steps will be taken for removing encroachments from AAI land and if necessary, comprehensive rehabilitation package will be formulated.

14. Cargo handling

    (i) Infrastructure like satellite freight cities with multi-modal transport, cargo terminals, cold storage centers, automatic storage and retrieval systems, mechanized transport of cargo, dedicated express cargo terminals with airside and city side openings, computerization and automation etc. will be set up on priority basis.

    (ii) Private sector participation in cargo handling will be encouraged.

    (iii) Efficient Electronic Data Interchange systems will be developed and linked amongst all stakeholders in the trade.

    (iv) Air cargo complexes and dedicated express cargo terminals (with airside and city-side openings) will be integral part of all major airports.

15. Operation of airports would be in accordance with the provisions relating to prevention of air, water and noise pollution.

16. Guidelines for naming of airports will be formulated to ensure that the airports are named after the cities they are situated in as per international norms.

17. Air Traffic services

    (i) Air Traffic controllers will be licensed by CAA.

    (ii) AAI will continue to provide Air Traffic Services over the Indian air Space as per standards set by CAA in accordance with ICAO norms.

    (iii) Approach and aerodrome control services may be provided by licensed ATCs engaged by the airport operators

(iv) New satellite based CNS/ATM systems will be introduced as per ICAO's Regional Plan

(v) India to have a significant say in the provision of new satellite based CNS/ATM services in Asia-pacific/ SAARC regional airspace

(vi) Fresh Air traffic Services and Controlling (Departure, holding and approach) procedures will be evolved for helicopters and small aircraft to exploit their inherent advantages and to reduce the cost of their operations and efficient use of airspace without compromising safety. This will also give boost to Flying Clubs.

(vii) Efforts will be made for Civil-Military co-ordination for

(a) Greater sharing of civil and military airspace for unidirectional air-corridors and straightening of air-routes to save fuel and time,

(b) Uniform air-traffic procedures,

(c) Additional slots for civilian flights at military airports,

(d) Sharing of revenues at civil enclaves

Domestic Passenger and Cargo Air Transport

1. The government will encourage provision of safe passenger and cargo air transport services to every region of the country at economic prices.
2. It is necessary that both airline operations as well as airport infrastructure be treated as mutually dependent and complementary and given similar concessions to promote a balanced growth of the sector. Therefore, airline operations and acquisition of aircraft should be given the status of "infrastructure"

3. Private sector participation in providing domestic passengers and cargo air transport services will be encouraged.
4. Permission to start scheduled passenger and cargo air transport service would be given by government on demonstration of competency, minimum capital requirement and viability of the company to provide a safe and reliable service. CAA may also fix a minimum number of aircraft for scheduled operators permit.
5. Capacity induction will be regulated with a view to ensuring safety, security and preventing unhealthy levels of capacity.
6. Government and CAA will ensure that there is no discrimination between different passenger and cargo air-operators.
7. Foreign equity up to 25% and Non-Resident Indian investment up to 100% will be permitted for domestic passenger transport services. However, participation from foreign airlines either directly or indirectly will not be permitted. Substantive ownership and effective control by Indians will be a pre-requisite.
8. Wet leasing of foreign registered aircraft by operators will be permitted only in special circumstances like grounding of aircraft, augmentation of capacity for short term, to meet the capacity requirements for handling natural calamities, etc.
9. ATF will be taken out from administered price mechanism for petroleum prices. The price of ATF for domestic airline will, therefore, be governed by market and customs duty. Airlines will also be permitted import of ATF.
10. There will be freedom to operate non-revenue and passenger charter and cargo flights to any foreign

destinations. Indian passport holders will also be allowed to travel on these flights.

11. Helicopter operations will be given a new boost by a total change in outlook. At present, fixed wing norms with minor changes are broadly applied to rotary wing aircraft. Fresh guidelines will be formulated in consultation with user industry from the point of view of rotary wing aircraft. Fresh Air Traffic Services and controlling procedures, which exploit the inherent advantages of helicopter without compromising safety, will be evolved. This will also reduce the cost of operations of helicopters and efficient use of airspace. Encouragement will be given to use of helicopters in the areas of heli-tourism, adventure sports, mountaineering/ trekking, point-to-point heli-services to bypass traffic congestion on the road, connecting remote areas and islands in Northeast, Andaman and Nicobar and Lakshdweep, religious places, sky crane for construction/ laying of transmission lines etc.

12. Flying clubs, Aerosports like hang-gliding, ballooning, heli-skiing, para-jumping etc. will be promoted by encouraging private investment and formulating liberalized guidelines in consultation with users. This will include rationalized Avgas prices and liberalized air space control.

13. Special consideration will also be given to Private operators and Corporate operators by way of rationalized Avgas prices, encouragement for construction of smaller airstrips/helipad et. in private sector.

Promotion of General Aviation and Small Aircraft Operation

1. There is need to open up the country and tap the latent demand for air services in many parts of the country currently not on the air map. However, the

traffic profile in these areas does not permit viable operations of jet. Even smaller aircraft operations are not viable because of the high cost of operation and high break-even factor.

2. While Route-Dispersal Guidelines do help in providing air services in the remote and inaccessible areas, further measures are required to encourage widespread air-connectivity. Passenger and cargo air transport services to many regions will not be possible unless operation of small aircraft is made economically viable either on stand alone basis or in conjunction with major trunk routes.
3. Therefore, Aviation Turbine Fuel (ATF) for turbo prop aircraft operations will be provided at par with price for international air services, with a cap of 4% on sales tax. Operation of smaller aircraft/ charters will be further encouraged through rationalization of airport charges, Inland Air Travel Tax (IATT) and Avgas prices. For the NorthEast region, IATT has been fully exempted on all routes. Government will consider extending similar facilities to other category II areas.
4. There is a need to change the traditional concept of airport development, ownership and operations in view of the economics of small aircraft/charters operations. Participation of state Government, urban local bodies, airline/ aircraft operators, other private investors will be encouraged in development, upgradation and management of small airports/ airstrips. These airports will be distinct from traditional airport and will be bare-bone type with no frills. Such airports need not be mandatorily manned and onus of ensuring security and safety of operations will rest on the aircraft operator in conjunction with the local administration/ bodies, etc. This will encourage the operation of small aircraft/ air taxis,

as operators themselves or in collaboration with State Government / Urban local bodies/ residents of a specific locality, factory, nearby factories, tourist operators will be able to manage such airports/airstrip flexibly and efficiency at reduced cost. This will boost passenger transport and tourism

5. Single engine aircraft of seating capacity upto 10 seats can be permitted for passenger charter and cargo flights. Such operations shall be in accordance with the single engine operation guidelines and over land areas having no hilly terrain or other obstructions.

International Air Transport

1. The Government will aim at ensuring adequate capacity to fully meet the requirement of international trade and tourism.
2. Liberal bilateral rights will be given for promoting international operations to less developed regions of the country as well as to ill-connected far away countries (e.g. Latin America) to promote trade and tourism in those regions.
3. Government will ensure that traffic rights are utilized to the maximum extent possible through direct operations, creation of virtual equipment by way of joint flights, code sharing arrangements etc. by the two national carriers i.e. Air India and Indian Airlines. Other domestic carriers who fulfill the minimum criteria for designation as Indian carrier to operate international passenger flights will also be permitted to meet this objective. Initially, they may be permitted to fly to neighbouring countries against unutilised rights subject to right of first refusal by national carriers. The requirement of substantial ownership and effective control of the airlines by Indians would continue to be operative.

4. There will be freedom to international tourist Charter operation to different custom airports.
5. Government will also establish, in the long run, an objective and well-defined mechanism for sharing of international traffic rights amongst all airlines in a transparent manner.
6. Government will ensure that there will be no discrimination between different airport operators in allotting capacity to foreign carriers as per bilateral agreements if demand exists.
7. Efforts will be made by national carriers to join global alliances in their own commercial interest and in the interest of travelling passengers through code-sharing, exchange of frequent- flier programs etc.
8. There will be no restriction on international cargo flights. However, they will not be allowed to carry domestic cargo on their flights within the country.
9. Tourist charters from domestic airports to foreign destinations will also be permitted subject to safeguards for scheduled operations.
10. Air India and Indian Airlines would be guaranteed the use of traffic rights actually being utilised by them for five years following privatisation.

Information Technology Plan

1. The government will give thrust on use of Information technology in all aspects of civil aviation sector. Each organisation will have time-bound IT action plan.
2. The following information will be made available by CAA on internet
   (i) Policies/ Rules/ Regulations related to aviation sector
   (ii) Status of various pending proposal and applications

(iii) Syllabi, schedule and results of various examinations conducted by the CAA

3. Increasing use of Intranet/ video-conferencing facilities for consultation for quick decision making and reducing administrative costs.

4. In the national carriers, revenue yield management systems will be increasingly used for flexible tariffs and maximisation of revenue

5. Internet based flight reservation, inquiry and status information system will be introduced.

6. There will be web-site for all major airports where information required by various users like passenger facilitation,transport facilities to and from city, duty free shops, car parking, cargo, guide map etc. will be available

7. Electronic data interchange (EDI) system will be introduced in cargo terminals linking all stakeholders for quick transactions and availability of latest information about the status of cargo movement.

Promotion of Aviation in North-East and Remote Areas

1. In the Northeast region and other remote areas, the management of airport infrastructure as well as air services is not economically viable because of low utilisation and low fare structures etc. However, given the topography and inaccessability of the region, the need for such infrastructure and air services is much greater. But at the same time, forcing commercial airlines and airport operators to invest in these areas, distort the functioning in other areas also and affect their efficient functioning commercially. Therefore, there is need to correct these imbalances.

2. It has been decided to exempt all the currently operated routes in the North-East from payment of

Inland Air Travel Tax (IATT). The decisions to provide ATF to turbo prop aircraft operations at par with price for international air services and capping of sales tax at 4% would also encourage new air services in the North-East. Operation of smaller aircraft and helicopters for passenger and cargo flights will be further encouraged through rationalisation of airport charges and Avgas prices.

3. Airport Infrastructure will be upgraded wherever necessary keeping in mind the linkage with the aircraft type and traffic profile.
4. Adequate funds as grant-in-aid through North East Council (NEC) will be made available for the infrastructure development work needed to be carried out in the North-East region.
5. The air-links between the capitals of the States in the North-East region and between major stations on both sides of the Brahmaputra river will be encouraged.
6. Guwahati and Calcutta will be developed as hub station and main base of turbo-prop aircraft operations by the airlines
7. Regular airservices will be encouraged at convenient timings to enable onward connections to other parts of the country without involving night stop.
8. Suitable infrastructure like hotels, organised taxi-services at the airports and tourist spots in the North-East will be encouraged to help growth in tourism in the region.

Tourism and Trade Promotion

1. Tourism and trade sectors are closely linked to civil aviation sector. Therefore it is important that airport infrastructure and air services are planned keeping in view the requirement and promotion of these sectors.

Multi-modal approach will be used for planning to ensure better connectivity.

2. A thrust for international tourism in India will be given by

   (i) Providing freedom to International Tourist Charters to all airports linking places of tourist interest

   (ii) Declaring additional airports as international airports resulting in easy connectivity and better services,

   (iii) Upgradation of airports at places of Tourist interest like Buddhist circuit, sanctuaries, beach resorts etc.

   (iv) Encouraging private sector participation in building tourist infrastructure near airports like transport services from airports to nearby cities, golf courses, amusement park, business centres, duty free shopping complexes of international class, aviation recreation activities, adventure aviation, hang-gliding, microlight aircraft, parachuting etc

   (v) Efforts will be made to issue visa on arrival at the airport in larger number of cases.

   (vi) Improvement in passenger facilitation and sensitisation of personnel of immigration, customs, security and AAI at airport to make them more courteous and passenger friendly.

12.3. For promotion to trade and industries, following steps will be undertaken :

(i) Abolition of On-Board Courier Scheme to facilitate courier trade

(ii) Introduction of "Known Shipper " scheme for reducing dwell time in exports by doing away with "cooling off" requirement

(iii) Introduction of EDI (Electronic Data Interchange) interlinking trade agencies, customs, immigration for faster efficient trade transactions

(iv) Private sector participation in cargo handling for increasing competition and improved services.

Safety

1. Standards for civil aviation safety for all agencies will be set as per international norms prescribed by ICAO and enforced by CAA
2. New Communication, Navigation Surveillance/ Air Traffic Management (CNS/ATM) system will be introduced on a priority basis as per ICAO's regional plan.
3. Safety audit of various agencies in the civil aviation sector will be carried out by CAA.
4. Installation of Airborne Collision Avoidance system (ACAS), Ground Proximity Warning System (GPWS) and transponders will be mandatory on specific categories of aircraft to enhance safety in civil aviation.
5. Regular Flight Inspections will be carried out by CAA
6. Regular and systematic monitoring of recordings of Flight Recorder shall be mandatorily carried out by the operators as part of accident/ incident prevention programme. Random monitoring by CAA shall also be carried out.
7. Minimum Safe Altitude Warning (MSAW) system shall be provided in all secondary surveillance radars in the country to prevent Controlled Flights Into Terrain (CFIT) accidents.
8. Excellence in maintenance of equipment would be accorded high priority and system will be further refined to safeguard against any malfunctioning leading to loss of life or property.

9. The personnel should be specifically trained in responding to any safety-related emergency situation and roie and responsibility of every functionary should be clearly specified. Regular mock exercises will be conducted to deal with various possible emergencies.

Security

1. A strict national civil aviation security programme to safeguard civil aviation operations against acts of unlawful interference will be established through regulations, practices and procedures, which take account of the safety, regularity and efficiency of flights.
2. Periodic review of threat perception will be carried out taking into account the international situation, internal security scenario and other relevant inputs. Security arrangements and drills will be updated and upgraded regularly on this basis.
3. Strict security standards/ security programme will be set by BCAS (Bureau of Civil Aviation Security) under CAA as per ICAO Standards and recommended Practices with periodical review and enforced by them through regular security audit of various agencies involved.
4. Airport Security will be primary responsibility of AAI in all the airports whether managed by AAI or by private operators, as per the standards set by CAA. AAI will reorient its structure and processes suitably for the purpose.
5. Aircraft security will be primary responsibility of Airline-operator as per the standards set by CAA. Suitable manpower, training and procedures will be provided and set up by the airline operators to ensure this.

6. All arrangements made and personnel engaged for security functions will have to be licensed/ cleared by BCAS.
7. Evolving technologies and equipments will be constantly scanned for identifying those more suited to our secuity needs and their use will be encouraged thereby resulting in more effective security arrangements with leaner organisations.
8. Emphasis will be given on unobtrusive, effective, passenger-friendly security.
9. Emphasis will be given for state-of-art training of personnel engaged in security functions including in the areas of use of modern technology, passenger friendliness, specific requirements of aviation security. Special training modules will be developed for all types of possible emergencies, with clear analysis of different parameters, options available with consequent implications, and tune to developing requisite mindset and skills to act effectively
10. Contingency plans will be developed, kept up-to-date and the resources will be made available to safeguard airport and ground facilities used in civil aviation against acts of unlawful interference
11. Effective measures relating to passengers and their cabin luggage, checked baggage, cargo and other goods and access control will be taken as per international standards and recommended practices to prevent weapons, explosives or any other dangerous devices which may be used to commit an act of unlawful interference, the carriage or bearing of which is not authorised from being introduced, by any means whatsoever, on-board an aircraft engaged in civil aviation.
12. The plans and procedures for management of response to acts of unlawful interference in civil aviation

operations would be reviewed and suitably modified from time to time.

Aviation Support Services

1. The role of aviation support services like human resource development, maintenance facilities and manufacture of aircraft is very important, as these are the backbone of civil aviation services. These services should be available in state-of-art condition in adequate supply in accordance with demand. For this, the role of private sector needs to be emphasised.
2. Training
   (i) Standards and guidelines for training institutions will be prescribed and enforced by CAA.
   (ii) Private sector participation will be encouraged in training institution for pilots, maintenance personnel, security staff and air-traffic controllers.
   (iii) Existing training and management institutes like Indira Gandhi Rashtriya Uran Akademi (IGRUA), National Institute of Aviation Management and Research (NIAMR), Civil Aviation Training College (CATC), Central Training Establishment (CTE), Flying Clubs etc. will be strengthened by involvement of private sector.
   (iv) Emphasis will be given for training of personnel for customer service including safety aspects of various equipment at the work places.
3. Maintenance
   (i) Private sector participation will be encouraged in existing maintenance infrastructure of Indian Airlines and Air India like Jet Engine Overhaul Complex (JEOC) and new maintenance facilities including engine overhaul and repairs with up to 100 % foreign equity.

4. Manufacture of Aircraft/ Engine
   (i) Indigenous design, development and manufacture of light trainer and small transport aircraft, engine, components and spares etc will be encouraged.
   (ii) Offset clauses for sourcing aviation products/ services from India will be incorporated in the RFQ itself for import of aircraft by national carriers.
   (iii) private sector participation will be encouraged.
   (iv) Co-ordination with Department of Defence Production, Defence Research and Development Organization (DRDO), Hindustan Aeronautics Limited (HAL), Bharat Heavy Electrical Limited (BHEL) and other organisations will be strengthened.

Role of Regional and International Civil Aviation

1. India will continue to take active interest in the formulation of global policies on civil aviation and promote international cooperation between member states of International Civil Aviation Organisation (ICAO) to develop global aviation and infrastructure. India will continue its efforts to strengthen cooperation in the field of civil aviation in the region.
2. India will ensure participation in International Co-operation programmes like
   (i) Co-operative development of Operational Safety and Continued Airworthiness Programme (COSCAP) for training by international experts
   (ii) European Union Project for cooperation in civil aviation sector with European countries
   (iii) Regional Co-operation with for development/ provision of satellite based CNS / ATM systems as per ICAO plan

Co-ordination

1. A number of department/agencies are involved in the development of civil aviation infrastructure and facilitating the convenience of the traveling public. Inter-linkages with other modes of transport for travel and trade need to be emphasised.
2. An Inter-Ministerial Standing Committee will be constituted for coordination with Ministries of Commerce, Tourism, Industry, Railways, Surface Transport, Defence, Home Affairs (Immigration and Security), Finance (Customs) and External Affairs.

Bibliography

Atkinson, H. Berry, A. and Jarvis, R., *Business Accounting for Hospitality and Tourism*, ITBP: UK, PB, 1995.

Baum, T., *Human Resource Issues in International Tourism*, Butterworth Heinemann: UK, PB, 1993.

Boella, M.J., *Human Resource Management in the Hospitality Industry*, Stanley Thornes: UK, PB, 1996.

Boissevain, J., *Coping with Tourists: European Reactions to Mass Tourism*, Berghahn Books: UK, PB, 1996,

Briggs, S., *Successful Tourism Marketing*, Kogan Page: UK, PB, 1997.

Buttle, F., *Hotel and Food service marketing: A managerial approach*, Cassell: UK, HB, 1986.

Butler, R. and Hinch, T., *Tourism and Indigenous Peoples*, ITBP: UK, HB, 1996.

Clift, S. and Grabowski, P., *Tourism and Health: Risks, Research and Responses*, Pinter: UK, HB, 1997.

Coccossis, H. and Nijkamp, P., *Sustainable Tourism Development*, Ashgate: UK, HB, 1995.

Cooper, C. and Wanhill, S., *Tourism Development: Environmental and Community Issues*, Wiley: UK, PB, 1997.

Corke, J., *Tourism Law*, Elm: UK, PB, 1993.

Davidson, R. and Maitland, R., *Tourism Destinations*, Hodder and Stoughton, UK, PB, 1997.

Deegan, J. and Dineen, D.A., *Tourism Policy and Performance: The Irish Experience*, ITBP: UK, HB, 1997.

Downes, J. and Paton, T., *Travel Agency Law*, Longman: UK, PB, 1993.

Foster, D.L., *An Introduction to Travel and Tourism: First Class*, McGraw Hill: UK, PB, 1995.

Gee, CY., *International Tourism: A global perspective*, World Tourism Organisation: Spain, PB, 1997.

Goodall, B. and Ashworth, G., *Marketing in the Tourism Industry: The Promotion of Destination Regions*, ITBP: UK, HB, 1988.

Hall, C.M. and Jenkins, J.M., *Tourism and Public Policy*, ITBP: UK, PB, 1995.

Johnson, P. and Thomas, B., *Perspectives on Tourism Policy*, Mansell: UK, PB, 1992.

Kemp, K. and Pearson, S., *Leisure and Tourism: GNVQ Intermediate*, Addison Wesley Longman: UK, PB, 1997.

Kotas, R. and Conlan, M., *Hospitality Accounting*, ITBP: UK, PB, 1997.

Laws, E., *Tourist Destination Management: Issues, Analysis and Policies*, ITBP: UK, PB, 1995.

Lawson, F., *Hotels and Resorts: Planning, Design and Refurbishment*, Architectural Press: UK, PB, 1995.

Medlik, S., *Understanding Tourism*, Butterworth Heinemann: UK, PB, 1997.

Middleton, V.T.C., *Marketing in Travel and Tourism*, Butterworth Heinemann: UK, PB, 1994.

Morrison, A.M., *Hospitality and Travel Marketing*, Delmar: UK, HB, 1996.

Pannett, A. and Boella, M., *Principles of Hospitality Law*, Cassell: UK, PB, 1996.

Sharpley, R. *Tourism, Tourists and Society*, Elm: UK, PB, 1994.

Sheldon, P.J., *Tourism Information Technology*, CAB International: UK, PB, 1997.

Smith, S.L.J., *Tourism Analysis: A Handbook*, Longman: UK, PB, 1995.

Taneja, N.K., *Introduction To Civil Aviation*, Lexington Books: UK, HB, 1989.

Vellas, F. and Becherel, L., *International Tourism*, Macmillan: UK, PB, 1995.

Wahab, S. and Pigram, J.J., *Tourism, Development and Growth: The Challenge of Sustainability*, Routledge: UK, PB, 1997.

Wheatcroft, S., *Aviation and Tourism Policies: Balancing the Benefits*, ITBP: UK, PB, 1994.

Index